esther

it's tough being a woman

BETH MOORE

LifeWay Press®
Nashville, Tennessee

Published by LifeWay Press®
© 2008 • Beth Moore
Fifth printing January 2010

ISBN 9781415852897
Item 005162885

Dewey Decimal classification: 248.843
Subject heading: BIBLE. O.T. ESTHER—STUDY \WOMEN \ CHRISTIAN LIFE

To order additional copies of this resource:
Write LifeWay Church Resources Customer Service; One LifeWay Plaza;
Nashville, TN 37234-0113; fax order to (615) 251-5933; call toll free 1-800-458-2772;
e-mail orderentry@lifeway.com; order online at www.lifeway.com;
or visit the LifeWay Christian Store serving you.

Printed in the United States of America

Leadership and Adult Publishing
LifeWay Church Resources
One LifeWay Plaza
Nashville, Tennessee 37234-0175

To my wonderful daughters,
Amanda and Melissa—

If what you hold in your hands is a book, then you are its bookends.

Melissa, your hard work came before every lesson I wrote.
Your brilliant research through countless resources in my behalf was incomparable.
Your scholarship was impeccable. Your love of Scripture, remarkable.
Every author on earth should be clamoring to take you from me.
Your sister is right. You are a rock star.

Amanda, your hard work came after every lesson I wrote.
Yours were the first eyes I trusted to read and work each lesson.
Your encouragement kept me going when the months grew long
and the process grew inevitably—appropriately—hard.
Your gentle spirit, sharp eye, and love for a word fitly spoken
make you irreplaceable in this ministry.
Your sister is right. You are a rock star.

Through the nine chapters that follow,
we three have worked as an indivisible team with one unwavering goal:
to see hearts explode with love for Christ
through the thrilling exploration of His Word.
I have waited all these years to dedicate
just the right Bible study to you.
None could have been more appropriate than this one.
You are, hands down, the two most wonderful women I know.
My darling Esthers.
Streams of mercy never ceasing call for songs of loudest praise.

No words big enough.
mom

About the Author

Beth Moore has written best-selling Bible studies on David, Moses, Paul, Isaiah, Daniel, John, and Jesus. Her books *Breaking Free, Praying God's Word,* and *When Godly People Do Ungodly Things* have all focused on the battle Satan is waging against Christians. *Believing God, Loving Well,* and *Living Beyond Yourself* have focused on how Christians can live triumphantly in today's world. *Stepping Up* explores worship and invites us to reach a new level of relationship and intimacy with God.

Beth has a passion for Christ, a passion for Bible study, and a passion to see Christians living the lives Christ intended. God bless you as you join Beth and explore *Esther: It's Tough Being a Woman.*

CONTENTS

FOREWORD

Welcome to Bible Study! Today marks the 82nd week I have spent obsessing over the Book of Esther. I'd give anything to embark on this journey with you, but my journey as research assistant ends where yours begins. I have a few things I'd like to leave you before I reluctantly turn the last page of a cherished chapter in my life.

First, this is not a typical study because Esther is not a typical book. Unique in character and contribution to the canon, Esther is an amazing narrative complete with tragedy and triumph. You'll encounter intrigue, ambiguity, and excess, all in theatrical form. The thread of mystery that runs through the story will leave your mind spinning. If you frequently end a portion with more questions than you started, you'll know you're on the right interpretive track.

Second, Esther neither mentions the name of God nor gives us explanations on how we might live the Christian life. Be assured of many timely words in Esther, but the most significant things we learn will likely concern the nature of God and His activity in human history. Esther calls us to think beyond our individual lives. The book provides a greater and more awe-inspired view that will strengthen our individual lives and deepen our personal relationships with God.

Third and most importantly, I hope you will take Esther personally. You may wonder what Xerxes' extravagant empire has to do with our lives. Esther relates the dramatic preservation of Persian Jews in the face of annihilation. The threat should hit close to home since not even 70 years ago six million Jews were murdered in Nazi Germany. Esther concludes with the establishment of the Feast of Purim, still wildly and joyously celebrated by Jews all over the world. The significance of the book, however, should not be left exclusively for the Jews.

In light of Jesus we read Esther not as strangers but as fellow citizens of God's household. Haman threatened to annihilate the people of God. If the Persian Jews had been annihilated, our Savior Jesus Christ never would have been born. Let that sink in; and please feel free, if not obliged, to take Haman's offense seriously.

I have been privileged to spend the past year and a half poring over the Book of Esther and among the first to read this Bible Study. I believe it's a God-given and culturally-relevant *supplement* to the inspired text of Esther. Knowing the author fairly well, I can assure you that each of these Bible Studies was written to bring us back to the Scriptures, never to replace or overshadow them. They're meant to exalt the power of God through the biblical text. I hope they remind you afresh of the wonder of Holy Writ these next 10 weeks. No other book is like the Bible, for it alone has the ability to accurately convey God's nature and character. It alone was meant to nourish our souls, for "we are not to live by bread alone, but by every word that proceeds from the mouth of God" (Matt. 4:4).

Cheers to the only Wise God, the Lord Jesus Christ who gives us hope, and the Holy Spirit who empowers us!

With love and respect,
Melissa Moore Fitzpatrick
Research Assistant to Beth Moore

THE WHOLE MEGILLAH
An Introduction to the Study of Esther

What greater joy could I have than to welcome you to an adventure with God in His Word? The best page-turner on my nightstand never thrilled me like the book God breathed. If this is your very first in-depth journey through His Word, I offer a wonderful warning: You may be about to start something you can't stop. The Bible differs from anything else you'll ever study. Penned by God Himself in perfectly timed progressive revelation over hundreds of years and sixty-six books, it is far more than history or literature. It is a divinely-inspired meeting place where God reveals Himself and invites us into relationship.

Scripture cannot come without effect to the receptive soul. God is up to something profound in your life or you wouldn't be holding this Bible study in your hands. He not only desires to teach you but to transform you. His Word is living, healing, restoring, enlightening, directing, and empowering. It invades every part of our lives if we'll let it. Nothing except salvation has had a more profound effect on this former pit-dweller's life. I'm simply not who I was, and that's one reason I'm so passionate about Bible study. I make you this promise: You will never waste a moment you spend with an open heart in God's Word.

The Bible is unique, so to say Esther is unique within its pages might suggest the distinctive adventure we have ahead. Before we discover the book's placement in the hearts of the Jewish people, let's consider its placement in the Jewish Bible, traditionally called the *Tanakh*. The word *Tanakh* is an acronym for three words representing its three sections:

Torah (pronounced *to–RAH*)—The Books of Moses, also called the Law
Nevi'im (pronounced *neh–VEEM*)—The Book of the Prophets
Ketuvim (pronounced *KET–to–veem*)—The Writings

To find Esther, we'd open the Jewish Bible to the *Ketuvim* or *Writings*. Five books comprise this section: Song of Songs, Ruth, Lamentations, Ecclesiastes, and, lastly, Esther. This collection of books is known as *The Five Scrolls* or, in Hebrew terminology, the *Megillot* (pronounced *MEG-eh-lote*).

Each of the scrolls is read publicly in synagogues at certain times of the year but, of the five, none is dearer to the Jew than Esther. In fact, it is commonly called the *Megillah* or "the Scroll, par excellence." Every word is read aloud in synagogues during Purim. In fact, the long public reading inspired a figure of speech. You'd use the figure of speech if you were late meeting someone after class and said, "Beth had to give us the whole *Megillah*!"

So, here you have it, Beloved and we won't complete the journey until we've studied the whole *Megillah*! Don't worry though. You're not likely to get bored. We are about to have one of the best times of our lives. I promise we won't read all 10 chapters in one sitting. Quite the contrary, we'll have the joy of taking one brief segment of Scripture at a time, poring over it, musing over it, and learning what on earth to do with it. When we turn the last page, you will know this fascinating story like the back of your hand. You'll also find your own story within it ... if you're willing. I'm game. Are you? Then let's get started!

Beth

esther

viewer guide ☙ introduction

The Background of Esther in the Hebrew Bible and Tradition

The Book of Esther is also known as the _____.

Historical Background

Like the Book of Daniel, Esther is a _____ story.

The Uniqueness of the Book of Esther

1. The total _____ of any _____ to _____

   Why study the Book of Esther?

   • It's part of _____ _____.

   • Based on Psalm 138:2b God's name may not be _____ _____,

     but _____ _____ _____ _____.

   • It offers tremendous _____.

   • It extends a vital perspective on the _____ ____ _____.
     Merriam Webster's definition of *providence:* "God conceived as the

     power _____ _____ _____ _____

     _____." *Holman Illustrated Bible Dictionary* adds, "In so

     doing [in His providence] God attends not only to apparently

     momentous events and people but also to those that seem both

     _____ and _____. … Indeed, so all encompassing

     is God's attention to events within creation that nothing …

     _____ by _____."

Ephesians 1:11—Even when we're blind to the evidence, God "_____ _____ _____ in conformity with the _____ of His will."

Philippians 2:13—God "_____ ___ _____ to will and to act according to His good _____."

2. **The title bears a _____ _____.**

Throughout the next nine weeks we'll consider different scenarios to underscore the concept captured in our study's title.

Scenario #1

It's tough being a woman ___ _____ _____ _____.

3. **The God-ordained emphasis on _____ _____**

According to *Word Biblical Commentary*, the inspired author of Esther "lays all the stress on the _____ _____ to the divine-human _____" [combined or shared energy].

week one

A Royal Mess

Enter Vashti, the crowned Queen of Persia. Think of the most beautiful woman you've ever seen, and don't act like you don't notice because we're probably more aware of the appearance of other women than men are.

Principal Questions

1. What was the timing and political climate of the story Esther would soon enter?
2. In Esther 1, who attended Xerxes' banquet?
3. From your perspective, for what three possible reasons might Vashti have refused King Xerxes' order?
4. What did Memucan advise the king to do?
5. How might the thought that "it's tough being a woman in another woman's shadow" have proved especially true for wives all over Persia?

Day One
This Is What Happened

TODAY'S TREASURE

"This is what happened during the time of Xerxes, the Xerxes who ruled over 127 provinces stretching from India to Cush." Esther 1:1

"There is something delicious about writing the first words of a story."[1] Perhaps the anonymous writer picked by God to pen the words of Esther thought something similar to Rene Zellweger's opening line in the movie *Miss Potter*. At first glance, the genesis-words to Esther's story don't seem delicious at all. Not even noteworthy. *This is what happened.* So what? "But, although it seems perfectly natural to open a narrative in this manner, it is actually rare. Biblical narratives commonly begin with 'it happened' but omit 'in the days of.' On the other hand, prophetic writings are often introduced as having occurred 'in the days of King. ...' The Book of Esther unfolds, however, with the two intertwining. The result according to some scholars is an opening 'more like the opening of a folktale, with the aura of "Once upon a time, in the days of the great and glorious Ahasuerus, King of the vast Persian empire." ' "[2]

Esther resembles the opening of a folktale because it tells such a great and true story. Indeed, God's love of a great story is extravagantly evident in the narrative that makes up over 40 percent of the Bible.

In *How to Read the Bible for All Its Worth* Fee and Stuart note the crucial difference between the biblical narratives and all others because inspired by the Holy Spirit, "the story they tell is not so much our story as it is God's story—and it becomes ours as he 'writes' us into it. The biblical narratives thus tell the ultimate story, a story that, even though often complex, is utterly true and crucially important. Indeed, it is a magnificent story, grander than the greatest epic, richer in plot and more significant in its characters and descriptions than any humanly composed story could ever be."[3]

According to Fee and Stuart, how do biblical narratives such as Esther differ from all others?

Open your Bible and your mind to the Book of Esther. Invite every sense of your imagination to be kindled with color, texture, scent, and sound until you can smell the fear, then hear the cheer. There on the sacred page God overtook a human hand and scripted a young woman's story into His own.

For information on end-notes, see page 224.

Ahasuerus

the Hebrew name for Xerxes

There on the sacred pages of Esther God overtook a human hand and scripted a young woman's story into His own.

Marvelously, even miraculously, as you and I spend the next nine weeks with Him in the pages of Esther's story, God will write something new and unexpected of our own into His. Your personal story written into God's epic annals of human history will be different because you chose to meet Him in 10 of the most distinctive chapters of His Word.

Principal Question

If once upon a time, what was the time? Read Esther 1:1-3 and write in the margin everything you can glean about the timing and political climate of the story she would soon enter.

The year was 483 B.C., the third year of Xerxes' reign and the thirty-fifth year of his privileged life. His route to the throne is significant to our story. He was not the first son of Darius I, but he was the first son born to Darius after being crowned king. Xerxes' veins were plump and purple with a double portion of royal blood. His mother was Atossa, the daughter of a ruler who, among Gentiles, could hardly have had more Jewish significance in the era encircled by his crown. The first part of the Book of Ezra records the identity and actions of the man Atossa called "Father" and Xerxes called "Grandfather."

Please read Ezra 1:1–2:1. Look to the end of the segment first. What had happened to the Israelites according to Ezra 2:1?

Who is the king identified and quoted in Ezra 1? (Circle one.)

Cyrus   Belshazzar   Nebuchadnezzar   Artaxerxes

What tremendous significance did his actions have on the Israelites?

Cyrus the Great was born into conditions that would ultimately turn to his titanic political favor. His mother was a Mede and his father a Persian, making him a palatable choice to blend a Medo-Persian people. With shocking ease in 539 B.C. Cyrus conquered Babylon, the home of exiled Israelites. He then issued the decree in Ezra 1 that allowed the exiles to return to Jerusalem. Some never returned, a fact that becomes pivotal to the story of Esther. Many historians through the centuries explain away Cyrus's apparent benevolence as a simple and wise political move to garner the favor of foreigners.

Regardless of why Cyrus thought he issued the decree, how does Isaiah 44:24-28 explain his actions?

As we return to Xerxes' "once upon a time," recap the three royal generations leading up to our time frame in Esther 1:1.

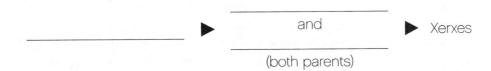

The Greek historian Herodotus wrote *History of the Persian Wars* only 25 years after Xerxes' reign. Although we don't have adequate parallel sources to verify everything he wrote as completely accurate and unbiased, his writings shed colorful light on the king and kingdom in Persia during the "once upon a time" of Esther. According to Herodotus, Xerxes was not just tall, dark, and handsome. He was the tallest and most handsome Persian of all. And a spoiled playboy at that. If you, like most of us, wish you had a godly outlet for gazing at the lifestyles of the rich, famous, and shockingly overindulgent, you'll want to stay tuned. Lean over here closely while I whisper: *I will too.*

In all the gazing, don't forget to look for something of yourself within these pages. At first glance, Xerxes' and Esther's lives and stories may seem to have little to do with yours, but if that were true, the Book of Esther might be the solitary Old Testament case where Romans 15:4 simply doesn't apply.

In our introductory session we talked about this verse. Whether or not you could join us, concerning Esther, what does Romans 15:4 mean?

Beloved, what are you hoping for as you begin this Bible study?

Don't forget to look for something of yourself within these pages.

Personal Question

Has a negative event or a near-eternal wait recently made you lose hope about something important to you? Do you have any natural reasons to think that whatever your "once upon a time" might have been, it can never be now?

Remember the first words of Esther, "this is what happened during the time of Xerxes," and their similarity to "once upon a time, in the days of the great and glorious Ahasuerus"? I learned in my research that those Hebrew words *wayhi bime* occur five times in Scripture. Brace yourself for a moment. Without exception all "introduce impending catastrophe or doom."[4]

Our first reaction may be the thought, *Then who wants a great story? Forget once upon a time!* But I'd like to suggest that the nature of life on planet Earth swirls a certain air of impending catastrophe in every hospital nursery in the world. Stick with me here a moment because this perspective could make you feel better instead of worse.

Unless you've lived in a place I've never found, with all your heart's desires met and without a soul who annoys you, Job was pretty accurate when he said, "Man [or woman] born of woman is of few days and full of trouble" (Job 14:1).

Case in point: I often run into people who tell me they've been prompted to pray for me "lately" and invariably ask, "Has anything been wrong?"

Beloved, *something* is always wrong! I still live in the real world where I get my feelings hurt, go to funerals, get rejected, catch stomach viruses, and age overnight. Life here is full of trouble whether in a sky-high mountain of small annoyances or an earth-splitting canyon of crisis. There's no escaping it until we escape these mortal bodies. But here's the good news. I also learned that in all five occasions where those same Hebrew words were associated with impending catastrophe, "the ending to each story is happy, but before that happy ending is realized, much grief occurs."[5]

I think we know the part about "much grief," but in the weeks to come I'm hoping for us to grasp that no life is free of troubles, regardless of religion, race, or nation. In fact, as Job said, every life is full of it. When we trust our lives to the hand *and pen* of an unseen but ever-present God, He will write our lives into His story and every last one of them will turn out to be a great read. With a grand ending. And not just in spite of those catastrophes. Often because of them. Don't just wait and see. Live and see.

> When we trust our lives to the unseen but ever-present God, He will write our lives into His story and every last one of them will turn out to be a great read. With a grand ending.

Day Two
Pitch a Royal Party

TODAY'S TREASURE

"For a full 180 days he displayed the vast wealth of his kingdom and the splendor and glory of his majesty." Esther 1:4

Mind your watch today because we've got a party to attend and don't want to be late. Esther's the wrong book for a Bible student too pious for a party. Seven of Esther's ten chapters refer to somebody throwing a party. That's not to say all of the festivities will be fun. Not all parties are, even when we pretend to the contrary and eat our weight in onion dip. We can count on some drama, however, and if you have my kind of taste, that's your kind of fun anyway.

Just in case you still aren't sure you can relish a plate of Bible study served up with a side of amusement, maybe the following quote will offer permission: "The Book of Esther is by any standards a brilliantly written story,

to be savoured—even chuckled over. The reader who wishes to learn may mix business and pleasure here."[6] Beautiful words to any sanguine! May they be intriguing words to all of us until the story line captivates us enough to agree.

What do you think the writer meant about savoring and chuckling over Esther?

The study of God's Word is serious business to me. He made it my lifeline. Medicine for my broken mind. Salve to my wounded soul. But God also made it one of the sheerest delights of my entire life. Encounters with Christ on the pages of Scripture have run the gamut with me. How many times in one paragraph of Scripture have I been rebuked only to be restored in the next? How many times have I sighed with reluctant acceptance over one portion and swung to heights of exhilaration in the next?

You may know exactly what I'm talking about, or you may never have experienced anything more than a stale read of a stiff, archaic book that you opened mainly because good people are supposed to read the Bible. If reading Scripture has been more like law than life to you, you are twice the candidate for the study of Esther. You're about to find out about mixing business and pleasure on the pages of the world's most sacred text.

Please read Esther 1:1-8.

Before we bask in the scene, let's see if we can determine the occasion. A closer look at who was present at the "banquet" in verse 3 can offer some clues.

Who was in attendance?

Principal Question

At this point in Xerxes' reign, Greece was the only part of the world that wasn't already under his thumb. The history books, the evening news, and our own personal experience suggest how wildly obsessed we can become over something tauntingly unattainable. Xerxes wanted Greece, and he needed enormous support to get it.

Since the timing corresponds with the great war council of 483 B.C., a number of scholars suggest that Xerxes may have thrown a 180-day expo of his vast wealth and power "to inspire Persians with confidence in preparation for the massive—and ultimately disastrous—military campaign against Greece ... which began in the same year as the banquet (483 B.C.)."[7] According to the Greek historian Herodotus, Xerxes promised copious rewards to those who would help him take Athens, and the excess he placed on exhibit was to prove he could make good on the promise.[8]

> The study of God's
> Word is serious
> business to me ...
> and one of the
> sheerest delights of
> my entire life.

If you look closely in verses 4 and 5, you'll find two time references to Xerxes' festivities. To what does each refer?

The seven-day public party was probably the culmination of the 180-day exhibit. Imagine how exhausting a seven-day party would be, particularly after the drama of tearing through our closets, trying to decide what to wear. Think how our feet would kill us because we'd choose cute over comfortable shoes. But if you could stand those three-inch heels, you were in for a sight.

Relish this quote by Michael V. Fox in his commentary on Esther. "The opening scene is unusually expansive for biblical narrative. Instead of reporting actions and words, the author scans the venue like a cinematographer, moving at a leisurely pace and describing in lavish detail what one present in the palace would have witnessed."[9]

I love Fox's comparison of the text's perspective to a movie-maker. Long before the movie projector married the big screen and manipulated our imaginations, there were books like Esther. Imaginations have to be exercised to be tantalized, and the reward was infinitely richer.

Read verses 5-8 once more, but this time read it like a cinematographer would have you see it. Imagine the scene in high definition and the camera moving just as Fox described: slowly, deliberately from one angle to the next. Let your mind's eye fix on one dimension then another. Take your time, mixing business with pleasure. Imagine the colors and the textures. Enter into one of the highest-budget sets in the entire world of Scripture.

List in the margin some details you would have found most impressive had you attended the great garden party of King Xerxes.

The original language is far more impressive than our English translations. Fox says the description in verses 6-7 is an unusual Hebrew form, a single long exclamation-like sentence that conveys the *narrator's* wonder and creates a mass of images that overwhelm the senses.[10] *Word Biblical Commentary* nods in agreement with the following translation of the portion: "Oh, the white and violet hangings of linen and cotton, held by white and purple cords of fine linen on silver rods and alabaster columns; the couches of gold and silver on a mosaic pavement of porphyry, alabaster, shell-marble, and turquoise! And, oh, the drinks that were served … in royal style!"[11]

Freeze-frame on those drinks for a moment. Imagine serving your guests beverages out of glasses that were different on purpose! Until our recent remodel, no two of my glasses were alike either—but not because of the finery of my kitchen. The glasses we'd received for wedding gifts had long disappeared and been replaced by the strangest concoction of table-surprise you've ever seen. But I've seen a few houses in my day that wouldn't put a sippy cup

with the dog-gnawed lid on the table for anything in Texas. You know the kind. When, as *Word Biblical Commentary* says, all that will come out of your mouth is "Oh!"

One of my coworkers and I saw an "Oh!" kind of home not long ago. I'd been invited to speak at a dinner party given by the gorgeous—and, at the risk of causing bitterness, *godly*—wife of a professional athlete. I have been in some beautiful homes in my day, but I have never in my life seen anything like that one. Had the Holy Spirit not shown up, I don't think I could have picked up my jaw enough to utter an intelligible word.

The experience was much more fun because my girlfriend was with me. We caught each other's eye a few times with expressions that said, "Are you believing this?" God completely stole the show, but He left us with some asides that still make us laugh. For instance, just before we left that evening, our good-humored host, amused by our poorly hidden giddiness, knew she'd send us over the edge by asking, "Would you girls like to see my closet?" We nearly jumped out of our pumps. Oh, the shoes! Oh, the purses! Oh, the capris! We were like two six-year-old girls leaving Cinderella's castle in a pumpkin—squealing like mice all the way home.

Describe a time when you toured an estate or attended a party that left you saying something like, "Oh, the _____!"

No doubt it was even more fun if you had an unspoiled girlfriend with you to share it. Now, let's take our experiences, throw them together, and multiply the grandeur by 100 and maybe we'll grasp the scene of Xerxes' garden party. The Persians were famous for their luxurious gardens. In fact, our word *paradise* comes from the same word they used for their gardens, *paradeisoi*. Rather than picture well-manicured yards, most Persian royal gardens were more like "large parks with trees, wild animals, and sources of water."[12]

Amid the beauty, the exiles who remained in Susa also may have had a constant reminder of defeat. According to Hebrew *midrash*, the marble pillars in verse 6 had been removed from Solomon's temple in Jerusalem and carried off by Nebuchadnezzar as part of the spoils almost a century earlier.[13]

The professional athlete's wife used her mansion to showcase God's glory. King Xerxes threw a party to display his own. Incidentally, Xerxes didn't earn an ounce of his fortune. He inherited it from dear old dad, Darius. We'll soon discover that Ahasuerus was "Exhibit A" of what happens when everything is handed to you in a golden goblet. Still, he had it and he chose to flaunt it.

Fill in the blank according to verse 4: "He displayed the vast _____ of his _____ and the _____ and _____ of his _____."

For those of us who are familiar with God's Word, those descriptions are chilling. We are accustomed to stringing together words such as *splendor, glory,* and *majesty* for God alone. Xerxes would have done well to have rolled himself up in a scroll of Psalm 49 and stayed there until his ego shrunk, but his chance has come and gone. Ours hasn't.

Our culture's mountain-high-piece-of-the-pie premium on riches is not so different from ancient Persia's, and the wealth around us can become as intoxicating as Xerxes' royal wine. As we place today's lesson under a post-modern bulb's light, let's pour over the timeless words of Psalm 49:6-20.

In the margin list every reason in the psalm why prioritizing wealth and strutting riches are wastes of precious time.

I can tell you something that will never be a waste of time: ascribing to God His measureless worth. Oddly, the most freeing thing we can ever do is to abdicate the throne of our own miniature kingdoms. Our status is infinitely higher as a servant in God's kingdom than a ruler in ours.

Conclude by writing in your own words Psalm 96:4-6.

> Ascribing to God His measureless worth will never be a waste of time.

Day Three
Saying No to a King

TODAY'S TREASURE

"Queen Vashti refused to come. Then the king became furious and burned with anger." Esther 1:12

In our previous lesson the cinematographer's camera moved from the mosaic pavement to the marble pillars as we were visually enticed into the extravagant surroundings of Xerxes' seven-day banquet. But the best part of a party is not the location; it's the people. Today the camera shifts from fabrics to faces and where you have people—particularly intoxicated ones—you have problems.

In any good drama it takes at least two spoons to thicken the plot. That's exactly what we'll have today as a second character appears on the royal scene. If a fire gets turned up under a thickening plot, however, something's liable to boil over. This is a mess you won't want to miss.

Since we have the luxury of taking nine weeks to study the 10 chapters of Esther, our Scripture reading will often overlap to keep our context clear. Please read Esther 1:1-12. After you've read the entire segment, settle on verses 7 and 8. At first glance, the snapshots revolving around the wine don't seem significant, but we'll soon see that they suggest more than meets the eye.

In the margin list everything these two verses tell you about the wine.

The custom among ancients such as the Persians dictated that attendees of royal banquets raised their glasses at the invitation of the king. Xerxes forewent the custom and essentially offered an open wine bar. One translation of Esther 1:8 reads, "The drinking was according to the rule: let there be no restraining."[14] In other words, Xerxes' only rule for drinking was that there would be no rule at all. Without the insight of scholars and historians, we might assume he was simply generous. Consider another perspective:

"Although the king's declaration might appear to be an act of grace, it is in fact a subtle sign of weakness. Whereas other Persian rulers demanded unyielding adherence to this custom, Ahasuerus, perhaps being unsure of his power base, finds it necessary to relax this custom as part of his efforts to win the favor of his people."[15]

Xerxes was like a high school kid having a party while his parents were away and letting his guests do as they pleased because he was too insecure to lay down the law. Unfortunately, you and I don't have to be an adolescent to fall to the same temptation. Like Xerxes, all we have to do is act like one. Trying to win favor at the risk of smart boundaries is as tempting among coworkers as students. Imagine the pressure had you and I tried to be impressive for a solid seven days of entertaining. What an embarrassing prospect!

Just about the time we're getting bored with Xerxes and his drink-a-thon, a new character enters the narrative.

List everything you learn about her and can also infer about her based on verses 9-12, starting obviously with her name and position.

Enter Vashti, the crowned Queen of Persia. Think of the most beautiful woman you've ever seen, and don't act like you don't notice because virtually every woman does. We're probably more aware of the appearance of other women than men are.

Agree or disagree? _____ Why?

Vashti was the kind of beauty who turned every head in the room. Her profile was as favorable from the left as from the right. Her hips weren't out of proportion with her bustline. None of her toes was a half-inch longer than the others. She could probably wear any old thing and look fresh off the runway. Vashti was the kind of woman who didn't have a gap between her two front teeth or, if she did, she made people want to pry theirs apart. She was a woman whose hair worked despite a steamy climate only 150 miles off a gulf coast. *Queen Vashti.* A trophy wife if you'll ever meet one.

Some scholars suggest her beauty even surpassed our yet-to-be-introduced protagonist, Esther. Did I hear a gasp? One scholar said that the trouble with approaching very familiar stories like Esther is that we sometimes don't know them as well as we think. Let's be careful not to impose everything we thought we knew about this book on our present study. Let's allow ourselves to think outside the box if we have solid grounds for additional perspectives.

One reason some scholars surmise that Vashti's beauty may have even exceeded Esther's is that, in a genre where words mean the world, Vashti was twice attributed with beauty and Esther, once.[16] To our great relief, we're going to find that Esther was more than just a pretty face.

Glance at your book's cover for a moment. Then write the subtitle to our study: _____.

Throughout the next nine weeks we will add all sorts of scenarios to underscore the statement. I suggested one already in our introductory session. If you participated, please complete the following:

It's tough being a woman _____.

If you were unable to attend, you'll find the completed sentence at the end of today's lesson. A woman doesn't have to be stunning like Vashti to cast a shadow that becomes difficult for the woman who follows her. A mean-spirited woman can make life just as difficult on her "successor." Let's not minimize the hardship of following a classic "Vashti," however, particularly in our air-brushed, media-driven culture.

Why would it be tough for a woman to be in a "Vashti's" shadow?

I cannot imagine a society that breeds more comparison-driven insecurity than ours. Can you?

A woman doesn't have to be stunning to cast a shadow that becomes difficult for the woman who follows her.

On a scale of 1 to 10, how haunted are you by the pictures of physical perfection that loom nearby?

| 1 | 2 | 3 | 4 | 5 | 6 | 7 | 8 | 9 | 10 |

unaffected   greatly affected

Now, let's get more personal. Do you live, work, serve, or recreate near a woman who makes you feel tremendously insecure? If so, and without mentioning her name, in what ways?

I've been there too, and it was miserable. I vacillated woefully between hating her and hating myself. I don't doubt I'll be there again if I don't let God tend to my insecurities. One of the goals of our study is to let God heal our world-torn souls and make us experience His security in our reality. Stay open to all the ways He wants to speak to you about becoming more secure in your world over the next nine weeks. In the meantime, you'll be glad to know that Vashti had more than looks. Vashti had competence.

What was she doing in Esther 1:9? _____

> One goal of our study is to let God heal our world-torn souls and make us experience His security in our reality.

At this point in the seven-day banquet, Xerxes entertained the men and Vashti entertained the women. Since ancient Persian parties commonly included both genders, the segregation here was obviously intentional. The queen was hosting a girls-only grand affair when the king suddenly summoned her.

Check verse 10. Who did Xerxes send for her? (You don't need to list names.) _____

Why the sudden whim? Remember, the point of the entire six-month festivity was to display Xerxes' wealth. He had one unrivaled prize yet to exhibit.

"The beautiful Vashti, wearing her royal diadem, was a living trophy of his power and glory. He sent seven eunuchs to fetch her, perhaps the number needed to carry her seated in the royal litter."[17]

I can't resist interrupting the quote to interject that, where I come from, litter is litter, whether or not the cat lives in a palace. However, in the ancient world of royals, a litter was a curtained couch carried by shafts and used to transport a single passenger in grandest style.

"This would create a dramatic and majestic entrance for her before the men being asked to go to war for the empire. Perhaps the sight of the queen in her royal glory was intended to inspire patriotism and loyalty, as public appearances of the British queen do today."[18]

Perhaps we should give a king, decidedly under the influence of free-flowing wine, the benefit of the doubt (more on that topic in a moment). We've arrived at the point in the narrative when we realize that Vashti was not only beautiful and competent but she was also strong-willed.

What happened when the eunuchs issued the king's command?

Scripture answers some questions outright and leaves others hanging in the air.

Now that's royal rejection. The dramatic pomp of the fetch did nothing but add insult to injury. I love the way Scripture answers some questions outright and leaves others hanging in air so thick you could cut them with a knife. Through the centuries students of the Book of Esther have been left to do with Vashti's refusal exactly what we'll do today: wonder why. Before I propose traditional explanations ranging from the reasonable to the absurd, I want you to give the scenario some creative thought. Remember, Vashti was issued a command from the king.

Principal Question

Offer three possible reasons from your own independent perspective why Vashti might have refused King Xerxes' order:

1.

2.

3.

Consider a few of the more historically persistent explanations for Vashti's refusal:

1. She refused the indignity of appearing before a gathering comprised only of men and intoxicated ones at that.
2. "Vashti, being the granddaughter of King Nebuchadnezzar, considered herself to be the legitimate heir to the throne rather than Ahasuerus, whom she deemed to be a usurper."[19]
3. She simply had no respect for Xerxes as a king or a man.
4. The command was for her to appear unclothed, wearing *only* the royal crown.
5. Brace yourself for this one: She refused to appear because "Gabriel [the angelic messenger] had come and caused a tail to grow on her."[20] (After all, I'd like to suggest that under those conditions finding the right outfit for a public appearance can be challenging. You know how we women are about our hips.)

Which one of the five proposals is closest to what you'd surmise?

My guess is that for any number of reasons the queen considered the summons an affront to her dignity. I have to wonder if Xerxes was at a loss to come up with a climactic finish to a 7-day party on the tail end of a 180-day expo. Perhaps he grappled for something dramatic and, under the influence, reached beyond the boundaries of a queen with a mind of her own. "Undoubtedly, for a woman, pretentiousness and inebriation are not a comforting combination in a man."[21] Can anybody relate?

J. G. McConville suggests that the command stirred a divided loyalty in Vashti: "loyalty to the authority system at whose centre stood her demanding husband, and loyalty to her own dignity."[22]

My daughter Melissa remarked that Vashti was in a lose-lose situation. If we think long and hard enough, we can relate on some level. Most of us have had crises when being loyal—or even agreeable—to someone we cared about could cost us considerable dignity. I'd like to pose a question in a purposeful way that causes us to think of a similar occasion but keeps us from sharing (if applicable) something graphic.

Think of an example in your life when you were in a lose-lose situation; then, without describing it, relate what was at stake from both sides:

Whatever the queen's reason for refusing, the king's reaction was immediate. If he had a mouthful of wine when the eunuchs delivered the news, all seven of them likely ended up wearing it. One scholar feathers the scene with vivid color: "Ahasuerus is like a peacock who cannot get enough of having others admire his display. He sets no limits to his showing off; everything and everyone is *his* after all. When someone else provides a limit, it enrages him and the party is over."[23]

As I write this portion of today's lesson, I am in mid-air on a plane (yes, again). I just glanced across the aisle to see a woman's magazine opened to an article speckled with pictures of celebrity couples. It is aptly entitled, "Paging the Love Doctor." The pagers could have been heard for a country mile calling from the citadel of Susa.

(*Answer: It's tough being a woman in another woman's shadow.*)

Day Four
A Royal Fit

TODAY'S TREASURE
"This very day the Persian and Median women of the nobility who have heard about the queen's conduct will respond to all the king's nobles in the same way. There will be no end of disrespect and discord."
Esther 1:18

Welcome to the continuing mini-saga of Xerxes and Vashti, Susa's resident drama king and queen. Our previous segment of Scripture concluded with a plot so thick that it became a royal stew.

What had caused the drama, and how did Xerxes' moods change between Esther 1:10 and 1:12?

Behold the emotional equivalent of the Sky Screamer, an amusement park ride that creeps up 400+ feet, jolts to a stop, and drops with the velocity of a free fall. Add excessive drink to the equation and your emotional free fall doubles. That's what happened to Xerxes. The king wasn't just furious. He was burning alive inside. Many of us didn't need Xerxes to remind us that excessive drink can intensify a temper, did we? We've witnessed it—or experienced it.

In the margin list several additional reasons why you think the king may have been so enraged over Vashti's refusal.

God is faithful to remind us that He alone is Lord.

We probably agree that Xerxes felt publicly humiliated and feared appearing weak. The chink in the king's armor that appeared when he took no leadership over public consumption in verse 7 became a gaping hole when his own wife refused his summons in verse 12. I love how one scholar described the event as the unraveling of "the first stitch of thread in the king's 'power suit.' "[24]

Meditate on those words for a moment. At times we all put on a power suit of one kind or another. I don't mean assuming appropriate responsibility. We put on our power suit when we take advantage of someone else's false belief that they are inferior to us. Because God is faithful to remind us that He alone is Lord, one day the power suit begins to unravel even if we're the only one aware of the dangling thread. Today's text picks up exactly where our previous segment ended. Please read Esther 1:13-20.

To whom did King Xerxes turn for advice?_____

Who became the spokesperson among them? (Circle one.)

     Carshena   Shethar   Admatha

   Tarshish   Meres   Marsena   Memucan

His name sounds like a fiber supplement to me, but maybe the word association will make Memucan's odd name more memorable to us.

According to verse 16, whom had Vashti wronged in his opinion?

What effects did he think Vashti's refusal would have (vv. 17-18)?

What did he advise the king to do?   *Principal Question*

What do you think Memucan meant by someone "better than she"?

Consider the irony. Xerxes had shown off his vast wealth for 180 days,

"But he finds himself powerless to show off the beauty of his own wife: that comes with a *person* and requires human relations skills that he sadly and conspicuously lacks. What is still worse, he compounds the problem by treating his personal deficiency through official means, promoting an embarrassment into a state crisis and his problem with Queen Vashti into a problem of all men with their wives (vv. 13-20). The ludicrous outcome is that the man who cannot rule his wife becomes the all-powerful emperor who formally enjoins all his male subjects to rule their wives (vv. 21-22)."[25]

How had Xerxes compounded the problem?

Xerxes' advisors inadvertently treated his embarrassment with a double dose of the same. With experts like those, who needs enemies? Have you ever had an associate who, rather than helping you calm down and think clearly, fanned the flame on your fiery emotions and ended up talking you into double the trouble? Let's be careful not to Memucanize those who come to us for counsel.

What can you do to keep from giving someone else inflammatory advice when the temptation is strong?

The absurdity of the scene in Xerxes' advisory board meeting has an amusing side. Adele Berlin suggests that the arrangements of the seven eunuchs' names in verse 10 and now the seven advisors in verse 14 have the ring of "playful devices, like the names of the seven dwarfs in 'Snow White.' "[26] In light of the ridiculous reasoning they offered the king, the parallel is amusing. Another author went further to say that the sounds of the foreign names of the seven advisors "would have been ludicrous to Hebrew ears … giving 'the impression of a dumb chorus in an opera bouffe.' "[27]

Any of us who have lived or worked among a people of another language know how ridiculous some of our words can sound to each other. For instance, Beth is pronounced "Bet" in French and sounds like their word "bete," which means "idiot" or "imbecile." (The shoe fits on occasion.)

Do you have a similar example? If so, share it.

Humor is one way we cope with a tough situation.

You get the idea. Now, stick it in today's context. Enjoy discovering that "the Hebrew form of Xerxes' name (pronounced *Ahashwerosh*)" has a very comical sound when it is pronounced in Hebrew and "would correspond to something like King Headache in English."[28] You can be sure the word play wasn't lost on the Hebrew people. Can't you picture them on every street corner during a royal parade making fun of King Headache behind his back? Isn't humor, after all, one way we cope with a tough situation?

Personal Question When was the last time humor helped you cope?

Right or wrong, a comical view can be an effective coping skill because it resketches an imposing figure into a caricature of sorts that shrinks him or her to a more manageable size psychologically. You see it at work every time you glance at a political cartoon. The sketch in the second half of Esther's first chapter is intended to some degree to draw an ancient political cartoon. We can just picture King Headache and Snow White's Seven Dwarfs deliberating over what must be done about Vashti.

I learned something from my research that framed the consultation in an even stranger light. The Greek historian Herodotus wrote that the Persians would "deliberate about the gravest matters when they are drunk, and what they approve in their counsels is proposed to them the next day by the master of the house where they deliberate, when they are now sober and if being sober they still approve it, they act thereon, but if not, they cast it aside. And when they have taken counsel about a matter when sober, they decide upon it when they are drunk."[29] As strange as the idea is to us, the ancient Persians believed they could reach further into the spiritual world when they were

intoxicated. Before we find the thought too laughable, the same propaganda was spread about LSD in the 1960s.

Various scholars surmise that the meeting between Xerxes and his advisors took place when many of them were inebriated. In other words, they weren't only under the influence when the royal rejection occurred, but they were also under the influence when they determined what to do about it. Two commentators refer to the consort as "the drunk leading the drunk."[30]

Proverbs 31:4-5 conveys vastly different advice to kings or presumably those in powerful places of authority. What is it?

Xerxes' "experts" may not have advised such extreme measures only out of drunkenness, they may also have felt the need to nip a problem in the proverbial bud. Defiance against husbands may have become a bit trendy among various circles of wives around that time. Aristophanes wrote a popular Greek comedy called *Lysistrata* that circulated throughout their part of the world only a few decades later. The comedy centered on women banding together and going on conjugal strike against their husbands. Vashti's jaw-dropping refusal quite possibly happened in a world where a handful of insecure husbands were on the lookout for badly behaving wives.

Never think for a moment that the sudden surges of popular culture have no impact on what seems to be the immovable societal pillars of government and religion. The populace wields more power than either of those sturdy branches would ever choose to give away. A fierce swell of popular opinion is a force to be reckoned with in one way or another. Thankfully, we have a sovereign God who reigns over all and is threatened by none. Let the rich words of Michael V. Fox put the finishing touches on today's lesson:

"For now, however, the world exhibits a certain stability. The first disturbance to the stasis does not seem threatening; it is a phony crisis of little consequence. But in fact it exposes the seeds of danger. It reveals a society easily destabilized. It shows that beneath the jovial and trivial surface reside some dangerously tender egos. It introduces men whose need for honor can make them provoke the king into setting in motion the inexorable machinery of the empire. It shows us people who try to impose their will on others and who identify strength with rigidity, who fear that flexibility proves weakness and who regard obduracy as the essence of the law. Rigidity of this sort will place severe barriers before the book's heroes, who will be forced to work around them in a way that Vashti could not or would not."[31]

Underline in the preceding paragraph the phrase "dangerously tender egos" and be on the lookout within.

We have a sovereign God who reigns over all and is threatened by none.

Day Five
Dispatched Reprisals

"He sent dispatches ... proclaiming in each people's tongue that every man should be ruler over his own household." Esther 1:22

My middle school's P.E. coach high-jumped to the conclusion that I was a shoo-in for track because I had long legs. Both my older brother and sister were musical whiz kids, and since I held the dubious honor of next-to-last-chair flutist in a band overblown with flutists, I thought maybe my great talent had been discovered elsewhere.

Just before my first track meet one of my friends advised me how to take the advantage. She told me that if I really wanted to win the race, I should walk the first three-quarters of it and wait until the very last to take full flight. She reasoned that the others would run wildly from the start and wear themselves out, allowing me to take the lead. I did exactly what she said.

My coach yelled, "For heaven's sake, Beth, what are you doing? Run!" while I meandered along, musing to myself about how inexperienced she must be. While my opponents sailed into the horizon, I pictured how I'd ultimately leave them in the dust, tongues hanging, while I took the finish line like a gazelle. I looked to my right and left at the amazed observers and smiled knowingly. Reassuringly. I imagined them cheering madly at the end of the race and saying things like, "Isn't she the sneaky one? And such a natural athlete!" The plan might have worked had I ever gotten a chance to run.

About the time I was supposed to rev up my engine, my opponents crossed the finish line. Every time I tried to blame my friend, somebody said, "Exactly what made you think that plan would work?" Memucan's advice was bad enough. Xerxes' taking it was worse. The difference was no one had the courage to indict the king for thinking such a foolish plan would work. Read Esther 1:16-22, allowing its overlap to refresh your memory.

Compare Daniel 6:12b to Esther 1:19. What was distinctive about "the laws of Persia and Media"? Circle one. They could ...

not be repealed   include the death penalty   be unethical

What was proclaimed in every person's language (v. 22)?

Can you think of any potential misuses a proclamation like this one might have invited?

In our first week of study, we've suggested that it's tough being a woman in another woman's shadow. In the margin describe how this statement might have proved especially true for wives all over Persia.

Of all the repercussions Vashti experienced for her refusal, I wonder if she cared most about the royal license for harshness invited into households all across the kingdom. Ironically, her determination to exercise her own personal rights was exploited when the rights of others were taken away. The essence of oppression is punishing one by hurting many.

Glance back at verse 19. Can you think of anything particularly ironic about Vashti's punishment in this verse? Explain.

We don't know what happened to Vashti. Some scholars and rabbis believe that the death penalty was inherent in the banishment. All we know for certain is that she was never again in the presence of the king. Oddly, she received permanently what she desired temporarily. Refusal turned into reprisal.

The dust kicked up by the messengers spun like dirt devils all over Persia. As they arrived with the news in each corner of the kingdom, we arrive at the perfect place to make a monumental point: The conflicts we study in our journey through Esther will not become gender issues. Despite buckets of ink spilled in books with a feminist approach to Esther, we're not going to hang "Women vs. Men" on the marquis of this study. Turning the book into a gender war not only produces the wrong results. It misses the point.

The conflicts in Esther are those caught in the crossfire between wisdom and foolishness, modesty and licentiousness, bravery and cowardice, waiting and acting, living and dying. The genders are secondary and could as easily be reversed. Case in point: Queen Jezebel and the prophet Elijah in the Book of 1 Kings. Let's celebrate womanhood without emasculating manhood. With that said, the following excerpt sheds light on the real issue at hand:

"The king's decree that every man should be the ruler in his own home is not an affirmation of patriarchy, but a cynical commentary on the character of leadership in the Persian court. Indeed, the author portrays the demand of the men in power for the respect of the women as self-defeating. Memucan's view of respect and how to get it reveals the inner workings of Persian power as brute force, fueled by the need to control. He fears female 'disrespect' (v. 18) and apparently believes respect can be acquired through the brute force of a royal decree. However, such a tactic is hollow and self-defeating."[32]

Turning the Book of Esther into a gender war would miss the entire point.

Why might such a tactic be hollow and self-defeating?

The excerpt continues with further explanation: "for if a man has to command a woman to respect him, then whatever 'respect' is so rendered loses its meaning. Those who can gain respect and obedience only by holding enough power to command it live with the constant anxiety of losing it."[33]

Make no mistake. The Bible teaches wives to honor their husbands, but read Ephesians 5:22-30 carefully and list in the margin all the ways the New Testament segment paints a different picture than Esther 1:19-22.

Imagine being married to someone who had this inscription engraved about himself on one of his palaces: "I am Xerxes, the great king. The only king, the king of (all) countries (which speak) all kinds of languages, the king of this (entire) big and far-reaching earth—the son of King Darius, the Achaemenian, a Persian, son of a Persian, an Aryan of Aryan descent."[34]

Oh, the perils of believing your own earthly press! God exalted Jesus to the highest place and gave Him a name above all names, yet consider how differently the divine Son of God appropriates His authority over His bride.

Kings such as Xerxes saw women as objects to be displayed or dismissed on the least whim. Even when a wife was fortunate enough to retain her crown, the hope of fidelity was usually laughable. Xerxes' exploits with women are the stuff of history books, as were other bizarre actions that make one wonder what on earth drove the man. For example, once when a storm destroyed a bridge he'd had constructed across the Hellespont strait, he commanded that the body of water be given 300 lashes and that the engineers who designed it lose their heads.[35] God only knows if King Headache came up with the punishment or if it came from the seven dwarfs.

I am already captured by the story line. I hope you are too. As we spend the next eight weeks in the pages of Esther, our journey will become twice as rich as we look for certain features. Throughout each unit keep an eye out for the following repetitive concepts comprising the acrostic PURIM, and record them on the foldout chart inside the back cover.

Parties: Keep a record of every banquet, festival, or dinner party (public or private) in the Book of Esther and a brief synopsis of who attended and what happened. As we wrap up Esther 1, you already have several to note.

Unknowns: Record every instance when something is hidden or concealed, whether temporarily or permanently, in the Book of Esther. One of the most profound examples of something hidden in Esther is the hand of God, but as you keep watch you'll discover many more unknowns or concealments. (Hint: Keep an eye out for hidden identities and schemes!)

Rescues: Note every time a rescue of any kind—obvious or inferred— takes place in the chapters of Esther.

Purim =

Parties

Unknowns

Rescues

Ironies

or

Moments

Ironies: Ironies are sprinkled all over the story line. In fact, you don't have to wait until the next chapter. You should already have at least one irony to record: Xerxes commanded other husbands to do what he could not.

Moments: The Book of Esther is filled with single moments that may seem isolated and independent at the time but end up profoundly impacting destinies. These "moments" occur whenever a decision, encounter, or action becomes pivotal in the story line.

Watch for moments that have lasting impact in the study of Esther and record them under the acrostic, but not only as a study tool. Let them awaken you to moments in your own life that may have seemed unconnected to anything God was doing at the time but ended up crucial in your own story. Before our study is over we'll see how God's providence is at work through a multitude of life-moments strung together on the same strand. In His faithful sovereign hands, even negative moments of decision, encounter, or action can become treacherous steppingstones toward a grand Kingdom destiny.

Each time you discover a PURIM feature in the study, please turn to the diagram of the acrostic and record the occasion under the appropriate heading. As you begin each lesson, you might jot the acrostic on the top of the page so you'll remember to be on the lookout. By the end of our study your acrostic themes will comprise a photo album illustrating Purim's truest message: the providence of God. If, in years to come, you still associate Purim with God's providence, the study of Esther found its highest purpose in you.

Please keep in mind that our acrostic exercise will be somewhat subjective. At times you may recognize a different unknown, irony, or moment from someone else taking the study. Other times the concepts may overlap. Don't feel pressured toward exact answers. The idea is to stay alert and record the features in a way that enhances your learning process. Now let's stop talking about it and start doing it. Glance back over our first week of study and see if you have any Parties, Unknowns, Rescues, Ironies, or Moments that need to be recorded under the acrostic. Take the time to fill them in now. The exercise shouldn't take long and, from now on, you'll record them as you go.

The PURIM features are also meant to have a personal effect on you. Hopefully, they will train the eyes of your heart to see how an unseen God works in similar ways in your own life experiences and remind you that He is never more present than when He seems strangely absent. That's what providence is all about.

I am elated to study the Word of God with you, sister! As the first week of our journey draws to a close, we say good-bye to Queen Vashti as quickly as we said hello. Her whirlwind "once upon a time" on the sacred page was brief but monumental. Ironically, without Vashti, we'd have no Esther. Yes, it's tough being a woman in another's shadow, but sometimes, there in the hiddenness, God builds a woman she'd never otherwise become.

Today's session introduces our protagonist and most vital supporting actor. We will use these important "first mentions" to help us draw character sketches of each based on what we know and what we also might imagine.

Part One
A Character Sketch of Mordecai

- **He was a _____** (6:10; 8:7; 9:31; 10:3; 5:13).

    "Its significance is indicated by the fact that this is the _____ _____ in the whole Old Testament that a _____ _____ of the community of Israel is named and identified by a gentilic."[1]

- **He was an _____.**

    Esther 2:6 "employs the root of the word for exile (*glh*) in four distinct constructions, lest the full measure of the Jewish plight be overlooked."[2] View the repetition in the King James Version: "Who had been _____ _____ from Jerusalem with the _____ which had been _____ _____ with Jeconiah king of Judah whom Nebuchadnezzar the king of Babylon had _____ _____."

- **He was a _____ _____ to his _____.**

Part Two

A Character Sketch of Esther

• *She was named* _____.

   This Jewish name comes from the word for "_____"

   and means "_____."[3]

• *She was* _____.

• *She was* _____ _____ *by her male* _____.

• *She was* _____.

Scenario #2

It's tough being a woman in a _____ _____

_____ is a _____.

• *She was also _____ as _____.*

   This Persian name means "_____."

   Perhaps even more significantly, "the name Esther comes from the

   verbal root in Hebrew *str,* meaning 'to _____.' "[4]

week two

A Contest for a Queen

The Book of Esther will seem to pick the scabs off some of the wounds our culture has inflicted on us, but I believe God will also use it to clean those wounds so they can heal. We'll begin to see that something far greater than beauty positioned Esther as our protagonist in this narrative.

Principal Questions

1. What specific steps were proposed in verses 3-5 toward the selection of the new queen?
2. What facts does Esther 2:5-7 tell about Mordecai and Esther?
3. Why might Mordecai have wanted Esther's Judaism kept secret?
4. What three responses from Xerxes led to Esther's queenship?
5. What happened after Queen Esther gave Mordecai credit for exposing the plot?

Day One
When His Anger Subsided

TODAY'S TREASURE

"Let the girl who pleases the king be queen instead of Vashti." Esther 2:4

The dust of Vashti's rejection settled on a kingdom with no queen and on a crown with no consort. The chatter about King Headache's humiliation moved from the marketplace to the den like a merchant weaving his way home after a workday. The shocking news lost its luster except to the women determined to milk the cow of celebrity gossip dry. The rest kept their mouths shut except to say the Persian version of "Cursed be Vashti!" for the benefit of eavesdropping husbands. After all, things had tightened up considerably since the proclamation that "every man should be ruler over his own household" (1:22).

Session 1 catapulted us into the second chapter of the intriguing Book of Esther, and no matter how you turn it, the reality is jaw-dropping. You won't likely snore your way through Bible study this week. By the end of it, though, you may be on such estrogen overload that you need to go to a football game … with no cheerleaders. Today we will begin to take the chapter apart section by section in our homework. Please read Esther 2:1-4.

When did King Xerxes "remember" Vashti (v. 1)?

Since we can be certain he hadn't forgotten his own wife, particularly in light of the prior offense, what do you think this Old Testament passage (2:1) means by "he remembered Vashti"?

Who proposed the search for a new queen (v. 2)? Choose one.

    The king's eunuch   The seven nobles
    The guards   The personal attendants

List the specific steps proposed in verses 3-5 toward the selection of the new queen: (Hint: In almost all the major Bible translations the steps will be introduced with the word "let.")

Step 1	Step 2	Step 3	Step 4

Now look back at the time reference in verse 1—literally "after these things." A good place to launch our second week is to ask *what* things? The obvious conclusion may be the events in chapter 1, but a closer look at history against the inferred time line in Esther could suggest something more.

What years of Xerxes reign are specified in the following two Scriptures?
1:3 _____   2:16 _____

Surprisingly, Xerxes didn't crown the next pretty head that came around the political corner. Four years transpired between the banishment of Vashti and the selection of the new queen. During that time Xerxes made a disastrously unsuccessful expedition to Greece, suffered naval defeat at Salamis, and was chased like a girl out of Plataea. He failed at marriage and at war, but not until the second failure did the great Xerxes appear to wake up to the first.

That Xerxes may have experienced remorse or even a hint of grief may be suggested by several elements in today's segment. The Hebrew word *remembered* implies a note of compassion, "that Ahasuerus has become melancholy in the absence of his wife and regretful of the severity of her punishment."[1]

The language of the text suggests that Xerxes "thought about what had been decreed against" Vashti. The passive verb suggests that he is transferring blame to his advisers—a habit he will manifest again.[2]

Let the Hebrew draw a word picture for you. The word translated "subsided" in Esther 2:1 is the same word translated "receded" in Genesis 8:1. Interestingly, the verse also uses the same word for "remembered."

Look up Genesis 8:1 and describe the context of the word "receded."

Receding anger often reveals different emotions.

We've all been through enormous ordeals when we were swept up in the floodwaters of anger but discovered other emotions underneath when they finally receded. Think of a specific example in your own life. What other emotions were left on the shore once the anger receded?

When Xerxes' anger subsided, regret may have washed ashore in tangled weeds of loss and loneliness. In its wake, Xerxes didn't need what 100 concubines could give him. He needed a wife, and his personal attendants knew it.

The attendants' reaction suggests that Xerxes felt pain over the loss of Vashti. They were stewards who also waited on him behind the scenes. If anyone saw Xerxes showing a weakness or shedding a tear, they did. The sight of a high and mighty man feeling low made them scramble for solutions.

If you've ever caught a shocking glimpse of vulnerability in someone who wears a tough exterior, you know how overwhelming the temptation can be to find a quick fix. When the seemingly unshakeable shakes, we're twice as shaken. That's exactly how the compassion of Xerxes' personal attendants turned into a beauty contest.

If you participated in session 1, in the margin please complete the second scenario we introduced:

The Hebrew term translated "beauty treatments" in Esther 2:3 means "cosmetics, beauty treatments, precious ointments, soaps for bathing." If you're at home right now, go into your bathroom, look in the cabinets, and make a list of as many items as you can find that fall under these categories. Don't be shy. Yours truly could win this contest hands down. If you're not at home, compile your list as soon as you are, but please don't forget! And while you're at it, have a little fun!

Don't think I'm setting you up for condemnation. I'll spare you my hypocrisy. Just this morning I used face wash, refining lotion, moisturizer, makeup primer, foundation, highlighter, bronzer, blush, frosty beige eye shadow, frosty brown eye shadow, eyeliner, mascara, lip-stain, lipstick, and lip gloss. I was thankful for every bit of it, and so was my husband.

My goal is to suggest how thoroughly and literally we've bought in. Beauty is an estimated $29 billion business in the United States annually.[3] What's more, the big bucks aren't spent just by those who could use a little help. Ironically, no one feels more pressured to look good than those who already do. You and I both know beautiful women who are so insecure that they are painful to be around.

According to Esther 2:2, what kind of women were sought out to receive these beauty treatments? Check one.

☐ Those who really needed the help.
☐ Those who were already young and beautiful.

My point exactly. We will never be beautiful enough for our Persian-like world to leave well enough alone. We'll always need more treatment.

What might be a reasonable way to handle the pressure for those of us who are neither likely to nor under spiritual conviction to throw away all our cosmetics?

Beauty treatments weren't the half of it in Xerxes' kingdom. They were a means to an unsettling end. Unfortunately, the contest conjured up by his attendants can't be claimed as an archaic insult to modern sensibilities. To picture Esther 2:2-4, flip on the television to one of those reality shows where a bachelor holds try-outs with a group of sensual women. You'll get the idea in high definition. Like it or not, the purpose of the search in Esther 2 was to gather a harem. Parts of this story fly in our female faces, but it also teaches us volumes about womanhood. Sometimes that which ignites us with indignation burns a hole through the wall to a revelation.

It's tough being a woman in a world where

_____

is a

_____.

Personal Question

> God often makes the story line flow uninterrupted—even by interjections of moral judgments.

The remainder of our lesson underscores a fact about biblical narrative. God often makes the story line flow uninterrupted—*even by interjections of moral judgments.* Please read that statement again until you really hear it. God doesn't interrupt, for example, through much of the patriarchal narratives in Genesis. I sometimes want God to push hold on a story line and boldly state His opinion concerning what just happened.

I wanted God to stop and have an in-print fit about Jacob not only having two wives but also sleeping with their maidservants. I knew God didn't sanction the action but still graced the servants' sons with His loving-kindness by accepting them as legitimate heirs. Still, I wanted to stomp my feet until I got a divine statement—if not for me, for those who were new to Bible study.

Can you think of an example when you felt something similar?

God sometimes allows our confusion to coax us into further study of the entire Word. Only by measuring actions by other Scripture can we clarify right and wrong in certain morally ambiguous narratives. That's the way God meant for the Bible to work. All Scripture is God-breathed, but different parts—such as the Law, the Prophets, Psalms, Proverbs, the Gospels, and the Epistles—have different primary purposes. Only together are they complete.

To make matters more challenging, some events remain gray to us regardless of our search through other Scriptures, leaving us without definitive ways to measure them. At those times, we might assume that God means to teach us a historical or spiritual lesson more than an ethical or moral one. Sometimes God reserves the right to tell us what happened without telling us how He reacted to it. God is so wholly secure in His own spotless integrity that He feels perfectly comfortable giving us an account of something without making Himself accountable to us. We can always rest utterly assured that God never compromises His holiness or sighs at sin.

Why am I on such a tangent over a simple beauty contest? To prepare you for a handful of mystifying events that will transpire in the Book of Esther when you and I will want our heroes to be perfect and wonder in the back of our minds if maybe they weren't. Let's just go ahead and settle the issue now. *They weren't.* Even those rare times when Scripture doesn't tell us so. And neither are we. Even at our best.

Even those most serious about their pursuit of God and godliness fail to be perfect examples all the time. That's why God is busy conforming us into the likeness of Christ alone. None of the rest of us can bear the burden of constancy. The mystery is not that an earthly hero can still be flawed and fall to cultural pressures but that God, in His mercy, chooses at times to retain only the snapshots He took when they were standing firm. Then, when students like us flip through the photo album of biblical figures, we can take those *moments,* if not their entire lives, as beautiful examples.

Day Two
Winning Favor

TODAY'S TREASURE

"The girl pleased him and won his favor." Esther 2:9

Xerxes responded to his personal assistants' proposal: "The advice appealed to the king, and he followed it" (Esth. 2:4). To recapture the context for today's lesson, think back to their proposal to the king. The contest was actually a bit unorthodox even among the Persians of the time.

Theoretically, Xerxes' search for a queen should have been limited to seven noble families. Instead, a kingdomwide search for Persia's top model ensued. Apparently the primary qualification was looking best in the crown, to put it modestly. Maybe one or two of us taking the study are young, beautiful, and nauseating enough to picture getting selected, but the rest of us—yours truly included—are having an understandably indignant reaction.

The last thing I need is more affirmation that a woman is only as valuable as she is beautiful. Or, worse yet, that she is only as valuable as she is sensual. In fact, if I didn't know where these Scriptures and this study were headed, I'm not sure I'd want to proceed. After all, don't we get enough of this kind of pressure from the world? Who needs it from a Bible study?

Stay tuned. Yes, the Book of Esther will seem to pick the scabs off some of the wounds our culture has inflicted on us, but I believe God will also use it to clean those wounds so they can heal. We'll begin to see that something far greater than beauty positioned Esther as our protagonist in this narrative. Please read Esther 2:5-9. From session 1 you will recall that we have already discussed verses 5-7. Therefore, we will complete the following activity based on those three verses, but we will save our commentary for the ones that follow.

Mordecai:

Esther:

In the margin list every fact Esther 2:5-7 tells about Mordecai and Esther.

Principal Question

You have a perfect opportunity to record at least a rescue under your PURIM acronym. In Esther 2:8 we learn that the proposal of Xerxes' attendants turned into a royal order issued throughout Persia.

Don't take the decree lightly. Imagine the rippling reaction to the news spreading across the provinces, not to mention the actual sight of numerous girls—all dressed in their best—gathered up by the commissioners because they were pretty enough or brushed off because they were not. The thought makes my skin crawl.

Signing up for a beauty contest is one thing. Being forced into one is another. This scene wasn't like Prince Charming's fairy-tale charges searching high and low for the foot that fit the glass slipper. This was a prize cattle call. For all we know, the commissioners checked the girls' teeth like a buyer would check a horse's. Still, most of the girls were probably swept up in the dreamy romance and glamour of it all.

What might have been some positive reactions to the gathering of these beauty contestants?

What do you imagine some of the negative reactions might have been?

"Many girls were *brought* to the citadel of Susa." No sign-ups. No permission slips required. The large numbers were herded like coddled cattle to the stalls of Susa, no questions asked. They were taken captive as surely as the exiles of Judah years earlier, even if some were foolish enough to be happy about it.

Many of the girls and their families were undoubtedly thrilled. After all, what more could any little girl hope for than to be a queen? Think, however, about the shattered plans of betrothed couples and the panic of parents who feared their daughters could be as disposable as Vashti. Many of them would not only lose their virginity to a man who might never call for them again but they'd also forfeit the chance to raise a normal family. I'm sorry, but it's true.

No wonder commentator Joyce Baldwin describes their estate as "more like widowhood than marriage."[4] Baldwin also presents the flip side: "The prestige of living in the royal palace was small compensation for the king's neglect, though girls with a passion for luxury could no doubt indulge it to the full."[5] Fox says the girls lived out a "plush but pointless imprisonment."[6] He depicts events that include equal opportunity injustices: "Most oppressive—is that their will, whatever it may have been, is of no interest … They are handed around, from home, to harem, to the king's bed. Their bodies belong to others, so much so that they are not even pictured as being forced. But not only girls were treated this way. Herodotus (III 92) reports that five hundred boys were taken from Babylonia and Assyria each year and castrated for service in the Persian court. Everyone's sexuality, and not only women's was at the king's disposal. The brutality of the system in this regard was thus not what we recognize as sexism."[7]

Talk about royal entitlement! Who did the king and his commissioners think they were? Breathe a deep sigh of relief if you live under a democratic rule where we're supposed to be able to exercise certain inalienable rights. Those of us who know Jesus personally live under divine rule where all us girls get to be princesses anyway. Now let's find out what happened when the girls arrived in Susa.

Those of us who know Jesus personally live under divine rule where all us girls get to be princesses.

Who was Hegai? See Esther 2:3,8-9.

What were some of his obvious responsibilities?

To our considerable relief, Hegai is not unfavorably cast in the narrative. His most important role in the story line, however, is in relation to Esther—a Jewish girl swept up in a Persian harem and forced yet again to suffer the loss of a parent. Esther 2:9 offers us two keys that begin to unlock the mysteries beneath her mere beauty. "The girl pleased him and won his favor." Circle the phrases "pleased him" and "won his favor"; then consider the implications.

That a eunuch was pleased with Esther tells us volumes, not about her sensuality but about her winsomeness. He saw something much deeper than her physical desirability. The eunuch's willingness to make haste and increase Esther's chances of being chosen conveys exactly what the text described in Esther 2:9. She'd won his favor.

Pay close attention because the description of Esther developed by these terms will be crucial. When we read in Esther 2:9 that she "won [the eunuch's] favor," the Hebrew conveys that Esther pleased Hegai and "gained" or "took" kindness.[8] Write the words *gain* and *take* in the margin, then consider the rest of the quote: "This idiom (found only in Esther) holds a suggestion of activeness in 'gaining' rather than, as the usual idiom has it, 'finding' kindness. Gaining kindness is something she is doing, rather than something being done *to* her."[9] Let's nail down this concept.

Describe the difference you picture between "finding" and "gaining" favor.

Esther neither curled up in a corner and passively received the favor of Hegai nor blended in so thoroughly that his favor would have gotten lost trying to find her. Something actively and openly exuding from her won his favor.

What do you think it was?

Among the things you just mentioned, Esther had people skills. Never underestimate the impact of God-driven, Scripture-quickened people skills even in the most uncomfortable human encounters. Despite the scowled-faced disapproval of the unbearably religious, we neither have to be carnal to be likable nor insincere to be endearing. We can love God and still be liked by people.

Our study of Esther is not meant to teach us how to work people but how to *work well* with people. It's not the only book of the Bible that affords the opportunity. Proverbs is chock-full of the how-to's of human interaction.

How do each of these examples describe a people skill?

Proverbs 16:21,23

Proverbs 29:11

> Jesus grew in
> wisdom and stature,
> and in favor with
> God and men.
>
> LUKE 2:52

Both Old and New Testament concepts of wisdom include people skills drawn from wells of godly insight, judgment, prudence, and diplomacy. Perhaps the best way to define people skills from a scriptural point of view is godly wisdom expressed through relationship. Luke 2:52 describes wisdom expressed through relationship in the life of Jesus Christ, our ultimate example.

What Christ possessed in perfect fullness, Esther must have possessed in part. From the opening images of Esther favor flows her way like ink on a thirsty page. Could the key be that she didn't demand it? Something caused her to stand out amid hundreds of beautiful, pampered girls, each trying to be prettiest.

I don't know about you, but had I been Hegai, I'd have been twice as likely to go the extra mile for a humble, likeable person who threw down her defenses and drew my favor without demanding it. As we continue to see Scripture sketch Esther's likeness, I believe we will become increasingly convinced that an integral part of her skill with people was—to risk using an old-fashioned term—her manners.

Personal Question In your own words, how would you define the term "manners"?

What are a few opposite terms?

Manners. More important than defining them, I believe God can increase our favor by refining them. Social graces become a lost art in *assert-yourself, say-what-you-think* environments where what we think is sometimes better left unsaid … and certainly unheard. One good thing about living in an increasingly crude world is that a woman with manners, even one who simply knows how to make introductions or host a gathering (stay tuned for Esth. 5), can stand out like a rare gem in a barrel of coal. God can grant her favor that a woman with a wall covered in credentials may never gain.

On the pages of Esther, you and I have an inspired and engraved invitation to pure, unadulterated graciousness. My mama told me that girls with manners RSVP.

Répondez s'il vous plaît with a *yes*.

Day Three
Preparing for the King

TODAY'S TREASURE

"Esther had not revealed her nationality and family background, because Mordecai had forbidden her to do so." Esther 2:10

In my church I am blessed to love a whole passel of girls from about four to sixteen. One of them text messaged me this morning to remind me to pray for her because she was nervous. She was on the way to her first day of high school. Though I love that she thought to remind me, she needn't have. I'd already lifted her up with joy to our Father several times in the last 12 hours. After all, being a 14-year-old girl is hard. Our ability to remember being that age, even if it was decades ago, is proof of how hard. Others of us are only a few years removed, but I imagine all of us can recall the torturous self-doubt.

Do I look good enough? Act cool enough? Will everybody be able to tell how nervous I am? Will the upper classmen think I'm stupid? Will they see my mom drop me off? Will I have time to make it from my class on the first floor to the next one on the third? Where will I sit at lunch? Of all days on earth, why does my face have to be this broken out today? Just thinking back on inner turmoil stirs up some emotions, doesn't it?

Describe an insecurity you remember having around the time you started high school:

The highest social tightrope most teenage girls walk is balancing revealing what they hope to convey and hiding what they hope to keep secret. Change the venue from a high school to a harem. Take every ounce of emphasis off academics and set it squarely on the shoulders of appearance, and you see the pressure-cooker world of the crown contestants. They couldn't have been much older than my 14-year-old friend. Granted, the average marrying age was significantly younger in ancient cultures, but the contest factor in Esther's Persia virtually cancelled out any semblance of age normalcy.

If girls today walk a tightrope, Esther and the others walked a tight *thread.* As they competed for the crown, each undoubtedly gave ample—if not obsessive—consideration to what to reveal and what to hide. In today's segment we'll discover that few of the girls could have had more to hide than Esther. Read Esther 2:10-14. Then take a good look at Today's Treasure.

> If girls today walk a tightrope, Esther and the others walked a tight thread.

Esther was not only Jewish. She was a Jewish orphan. The fact that Mordecai vehemently opposed any revelation of Esther's nationality or family background sheds important light on both elements. Let's briefly consider each.

Principal Question

Why might Mordecai have wanted her Judaism kept secret?

Why do you think he didn't want her to share her family background?

Esther's nationality and family background meant she had two biographical strikes against her. Ancient royals valued family pedigree for political alliances and future offspring or heirs to the throne. Xerxes' search beyond certain noble families was risky enough. To choose a girl with no living parent was almost unheard of. Then Mordecai's demand that she keep her Jewishness secret shines light on two important elements of our story:

(1) Prejudice against Jews was obviously already in motion in Persia.

(2) Most of the Jews were culturally assimilated enough to blend in.

That Esther actually *could* hide her Jewishness tells us something important. Probably as a means of coping in a pagan kingdom, the Israelites for all practical purposes had lost their distinctiveness. (Hint: You have a great opportunity to fill in an "Unknown" in your PURIM acronym.)

> The Israelites for all practical purposes had lost their distinctiveness.

Adherents to the law of Moses would have been utterly conspicuous in dress, speech, diet, behavior, and custom. That Mordecai and Esther were not openly distinguishable does not take away from the story. It profoundly adds to it. Many of the Jews had all but forgotten God in their daily disciplines, but He had not forgotten them. God would soon prove He'd never taken His hand off of them. They may have forgotten their identity, but He hadn't.

We're much like them. We too can become so steeped in our culture that we are almost indistinguishable from the world. We too can lose our sense of identity and forget who we are. Indeed, the fact that we *can* hide our Christianity assumes a certain amount of assimilation. I believe one of God's purposes in this journey is to help us recapture both our identity and identification as His children—not so we can be obnoxious but so we can be influential.

Personal Question

Are you going through a time of not knowing or showing your identity? We've all been there. In the margin describe a few of the circumstances that make distinctiveness a challenge in your environment:

God used Esther's anonymity—but only as a means toward a far-from-anonymous end. Christians are a spiritual city set on a hill. We are called to be the light of the world so that God can reveal the radiance of His glory through our lives. Yes, feel the weighty responsibility of it, but also feel the privilege. Christ is not ashamed of us (Heb. 2:11). What honor! What relief!

What does Esther 2:11 imply to you about Mordecai?

Esther 2:11 sketches a man worried sick about his beloved charge. Esther was out of sight but never out of mind. Perhaps in Mordecai's most hopeful moments he wondered if she might be chosen and promoted to a position of influence on behalf of the Jews. In less hopeful moments, however, he probably just wanted her to survive in one piece. Goodness knows Mordecai had reason for all sorts of torturous thoughts. The implications of Esther 2:12-14 would not be comforting to any parental figure.

What was the troubling process for each girl's try-out?

Let's look first on the bright side. In all probability, the "special foods" in verse 9 involved fattening the girls up. What a refreshing thought! Forget the spa where you pay a fortune to eat like a bird! Esther and her cohorts were under royal command to eat! The fattening foods they were served, however, were probably not the Persian version of fried chicken, mashed potatoes, and gravy. Since they were intended to enhance beauty, their meals were probably rich in olive oil and the tables spread with assortments of nuts and higher density fruits and vegetables like our bananas, avocados, and yams.

In ancient cultures and even in American culture as recently as a century ago, thinness was associated with poverty. Not fitness and certainly not glamour. Bone-thinness implied that you didn't have the money for food. The association is still prevalent in many developing countries today. Something has changed dramatically in the West over the last five or six decades to shape a "thinner is better" attitude in so many of us.

What do you think may be responsible for the paradigm shift?

The girls were given a diet intended to beautify them from the inside out and baths in spices and oil treatments to beautify them from the outside in. One commentator pointed out that the language could suggest that the maidens' bodies were subjected to a chemical bath.[10] In current terms, imagine an extravagant exfoliating treatment.

I'll never forget the first time someone gave me a gift certificate for a facial. I could hardly wait to relax and let a professional pamper my skin. Instead I felt like someone set a forest fire to my face. I thought I was having an allergic reaction. The beauty technician knew better but held an electric fan in front of my face just the same. My skin turned as red as a beet and peeled for days. I didn't know until later that the gift certificate entitled me to a "chemical peel."

I've had a number of them since and haven't enjoyed a single one. Esther and the others might have had a similar sentiment.

The part of the story in today's segment that probably bothers us most is the assembly line of girls sent to the king one night at a time. To top it off, they returned to "another part of the harem" never to see him again unless "he was pleased with her and summoned her by name."

Describe some emotions you imagine the girls experienced as they collected in the second harem.

Praise God for a King who gives a woman dignity instead of taking it.

Yes, a number of them no doubt felt hopeful and strangely honored, but I imagine many of them felt used and rejected … and rightly so. I've never competed for a king's attention, but I certainly know what a person feels like who has given herself to someone in unhealthy and ungodly conditions and ended up feeling more rejected and misused than ever.

I said something to God from my knees on my back porch this morning that I want to share with you in light of today's lesson. I thanked Him for being the kind of King who gives a woman dignity instead of taking it, a righteous King whose commands are always for our good and whose ways are always toward our wholeness.

In contrast to the gods of many world religions, our God never asks anything perverse of us. Men who please Him are not promised a harem of virgins for their sexual enjoyment when they die. Our God views women with purity, not sensuality. Maybe my perverse background makes me sensitive, but I'm a woman who needs to know those things. How about you?

As I studied for today's lesson, God brought to my mind several Scriptures that paint a beautifully contrasting picture of our King, including our vastly different preparation for His kingdom.

Isaiah 61:10

Ephesians 5:25-27

Please look up the Scriptures in the margin and list every difference you can infer between our King and Persia's king, and our experience versus the girls of Xerxes' harem.

Revelation 19:7-8,16

In stark contrast to King Xerxes, King Jesus gave Himself in greatest love for His bride so that He could *cover* us with garments of salvation and robes of righteousness. We who comprise His bride will make ourselves ready for the King through nothing less than the soul-healing pursuit of purity. And where we're going, there will be no night. No darkness at all. We will dwell in the bright, broad daylight of Christ's glorious presence.

"My salvation *and my honor* depend on God" (Ps. 62:7, emphasis mine).

Day Four
A Royal Crown on Her Head

TODAY'S TREASURE

"The king loved Esther more than all the women, and she found favor and kindness with him more than all the virgins, so that he set the royal crown on her head and made her queen instead of Vashti." Esther 2:17, NASB

When was the last time it was your turn? You know the feeling I'm talking about: when you're next. You've dreamed about it. You've longed for it. You've dreaded it. You've run from it. You're so nervous that the butterflies in your stomach have become vultures, and you can feel their claws all the way to your toes. Your life is about to change … one way or the other. It could be your best day or your worst, but it cannot be a normal day. Destiny has not come knocking at your door. It's come mauling you like a bear.

So, is your stomach churning yet? In the margin describe the memory this description conjures up for you.

Enter the world of Esther. No. Enter the *day* of Esther. Meet me in Scripture on the day a Jewish maiden was summoned from the throng. Our lesson will be longer than usual because the event is so crucial to our story line. Read Esther 2:15-17 slowly and thoughtfully. Then answer the questions that follow.

What time had come for Esther? _____
(You have a priority "moment" to record under your P.U.R.I.M. acronym.)

Glance back at verse 12. About how long had Esther waited and prepared for her presentation to the king? _____

In the margin describe the feelings you think Esther had when she realized her turn had come.

Esther 2:13 (NIV) depicts the protocol for each of the girls who appeared before the king. We are told that "_____ she wanted was _____ her." (Fill in the blanks.)

What does verse 15 tell us about Esther in stark contrast to the others?

> The point is not that Esther abstained but rather was restrained

The girls could request any extravagance to make themselves more appealing, but Esther asked for nothing. Before we jump to conclusions, Scripture doesn't say she received nothing. "Esther does not reject all beauty aids, but only avoids asking for more than she is offered. Her virtue is not abstinence from heathen luxuries but self-effacing receptivity and passivity."[11] Somehow, I'm relieved. Please tell me I can still be a godly woman who can walk acceptably before her exalted King without abstaining from some well-earned beauty aids! The point is not that Esther abstained but rather was restrained.

Still, I'm convicted. After all, no one has ever said my middle name was Restraint. How about you? Do you tend to abstain, restrain, or obtain?

Esther's relative passivity begs an answer to the obvious question: *Why?* Let's take a look at some thought-provoking perspectives.

Read each excerpt and then describe the qualities inferred and what Esther must have been like if the author was on target.

"Having mysteriously won the favor of Hegai (2:9), she wisely relies on his expertise instead of her own instincts. This too may foreshadow her deference to another older man, Mordecai, in her moment of decision (4:16). Both texts imply that she was wise and forbearing rather than impulsive, prideful, and self-destructively independent."[12]

Qualities inferred:

"This young Jewish girl is obedient to her foster father and submissive to her Persian caretaker. She wins favor not by threatening the structures of leadership (as Vashti had), but by compliance, by listening to and pleasing those under whose care she finds herself. However, the word 'won' is a subtle hint that Esther is more independent than she might appear to be."[13]

Qualities inferred:

"Apparently some of the candidates used this occasion to gratify their own personal whims in jewelry and clothes; Esther, however, was wise enough to dress according to the king's taste rather than her own. Trusting Hegai's knowledge of the king's preference in feminine attire, Esther not only made herself more appealing to the king, but she also showed herself to be humble and cooperative, two qualities conspicuously lacking in Vashti."[14]

Qualities inferred:

Based on those explanations or your own thoughtful perspective, why do you think Esther only requested what Hegai suggested?

Whatever Esther's reasoning, Scripture pictures a very unusual woman. Somehow Esther "won the favor of everyone who saw her" (v. 15). Brace yourself for a shock: That included the other women. Beloved, you and I both know that a rare woman indeed is beautiful from a male perspective and favored by other women. Females tend to be highly threatened by a woman admired by men. Throw a horde of women competing for one man in the mix and you're sitting pretty for a cat fight. A woman who can win the man *and her female peers* is in a class almost by herself. Don't start feeling intimidated and forget that Esther was flawed just as we are. She wasn't the ultimate woman, but she possessed a rare ability worthy of discussion.

Personal Question

In the margin describe what kinds of qualities a woman must possess to win the favor of other women in spite of her appeal to men.

I would love to discuss answers to questions like these with you in a small group! I could run out of ink and space with my own conjecture, but I'll offer something concise since you did. I think Esther was as likeable as she was beautiful. She had looks a man liked, but she had a demeanor that women liked. Perhaps she was endearing and befriending to the others. Maybe she refused to get her toes tangled in their back-combed hair on her climb to the top and she was humble enough to accept the advice of a eunuch. Esther managed to walk the fine line of moderation without making others feel judged because they didn't. How often have you witnessed that kind of girl?

In the tenth month of the seventh year of King Xerxes' reign, Esther was escorted to the royal residence. Let's see what happened then.

> Esther managed to walk the fine line of moderation without making others feel judged.

Principal Question

Please read Esther 2:17-18. Now meditate on the New American Standard Bible's translation of verse 17 in Today's Treasure. Esther received three responses from Xerxes that led to her queenship. What were they?

You will surely relish knowing that the Hebrew word translated "attracted to" in the New International Version means "loved" as you see in Today's Treasure. While the term in this context may or may not encompass all the romantic elements we associate with love, clearly the word contrasts the phraseology in verse 14. "Pleasing" the king was the noted qualification for a second summons. Xerxes wasn't just "pleased" with Esther. He fell for her in a way no other woman had moved him.

The New American Standard Bible also tells us Esther found favor with the king. The term is not new to us in light of our recent lesson on the God-given gift of favor. Xerxes himself may not have known exactly why he was so taken with Esther that his search through the assembly line was over. The ways of the heart are mysterious, aren't they?

We also read that Esther captured the king's kindness. The Hebrew word expresses the kind of graciousness and blessing prompted by close kinship. This brand of kindness takes place when you treat someone with the loyal partiality of family, whether or not she is blood related. Again we must ask ourselves, *Why?* Why was Esther able to capture the king's love, favor, and kindness so thoroughly? The odds against Esther were staggering.

An overriding explanation appears in Proverbs 21:1, a verse that rarely applies more perfectly. Paraphrase the verse in the margin.

God may have also used something a pagan king found surprising, maybe even refreshing. Verse 15 may imply Esther appeared less overdone and desperate than her peers.

If you were a single woman picking one of several hundred handsome guys, wouldn't you start looking for a little substance after a while? Wouldn't your respect begin to wane after the hundredth contestant tried too hard? But what if one didn't seem quite as desperate? Would you be intrigued by him?

Remember, Xerxes wasn't looking for a concubine. He was looking for a queen. He could have had a night, but he chose a wife. As you formulate your own thoughts, here's what we know: Esther swept a king off his feet and a crown off its stand. The mystery only makes the story more captivating.

OK, it's your turn. Why do you think the king chose Esther?

Get a load of the last scene recorded in verse 18. What happened?

Perhaps Xerxes had learned a lesson. If you want to guarantee your queen's attendance at a public party for important people, you better give it in her behalf and call it by her name. Esther's banquet it was. The whole kingdom celebrated its new queen with a tax-free holiday and party favors. Stories don't get better than this one.

So, here's how we'll end today's lesson while our imaginations are stirred. You are Esther. You've been tucked into your royal bed in the queen's quarters by handmaidens acting like you're their job. Your feet are killing you and, frankly, your head's a little sore from parading around all day in that crown.

You've smiled until your cheeks are sore. Met more dignitaries than you'll ever remember. You're weary to the bone, but you're too excited to sleep. Every time you close your eyes, they pop open. Unless you just had the most vivid dream of your entire life, you were crowned queen of the entire Persian Empire today. You grab your journal to write down what you feel. And this is your first paragraph ...

Day Five
An Unsung Hero

TODAY'S TREASURE

"But Mordecai found out about the plot and told Queen Esther, who in turn reported it to the king, giving credit to Mordecai." Esther 2:22

Today we'll draw our second week and second chapter of Esther to a close. I love taking a journey through a book of the Bible this slowly and deliberately. Spending an entire week on one chapter allows us to soak in the events and develop the historical characters until we feel almost like eyewitnesses.

A Scripture narrative studied in small segments is literary heaven for a people-watcher like me. I like to picture the expressions on characters' faces in pivotal scenes and explore the dynamics in an emotionally charged environment. When God captures our imaginations and ignites a spirit of wisdom and revelation within us, these kinds of explorations make the Bible the ultimate pop-up book to me. The Holy Spirit breathes life and power into Scripture causing the biblical figures to leap to their feet and come alive in brilliant color again. I absolutely love studying God's Word, and I can't think of anyone I'd rather study alongside than you. Thank you so much for the privilege.

Today's segment adds a twist of intrigue to our developing story line that doesn't fully unfold until later in the study. Please read Esther 2:19-23.

At first glance, verses 19-20 seem to have little to do with verses 21-23. Describe each segment.

Esther 2:19-20

Esther 2:21-23

Before we study a common denominator between the two segments, let's camp momentarily on the deeper development of Esther's character.

By this point in the narrative Esther had been crowned queen of Persia, yet what hadn't changed about her (v. 20)?

We have been talking about the gift of favor and reasons why we think Esther was such a lavish recipient. We've considered her people skills, her manners, her compliance, and possibly her modesty. Today note, "she continued to follow ... instructions." Oh, the favor that can come our way in a workplace or elsewhere through our simple willingness to follow instructions. Impatient and self-promoting people don't win favor this way; those who respect authority, who aren't insulted by instruction, who practice the art of truly listening, and who follow through by doing what they're asked win it.

How we take instructions has titanic implications. People who resist following an earthly authority's instructions, hedging and minimizing behind the superior's back, aren't apt to follow God's commands either, despite an insistence to the contrary. Those who don't like to be told what to do aren't any crazier about the prospect when God is the boss.

Taking instructions well can seem an unattractive way to win favor, but it eventually pays off. Our rebellious human nature makes us resistant enough to doing what we're told that over time the effort to go against the grain—to choose the excellence of Christ over the minimalism of man—will distinguish us from countless peers.

Our culture has strangely confused significance with independence and subservience with weakness. On the contrary, only a person strong in character and steadfast in spirit can follow someone else's instructions for long. Ironically, her dependability earns her double the workplace significance of those who won't risk it. If long-term persistence doesn't win the favor of an earthly supervisor, trust the God who sees and who is by no means limited to one channel of favor toward you.

Only a person strong in character and steadfast in spirit can follow someone else's instructions for long.

In the meantime, Hebrews 6:10-12 is a great help. What fitting exhortations does it give toward our present subject matter?

Now let's view the common denominator that connects the two segments in today's Scripture reading. Similar strings introducing each brief vignette tie together verses 19-20 and verses 21-23.

In verse 19 and in verse 21, where was Mordecai?

The inspired writer of Esther meant to tell us something about Mordecai's position rather than his location. Those who sat at the king's gate were official governmental employees who acted as the eyes and ears of their ruler. What the gate was physically, Mordecai and his colleagues were positionally. They provided both a boundary and a connection between the populace and the palace. One commentator suggests, "It seems likely, given the context, that Mordecai is a member of the king's secret police."[15]

If so, he did his job well. What did Mordecai find out?

How about those two names, *Bigthana* and *Teresh?* Don't they sound like mobsters? Maybe I'm just making the association because Bigthana sounds like "Big Thug" to me and "Teresh" sounds like something in a garbage can.

What were their official positions according to verse 21?

With guards like these, who needs thieves? Mordecai took the assassination threat seriously and wisely so. If he'd only been around years later when a trusted official contrived a similar conspiracy, maybe Xerxes wouldn't have been assassinated in his very own bedchambers. We've arrived at a prime opportunity to record another irony in our P.U.R.I.M. acrostic. How ironic that a Jew would be the one at the king's gate to jump to Xerxes' defense!

Mordecai's action on the king's behalf shows that a Jew can also be an excellent citizen. "Those who, in modern times, deny any Christian interest in political processes cannot have read with sensitivity the stories of Mordecai, Joseph, and Daniel. A conflict of interest indeed may come, and *has* come to many. But each of us, until it does, can take to ourselves the exhortation which in God's name the prophet Jeremiah addressed to the exiles in Babylon to 'seek the welfare of the city where I have sent you' (Jer. 29:7)."[16]

Go back to Esther 2:21-23 and trace the journey the news took from Bigthana and Teresh to King Xerxes.

Here we see bits and pieces of relationship that help us add texture and color to our historical characters. Since we know that Mordecai, upon discovering the plot, shared it with Queen Esther, the two of them clearly found ways to communicate amid their secret ethnic connection.

Can you imagine how Mordecai felt on the day of Esther's banquet as the streets turned into dance floors and royal gifts flowed like wine? How about when he was finally able to catch a glimpse of his beloved charge from a distance with a crown on her head and a queen's robes on her shoulders? Do you think Mordecai thought she looked like a little girl in dress-ups or did he suddenly jolt to the sight of a grown-up?

As parents do, Mordecai thought about Esther day and night, wondering how she was treated away from the public eye and whether or not a girl raised the way he'd brought her up could be happy in such pomp and circumstance. Then again, hadn't he handed her over to it? Pointed her to it? He was proud of her. He was worried for her. Ambitious for her. Astounded by her. She was a child to him. A queen to them. Welcome to the warring soul of the parent figure who feels he or she has lost the last illusion of control.

Personal Question In the margin describe the last time you felt conflicting emotions of protectiveness and pride over someone you love.

Our text for today not only invites us to engrave deeper dimensions into Mordecai and Esther's relationship but we also get to see the first sketches of an authentic relationship developing between Xerxes and Esther. Imagine the urgency that flooded her soul when Mordecai told her about the conspiracy. Picture her finding a way through an endless entanglement of protocol to get to Xerxes before the conspirators did. Don't forget that Bigthana and Teresh had access. Those who guarded the door could also go through the door.

I wonder if this crisis constituted the first moment when something beyond obligation or admiration stirred in Esther's heart toward Xerxes. After all, if you want to make a woman jump to her man's defense, just threaten him in some way. If you want to make her feel something for him, just make her wonder what she'd do if she lost him.

Don't think for a moment that, just because Xerxes and Esther were king and queen, they had what we consider a traditional husband and wife relationship. Nothing was normal about the way they began their life together or, as we'll soon see, how they'd sustain it. They didn't cook and clean up the kitchen together like Keith and I did last night or walk the royal canines like we did this morning. They did, however, have moments when something

While we can't consider Xerxes and Esther's relationship traditional, they did have unique moments that might be considered normal for royalty.

happened that impressed the crimson seal of the one on the other. I believe this may have been one of those moments.

When Queen Esther told the king about the plot, she gave "credit to Mordecai" (v. 22). Then, what happened according to verse 23?

Our culturally unconditioned eyes might miss an important oversight on the part of Xerxes. Though Mordecai's report was investigated and confirmed and the conspirators hanged, a reward was conspicuously overlooked. We read that a record of the events was written "in the book of the annals in the presence of the king," yet Xerxes inadvertently failed to make compensation to a man who'd saved his life.

The Greek historian "Herodotus remarks that the Persian rulers were well-known for rewarding benefactors (His. 3.139-141, 153; 5.11; 9.107). For such an act of bravery and loyalty, one could expect any number of benefits—including a significant promotion and tax exemption. *Orosangai*, as these heroes were called, were often exempted from bowing to other nobles! Although all this was recorded … in the presence of the king (v. 23), the king failed to reward him. For no apparent reason and to the king's embarrassment in chapter 6—Mordecai was passed over. Chapter 3 begins with awkward unfairness as the king promotes a rival of Mordecai's (and the king's!) instead of his true benefactor."[17]

Let the hold button flash on that last statement and your curiosity pique concerning this twist in the story line. I can't resist wondering with you if the end of chapter 2 finds Esther frustrated. Certainly she was greatly relieved that disaster was averted, but after going to great lengths to give Mordecai the credit for the revelation, Xerxes seemed to overlook him completely. Esther led that royal horse to water, but she couldn't make him drink.

Can anyone besides me relate? Has anyone except me noticed that sometimes you can force a man's ear but you can't force his hand? Sometimes I tell something to my husband for more than the benefit of his knowing. Secretly, I'm hoping to control what he's doing. At times nothing takes more discipline than giving someone information without telling them what to do with it. Test the theory for a while and see. Information served with a heaping side of personal agenda almost never turns into the meal we planned. Somehow we're left sitting at that table wondering, *What just happened?* while they're out on the golf course acting like they didn't get it. Because they didn't. Yep, it's tough being a woman.

Sometimes providence can be defined as times when God trumps your perfectly good plan with one of His own … then seems to disappear from it. Take heart, Beloved! He's right there and He's there right.

> Information served with a heaping side of personal agenda almost never turns into the meal we planned.

55

esther 3:1-5

Scenario #3

It's tough being a woman ____ ___ _____ _____.

1. _____ always has a _____.

Consider the history of these two rivals.

Mordecai,	Haman,
a _____ from the tribe of Benjamin and a descendant of _____ _____	a presumed Amalekite and descendant of _____, their king during _____ reign

The _____

instruction:

1 Samuel 15:10-23,30

The revealed

_____:

Deuteronomy 25:17-19

(Referring to Ex. 17:8-16.)

Exodus 17:16—"_____ _____ will be at war against the Amalekites from generation to generation."

2. _____ *perceives a* _____ *(2 Cor. 10:12).*

3. _____ *catches like a* _____.

• The word *Agag* is believed to be related to an Assyrian term (*agagu*) that means "to be _____, vehement, _____."[5]

• The name "Haman" sounds similar to the Hebrew word for _____ (Hebrew, *heman*).[6] (Compare Prov. 22:24-25.)

Consider the following quote

"Surely as Christians we must recognize the '_____ _____ _____' not only in our world but _____ _____."[7]

4. _____ *is* _____ *(Rom. 12:17-21).*

week three
A Raging Passion for Honor

Life sometimes isn't pretty. We aren't plastic ponies, and this isn't pretend.

No matter how we sparkle at church or Bible study, on earth we still have

pain. Instead of going ahead and feeling the pain, processing it before God,

and letting Him heal us, sometimes we opt for a trade-in.

Principal Questions

1. Mordecai did not slander, but he also did not kneel. How do we know Mordecai continued his stance?
2. Haman's shrewd rage turned into careful calculation. How did Haman choose a day for Jewish destruction?
3. Haman was obviously adept at psychological warfare. In what ways did he apply psychological tactics to get what he wanted from King Xerxes?
4. How does John 8:44 offer all the permission we could need to identify the Devil as Haman's "father"?
5. How do you picture the people of Susa reacting to the edict?

Day One
Refusing to Bow

TODAY'S TREASURE

"All the royal officials at the king's gate knelt down and paid honor to Haman, for the king had commanded this concerning him. But Mordecai would not kneel down or pay him honor." Esther 3:2

Recently I got to share the company of a darling six-year-old named Allison. She is a blessed child because all her life she's watched her mom study the Word in small-group Bible studies. Allison stole my heart when I learned she plays Bible study with her My Little Ponies®. I have a picture of the small group in action. The ponies are gathered in a semi-circle with one up front teaching the lesson. Allison wanted me to know that the one up front with the "sparkly wings" was me. I thought I recognized the extra poofy mane. Joy surged through my soul and spilled over with laughter.

Many of you are leaders of Bible studies. I am deeply grateful for your willingness to invest in those God has entrusted to you. Your labor is not in vain. God's Word really does renew minds and transform lives. Heaven alone can testify how one woman overtaken by the love of Christ can reach past her limited vision. So, small-group leader, stay the course! When the work gets hard, remember Allison. You're the one with the sparkly wings.

Our third scenario appears in the margin. It's tough being a woman in a mean world. The toughest part can be not getting mean with it. Goodness knows, we get ample opportunity. You and I are learning that we have to deal with our mean streak every time it rears its ugly head. If we don't, "mean" won't just streak. It will stick.

What spoke to you most personally about meanness in session 2?

Life sometimes isn't pretty. We aren't plastic ponies, and this isn't pretend. No matter how we sparkle at church or Bible study, on earth we still have pain. Instead of going ahead and feeling the pain, processing it before God, and letting Him heal us, sometimes we opt for a trade-in. We swap pain for anger because it's easier for a while, and, boy, can it be energizing! Soon mad turns to mean. Friends turn to enemies. And Agags turn to Hamans.

Please read Esther 3:1-4. In session 2 we studied the ancient rivalry between Jews and Amalekites. Today we'll view the segment as a whole.

Scenario 3:
It's tough being
a woman in a
mean world.

59

According to Esther 3:1-2, what two actions had King Xerxes taken as this portion of the narrative unfolds? He ...

- gave Mordecai the highest seat of honor among the nobles.
- gave Haman the highest seat of honor among the nobles.
- commanded all royal officials to kneel and pay honor to Haman.
- commanded all wives to kneel and pay honor to their husbands.

What drew attention to Mordecai? _____

God is as purposeful in what He *doesn't* reveal in His Word as in what He *does*. He doesn't tell us why Mordecai refused to bow. He may have concluded that the king was asking them, in effect, to worship Haman. If that were the case, kneeling would have been idolatrous.

Many scholars lean more heavily toward the persisting generational rivalry as the cause for Mordecai's refusal. His office at the city gate made him an insider to all sorts of information. Mordecai knew Haman's heritage. I think Mordecai saw through Haman's clever conniving and slick exterior into the malice rumbling below the surface.

I'm not sure we're ever in a more uncomfortable predicament than when we discern evil in someone who other people esteem. At no time should we be more prayerful or careful to search our own sin-driven souls.

The ramifications of a wrong or overblown judgment are enormous. In the margin describe a few things that could happen if we are wrong.

Among the ramifications on your list, you probably noted that we could find ourselves in a serious chastisement of God. I'd just as soon avoid asking for that kind of trouble. Also imagine the terrible guilt of a retraction proving insufficient. Surely we have all strongly misjudged someone.

With no names, describe a time when someone proved you wrong.

Which of the following words best describes how you felt?
- Relieved
- Shocked
- Embarrassed
- Puzzled
- Thankful
- Defensive

One reason why we must take care not to slander is because we can't control where our words will go. Humans eat gossip like frogs eat flies.

What does Proverbs 18:7-8 say about the process?

Gossip finds an easy ear because our human nature, left to itself, finds sick satisfaction in the deluded discovery that someone who seemed superior was inferior. We who have trusted Christ are partakers of a different nature (2 Pet. 1:4). If we discern something evil or suspicious, God calls us to take our concerns to Him with deepest humility, intercede earnestly, and ask Him what—if anything—we should do. Yes, Scripture tells us to expose "fruitless deeds of darkness" (Eph. 5:11), but all is conjecture until we're certain we're seeing darkness through eyes of light.

Often the matter involved is not urgent and time simply tells. If our judgment proves right, our internal reaction is the best indicator of whether or not our hearts were equally right. If we were smug, our hearts were wrong. If we were humbled and driven to our faces, our hearts were probably pure.

We see no evidence that Mordecai slandered Haman. In fact, his being the only pair of knees not to bow indicates that this man of considerable position didn't persuade others to join him in a public protest. Mordecai did not slander, but he also did not kneel. To Mordecai, Haman was a seed of evil buried in the soil of a hatred that heaped with every passing generation. Every pair of knees that hit the ground tilled the soil. With the least provocation, the seed would germinate … yet Mordecai stayed on his feet. And not just once.

> Mordecai did not slander, but he also did not kneel.

How do we know Mordecai continued his stance (Esth. 3:4)?

Principal Question

I can hardly wait to show you something. The language of the royal officials about Mordecai not bowing to Haman is strikingly close to the language of only one other verse in the Hebrew Bible.[1] Let's take a look at the verse along with its context.

Read Genesis 39:2-10. Like Mordecai, Joseph also refused to do what someone in a powerful position insisted upon. What was it?

The Hebrew wording describing how Potiphar's wife "spoke to Joseph day after day" but "he refused" is strikingly similar to Esther 3:4: "Day after day they spoke to him but he refused to comply."

Consider the two scenarios for a moment. In these references, we find two titanic temptations: giving over to illicit sexual gratification and bowing to a big ego to save our own skin. Each temptation is difficult enough to resist the first time it knocks, but keep in mind that for Joseph and Mordecai, the opportunity pounded at the fleshy gates of their souls like battering rams.

Reflect for a moment on a time when you were battered incessantly by a certain area of temptation until it was almost unbearable. If you're like me, you won't need to reach far for a

Personal Question

personal example. When was the last time you felt like an unseen enemy was trying to blast his way through your gate with the force and repetition of a battering ram? (Focus your response on when rather than what.)

Satan has a theory that he's banked his entire accuser's career on: Even the strong grow weak. True enough, but this, Beloved One, is also true: Even the weak grow strong if they set their minds to it. Take Joseph and Mordecai, for instance. How did they retain their stand so effectively that temptation's battering ram could not crash through the gates of their souls? I'll tell you what I think. Each responded out of his mind-set rather than his mood.

Joseph was a young, handsome single man. I don't think he wasn't in the mood every time Potiphar's wife made advances. After all, he didn't just walk away that last time. He ran. How did he succeed day after day?

Joseph's made-up mind was stronger than his mood. Likewise, the sight of Haman didn't just hit Mordecai the wrong way one day when he was feeling so contentious that he bucked the system and refused to bow. Even on the days when buckling his knees would have seemed easier than being harassed, Mordecai's made-up mind was stronger than his mood.

What do you think the apostle Paul meant by "set" in Colossians 3:2?

Sometimes you and I are simply out of sorts. Hormonal. Feeling carnal. Temptations come and we either cave in because we're in the mood to sin or we quick-draw from a mind-set that is stronger than our mood.

I spent years having a carnal mind-set and an occasional mood to resist temptation. You can imagine how much of the time I spent in the ditch. Praise God, He had the tenacious love to stick with me and help this chronic weakling grow stronger. To live some semblance of victory, I've had to learn to be intentional and determined about where I would "set" my mind.

We can't just depend on a good mood to get us through. After all, no one can have great hair, the right outfit, and a raise every day. But I'll tell you what we can have: a battering ram of relentless temptation … yes, day after day. We need more than a mood. We need a mind-set. Let's make a deal. I'll pray Deuteronomy 33:25 for you and you pray it for me:

> My beloved sister, may God be allowed to work such steadfastness
> of mind in you that "the bolts of your gates will be iron and bronze,
> and your strength will equal your days" (Deut. 33:25).

Day Two

The Lots of Rage and Scorn

TODAY'S TREASURE

"Having learned who Mordecai's people were, he scorned the idea of killing only Mordecai. Instead Haman looked for a way to destroy all Mordecai's people, the Jews, throughout the whole kingdom." Esther 3:6

Our previous lesson concluded with the spotlight on Mordecai's set mind and locked knees. Today our thoughts center on the chain reaction that followed his refusal to bow. I purposely saved comments on the fourth verse in yesterday's Scripture segment so we could view it in conjunction with today's scene.

Begin your lesson by reading Esther 3:4. What is the expressed reason why the royal officials told Haman about Mordecai?

Some people love a public fight so much they'll help book the venue. The royal officials approached Haman with the news precisely to see how he would react. Haman's distaste for the Jews appears to have been notorious among the officials since they assumed the piece of information would be inflammatory. How had they spotted his prejudice? The same way we spot the bigotries of those we work with or live around.

In the margin name a few specific ways we become aware of someone's prejudices.

Haman probably made remarks and stereotyped the Jews behind their backs. If he was like most bigots, he made fun of them when he was in a good mood and railed and raged about them when he wasn't. One thing seems clear: He had aired his opinion often enough for the officials to look for a reaction when he learned that the one person who wouldn't bow was a Jew. Haman was like a powder keg, but the officials' pressure for a reaction struck the match.

Have you ever felt compelled to react more dramatically to a situation because certain people were watching? Describe such an occasion.

I have enough problems not overreacting. The last thing I need is for someone to goad me into it. You too? Then let's start resisting the bait when we're feeling set up by people who are looking for vicarious drama. If the royal officials were looking for a reaction from Haman, they certainly got it.

Read Esther 3:5-6. What idea did Haman scorn?

The same question occurs to me over and over: What on earth makes a person think he or she has the right to take thousands, hundreds of thousands, or even millions of human lives?

How might any of history's dictators have answered that question?

Do you remember the third scenario we introduced in our last session? Fill in the blank accordingly:
It's tough being a woman _____.

I suggested in session 2 that the most disturbing part of living in a mean world is the people that make it mean. Circumstances may be hard, but "mean" requires a personality.

The harrowing twentieth century has come and gone, taking to its grave many of the dictators who laced their legacies with lethal poisons. Before we kid ourselves into thinking the world won't soon see another century with such wholesale slaughter, consider Christ's warning that religious persecution, wickedness, and war will only increase with the passage of time (Matt. 24:9-12).

Even now I shudder to think what our Christian brothers and sisters in North Korea are enduring while we sip coffee and turn the pages of our Bible studies. I'd despair without the assurance of Scripture that God sees injustice and suffering and will avenge the lives of His children.

"Hamans" have splattered trails of innocent blood all over history. None, however, contrived a more complete attack than the enemy of the Jews in the era of Queen Esther. He planned a holocaust in the most literal sense of the word. The term actually means *burnt whole, a thorough destruction and a sacrifice consumed by fire*. Surely only the Devil himself could be pleased by such horrific human sacrifice and the flames of hell the only fire that would dare consume it.

Scholar Jon Levenson suggests that Haman was driven to this course by his "gigantic self-regard and his exaggerated fear of disgrace."[2] You and I are not "Hamans," but we've each come face-to-face with our own mean streaks. As uncomfortable as the introspection may be, let's each reflect on times we've encountered hateful sides of ourselves.

> Circumstances may be hard, but "mean" requires a personality.

Think carefully. Can you see any connection between those times and a "gigantic self-regard [and/or an] exaggerated fear of disgrace"? If so, would you be willing to explain how they connect?

This process is not meant to incite self-condemnation. Instead, it could incite healing if we're willing to let God show us where meanness originates (remember, it always has a history!) and let Him tend to us in that area of brokenness. Meanness always identifies a threat, whether it's real or imagined.

How do you think Haman felt threatened by Mordecai?

According to verse 5, what overriding emotion did Haman experience when Mordecai refused to bow?

  Embarrassment   Fear   Hatred   Rage

"The Hebrew word *hamah* (anger) is a very strong term referring to 'an inner and emotional heat which rises and is fanned to varying degrees'—to 'a burning and consuming wrath.' Within the Book of Esther the term is used six times: four times of the king (1:12, 2:1; 7:7,10) and twice of Haman (3:5; 5:9). In reference to the king, anger is seen to arise quickly and then to subside. In regards to Haman, however, anger likewise bursts into existence, but there is no specific mention of it ever subsiding. In 3:5, Haman's anger rages because of Mordecai's direct affront."[3]

Have you ever known a person who got mad and never got over it? Whenever my brothers, sisters, or I got into an emotional tailspin about something, my grandmother used to say, "You can get glad in the same clothes you got mad in!" Some people never do get glad. They simply stay mad. We don't want to be among them no matter how we've been provoked. Anger that doesn't quickly subside always ends up burning innocent people.

What insight does Ephesians 4:26-27 give concerning anger?

Haman's shrewd rage turned into careful calculation. Read Esther 3:7. How did Haman choose a day for Jewish destruction?

Principal Question

Pur is the Babylonian word for dice-shaped clay cubes inscribed with prayers for good luck rather than dots. These specially marked stones or sticks were placed in a jar or the fold of a garment and shaken until one fell out, indicating the "divinely approved" answer to the question being posed.[4]

In certain specific circumstances, God allowed Israel to practice legitimate use of prescribed lots as a means of seeking His will. This means was not the normal daily practice, however. God's ancient people sought His will overwhelmingly more often through prayer and Scripture just as we do.

In Esther 3, Haman's use of lots was a means of determining the "lucky day" upon which his evil enterprise would be most successful. He sought the timing of pagan gods working through the favor of omens.[5] As we see the timing and irony of the events that will soon unfold, Proverbs 16:33 will rise from the scroll like a giant rising from his bed to eye the plans of a gnat.

What does Proverbs 16:33 say about the lot?

On what month were the lots cast in Haman's presence (Esth. 3:7a)?

☐ Nisan   ☐ May   ☐ January   ☐ Kislev

This timing will become momentous on day 4 of our present week, so keep it tucked in the back of your mind.

Now, on which month did the lot fall (Esth. 3:7b)?

☐ Nisan   ☐ Adar   ☐ Tammuz   ☐ October

The divinely inspired writer of Esther did something significant in Esther 3:7 that we don't want to miss. Back in Esther 2:16 he referred to the timing of Esther's summons to the king by using the name for a month (Tebeth) from the Persian calendar. Here in Esther 3:7, however, the writer suddenly switched to references of months from the Hebrew calendar: "Nisan" and "Adar." Why is the swap significant? The moment the Persian calendar posed a threat to the people of God, He switched their datebook for His own.

No matter how meticulously man plans, any evil scheme waged against a child of God is sketched right before divine eyes on a sacred calendar. God created time, and no human can take it from Him or use it against Him. Time is significant to God mostly because His children who are temporarily bound by its tenets are significant to God. Every man-scheduled date subjected upon one of His children is written, not just on a doctor's calendar, a hospital's calendar, or a trial judge's calendar. It is written on God's. For each person given one year to live, trust that time is God's alone to give.

Every date on your man-contrived schedule can be a date with Christ. He'll do the driving.

Trust that time is God's alone to give.

Day Three
Brilliant Evil

TODAY'S TREASURE

"There is a certain people dispersed and scattered among the peoples ... It is not in the king's best interest to tolerate them." Esther 3:8

Regardless of planning or lot casting, all things pertaining to God's people are marked on His calendar. We begin our present lesson with our gaze on the same Scripture but this time from an earthly perspective. Review Esther 3:7.

How many months fell between the casting of the lots and the time chosen for the annihilation?   11   6   12   2

The edict was announced almost immediately, leaving the Jews and even their Persian neighbors to dread and despair over the death sentence for 11 solid months. Can you imagine? Picture yourself and your closest loved ones living in a country where one day the TV anchorman announces a new and unchangeable law: As of this moment, Christianity is not only illegal, it's also lethal. You and those you love most have 11 months to live, after which time all of you will be murdered. The kingdom is so vast that no plane, train, or boat can take you far enough to cross the border. Would those 11 months be both the *shortest* and the *longest* of your entire life?

within the first 24 hours of the announcement

The prospect is horrible, isn't it? In Robert Gordis' words, imagine "living perpetually in the shadow of imminent catastrophe."[6]

six months from the announcement

In the margin describe where you think you'd find yourself emotionally in the three time frames listed.

Haman launched psychological weapons against the Jews, and we find ourselves in the crosshairs of the same weapon in the hands of our enemy who is trying to get back at God by attacking us. Because Satan has a limited leash where believers are concerned, his most powerful tactics are psychological. Though he can't possess our minds, he profoundly and destructively influences our thoughts.

the first day of the final month

Satan's most effective tactic with yours truly has been to trap me in mental torment. As recently as today, when I kissed my daughter and grandson goodbye and watched them drive off toward their home in another city, I realized how much the Devil would relish tormenting me with fear over their safety.

He would love nothing better than to see me forfeit my joy as a grandmother by taunting me to futile speculations (Rom. 1:21).

What situation most recently tempted you toward mental torment?

That, Beloved, is psychological warfare. We must catch the Enemy in the act, call it what it is, and keep from him what he wants. The Jews in Persia during the days of Haman didn't have the New Testament strategies we possess. The prospect of walking in the shadow of violent death for 11 months was virtually unbearable. The psalmist, David, knew what walking through the valley of the shadow of death was like and yet he pledged himself to fear no evil.

In Psalm 23:4 on what basis did David withstand mental torment?

One of the most complicated dimensions of the Esther narrative is that the Diaspora Jews, so far from Jerusalem and so at home in Persia, didn't know if God was with them or not. How I praise God for 2 Timothy 2:13 that says, "If we are faithless, he will remain faithful, for he cannot disown himself." Now, let's pick up with the next Scripture segment. Please read Esther 3:8-9.

Haman was obviously adept at psychological warfare. In what ways did he apply psychological tactics to get what he wanted from King Xerxes?

Haman didn't rise to the high places because he was stupid. How terrifying to face an evil heart mingled with an exceptional mind. His accusation proceeded from truth—a people scattered through the kingdom, to half truth—customs are different, to an outright lie—shouldn't tolerate them.

Observe the clever construction of Haman's approach. First he referred to the Jews as "a certain people." "Haman omits the name to keep the king from thinking in terms of specific persons, such as Mordecai the Jew, lest he recoil from killing known individuals. Haman alludes to the Jews in vague terms, making them anonymous, indefinite, and depersonalized. It is easier to kill an abstraction than a person."[7] God calls us by name. Satan and his hordes see us as numbers, illustrated chillingly by the identification tattoos of Jews in Hitler's death camps.

The phrase "a certain people" in Esther 3:8 can also be translated "one people." Haman's phraseology insinuates: "Your empire embraces many peoples. One of them (just one; no big deal) is peculiar and dangerous."[8] Haman conveys only one accurate piece of information to Xerxes. These "certain people" were indeed "dispersed and scattered." So much so, in fact, that they lacked the solidarity to be the threat Haman painted them to be.

Ironically, the edict would be the very thing to catapult them into the unification they severely lacked.

Second, Haman suggested the Jew's customs were intolerably different. Mind you, our narrative has thus far implicated God's people as so thoroughly assimilated in their culture that Esther's Jewishness was completely indistinguishable. Truth be known, the Jews in Persia were not nearly as different in custom as their God intended them to be. The particular custom Haman found objectionable, of course, was Mordecai's self-exemption from bowing.

One of the most profound ironies is the outright lie Haman told Xerxes regarding this "people's" unwillingness to obey his laws. In Esther 2:21-23, wasn't it Mordecai who protected the king's rule rather than his own Persian guards? Still, the king couldn't afford the humiliation of a sizable rebellion if Haman was right. He'd suffered the indignities of Vashti's rebellion, two Greek defeats, and an assassination plot within his own palace.

The last statement in verse 8 was Haman's clincher, however. Whose best interest was reportedly being served? _____

What did Haman suggest was not in Xerxes' best interest to do?

The Hebrew word translated *tolerate* means *to leave alone.* The word is spelled just like the word for *to give rest or give respite.*[9] Isn't one of Satan's primary agendas to not let us enjoy the rest Christ has given us? Matthew 9:36 tells us, "When [Jesus] saw the crowds, he had compassion on them, because they were harassed and helpless, like sheep without a shepherd."

Haman made a fatal mistake when he chose to harass the Jews and make them feel like sheep without a shepherd. All the enemy of the Jews would accomplish was to stir up compassion in the heart of God toward His scattered people and point divine hatred his own direction.

God showed compassion toward His scattered people.

Read Proverbs 6:16-19. In the margin list each of the things Haman had done that the Lord "hates."

Haman could have been the poster child for the Peoples Republic for Raising Divine Ire. Consider his offer to put money in the royal treasury for rewarding the hit men (3:9). He was willing to pay, but not in the way he planned.

Haman's hope through the bribe was to appeal "to the king's need to replenish the treasure depleted by Xerxes' disastrous war with Greece."[10] Haman planned to plunder the Jews (3:14), fatten the royal treasury and, undoubtedly, his own pocket.

What was Xerxes' response to the financial offer (3:10-11)?

"Xerxes makes the gesture of turning down the offer, but before you're too impressed, consider the gesture is understood to be false. In line with his self-image as giving liberally (see, for example, 1:7-8; 5:6; 9:12), his generosity is largely a pose, for all his decisions are governed by his concern for his ego."[11]

According to verse 10, Haman received something from Xerxes far greater than money. What was it? _____

What he received was obviously more than a piece of jewelry. What do you think it represented?

Haman could have desired nothing more than Xerxes' royal ring. He was much like the wretched creature Smeagol in J.R.R. Tolkien's fictional *Lord of the Rings*. To Smeagol the ring was "the precious." It was worth everything. Worth living for. Worth killing for. In the kingdoms of antiquity, the king's ring was used exactly like his official signature on any document. To give someone your signet ring was to give him carte blanche to use your name on any legal transaction as if the person were you.

Peek ahead at Esther 8:8, but try to resist reading the surrounding context. We'll fully explore it when the time comes, but it holds a piece of information that will impact our understanding of the ring now. The verse describes the enormity of anything done with the king's signet ring.

What does Esther 8:8 say about the signet ring?

Because the king handed Haman his ring, no man would be able to undo what the Agagite—the archenemy of the Jews—was about to do. The final statement of Xerxes in the end of Esther 3:11 is the most chilling.

What did Xerxes say Haman could do with the Jews?

Who on the face of the earth can be completely trusted to do with people as they please? Such unbridled power could corrupt even the most righteous. To those already cultivating the deep seeds of evil within them, it becomes license to steal, kill, and destroy.

The enemy of the Jews was a cunning man indeed. He succeeded in doing what his father, the Devil, has most savored doing: showing someone the good of doing evil. Today's segment ends, as one commentator so aptly described, "with the smell of the gas-chambers about it."[12]

Yes, there are a number of things the Lord hates. And Haman committed nearly the whole megillah.

Day Four
Destroy, Kill, and Annihilate

TODAY'S TREASURE

"Then on the thirteenth day of the first month the royal secretaries were summoned." Esther 3:12

A little while ago I ended my morning quiet time and set aside a prayer journal filled with a concoction of thanksgivings and pleadings. I thanked God for some miracles I knew He'd performed and begged Him for several more. Just like you, I have a list of people I'm praying for who are battling cancer. Others who desperately need deliverance. Others who have stunningly received it and propel me to practically break out in a praise-dance.

I don't know exactly how God perfects plans that seem so bleak to us in process, but these two things I know: He never takes His eyes off of us or off the clock ticking over us. I am praying right now that the lesson we have before us greatly encourages you to believe both of those things today.

Sweet One, God loves you so. He is hard at work in your life, and the same eye that's on the sparrow is on the wristwatch.

As we begin today's lesson, let's recapture our context. What permission had Xerxes given Haman in Esther 3:11?

Now read Esther 3:12-14. According to verse 12, how were the documents stating the edict prepared?

Esther 3:10 tells us who could have ordered the events and how. Feel the tremendous force of verse 13. Three words were used to describe what Haman wanted done with the Jews when only one would have been sufficient.

What three words were used?

Take this scene off the movie screen of your imagination and drop it into your own living room for a moment. I want you to remember these orders well when you're tempted later to feel sorry for Haman. Think for a moment of

God never takes His eyes off of us or off the clock ticking over us.

the unthinkable. Imagine that you have a brilliant maniac for an enemy. He is filled with such evil that planning your death and the deaths of your loved ones isn't enough for him. He won't be satisfied until you know what he has planned. *Word for word.*

One day you receive an envelope through certified mail. Inside is a copy of correspondence between your enemy and the hired hit man. You stare at the orders in complete disbelief. *"Destroy, kill,* and *annihilate* them—young and old, women and little children—on a single day." You and I can't even comprehend a hatred so thorough.

The threefold repetition of terms indicates something far beyond instruction. It waves the flag of furious passion, whipping the fabric with loathing and revenge. Haman's actions against the Jews were crimes of passion. Not just matters of royal housekeeping. The threat wasn't national. It was personal. *Emotional.* Like Hitler centuries later, Haman treated the Jews like animals whose lives held no intrinsic value in society.

The third word is annihilate. Offer a few synonyms from your own understanding of this term.

The Hebrew term translated "annihilate" in this verse is *abad.* Carefully read Revelation 9:11. This New Testament verse describes none other than Satan.

What is his Hebrew name in this verse? _____

Circle the part of the name that corresponds with the Hebrew term translated "annihilation."

Now, read John 10:10. Christ spoke of Satan as the "thief." What threefold agenda did Christ describe the thief as having?

Again, note the repetition of terms. Do you sense the crimes of passion driven by hatred and revenge? Our enemy seeks to steal our lives and everything of value to us. Don't miss the connection that the killers appointed by Haman were also told to plunder the goods of the Jews.

Satan's agenda is to kill and destroy anything dear to God. Satan has operated through the generations primarily through human agents. You need not even wonder if the Devil was at work in and through Haman. The tie between Haman and the Devil makes more than reasonable sense.

Read John 8:44. How does it offer all the permission we could need to identify the Devil as Haman's "father"?

The beautifully frustrating part of Satan's insatiable bloodlust is that ultimately he cannot have what he wants. In reality, he cannot destroy even one of us who belongs to God through Christ Jesus. Satan is bereft of the power he wants most. Even if he succeeded in murder, only our earthly bodies could be harmed. In a metaphorical sense, we'd simply unzip them and walk free of their encumbrance and, in perfect health and vitality, step straight into the lives we were saved to live.

Gather this into your soul: When all is said and done, Satan can't win and you can't lose.

Do those words mean anything special to you? If so, what?

God always trumps Satan. Never picture the two of them as equal but opposite authorities. Every hope and every victory the enemy thinks he has is maddeningly thwarted at the perfect time. All those centuries ago when the edict went out to the people of Persia, Satan should have known the plan would never work. His first giveaway should have been the timing.

I cannot wait to show you this. I hinted several days ago that something about the timing of the lots would be very significant, and several of you may have figured it out. The rest of us have a thrilling discovery to make together.

> Satan can't win and
> you can't lose.

Record the month when the lots were cast "in the presence of Haman" (3:7). Not the month chosen for implementation, but the month the lots were first thrown. _____

On what exact day were the royal secretaries summoned to draft the edict and dispatch the news (3:12)? _____

Read Leviticus 23:4-5. What connection do you see between the two dates?

Couriers were positioned in strategic locations to receive the royal mail and deliver it to their routes by pony express. Let the timing sink in for a moment: "The edict was written on the thirteenth of Nisan, so it began to be distributed on the fourteenth."[13]

From a divine perspective, the chronology was the furthest thing from coincidence. We have no idea how many of the seven annual feasts of Judaism were observed among the exiles of Persia. Of this we can be confident, however: If they celebrated only one, it was undoubtedly Passover. Even today very few people who count themselves Jewish are oblivious to the holiday or its significance, whether or not they commemorate it.

Picture this with me: The edict hit the provinces of Persia on exactly the day observing Jewish households were preparing their tables for Passover. The news swept across the cities and villages like wildfire. That very evening at dusk, in accordance with God's command, the fathers were to recount to their families the story of Israel's deliverance from the mighty Egyptians. They told about the terrible bondage and oppression, about Pharaoh and his arrogant unwillingness to release them, and about the 10 dreadful plagues. They also rehearsed every detail of the miraculous redemption in the ears of their wives and children, but this time no doubt choking back the tears and trying not to alarm the little ones. Celebration turned to shock and horror, but for those who were willing, perhaps also to hope.

Why today, the Jews of Persia must have wondered. *Why must we receive this terrifying news today of all days—on our own Passover?* The irony and sacrilege must have seemed at first almost unbearable. To God, however, the timing was perfect. Remember Proverbs 16:33? "The lot is cast into the lap but its every decision is from the LORD." More astonishingly, apparently so is the decision when to cast it.

What was meant to be a commemoration of a past event suddenly turned into a concert of imminent need. Decades earlier the Persian Jews had chosen not to take advantage of their deliverance under the decree of Cyrus and their permission to return to Jerusalem. They decided they liked Persian life and stayed put. Then came Haman. Maybe that's one reason God allows "Hamans" to come along in life—so we'll quit being so at home here.

Oh, the satisfaction Haman must have felt in knowing he'd spoiled the precious, peculiar feast of the people he hated with such passion. He must have smacked his lips, salivating with the words, "What perfect timing!"

"Indeed it is," God surely mused. That Passover night after the edict was posted in every province of the empire, the Jews were reminded who they were and what God had done for them.

The story of God's merciful redemption gave those who were willing a hope against hope. Could He who had delivered them from the Egyptians not also deliver them from the Persians?

You bet He can, Beloved. He who delivered you from drugs can deliver you from distraction. He who delivered you from bankruptcy can deliver you from bingeing. He who delivered you from infertility can deliver you from inconsistency. He who delivered you from the fire can deliver you from fear.

Sometimes God uses the winds of a new threat to blow the dust off a past miracle that has moved from our active file into the archives. Remember, Beloved! Remember what God has done for you! Rehearse the story again.

Find someone this week to retell it to.

Dear One, He who delivered you from a Pharaoh can deliver you from any Haman. Remember who you are.

Maybe God allows "Hamans" to come along so we'll quit being so at home here.

Day Five

A Casual Drink Over Chaos

TODAY'S TREASURE

"The king and Haman sat down to drink, but the city of Susa was bewildered." Esther 3:15

Today we drop the curtain on the third chapter of Esther, but not before we freeze the frame on a certain scene. Some scenes in movies, pictures, or in everyday life are memorable because they are entirely absurd. Take, for instance, the moment in the old movie *Junior* when Arnold Schwarzenegger, playing a pregnant man, is wheeled frantically to the labor and delivery room with a full-term belly. By that point in the movie, you've almost made the mental adjustment and accepted his delicate condition. When the baby is born, you nearly get misty-eyed. Ridiculous but hilarious.

The more serious the absurdity, however, the more disturbing the scene. Today we'll pull ourselves up to the table of two men jovially toasting a genocide. Scenes don't get more absurd than this one.

To keep our story line intact, we'll overlap today's reading with yesterday's. Please read Esther 3:13-15. What about verse 15 seems absurd?

One commentary suggests a better translation for the actions of the king and Haman: They sat down to *party*. They were "drinking—that is, partying—with its overtones of boisterousness and bawdiness"[14] while the entire city was thrown into an emotional earthquake.

In the following paragraph, circle every synonym for the Hebrew word translated "bewildered" (in Esth. 3:15).

The Hebrew word describing the reaction of the people of Susa "refers to a highly agitated, bewildered, and tumultuous state. Thus in Exodus 14:3 it refers to the agitated and bewildered state that Pharaoh attributes to the Israelites after the escape from Egypt when the desert 'hemmed them in.' In Joel 1:18 it refers to the agitated condition of cattle who have no pasture because of drought (the parallel clauses speak of the animals 'moaning' and 'suffering'). Hence, here it refers to a tumultuous and agitated state brought on by the enormity of what Haman's edict proposed."[15]

Based on these descriptions and the contexts of the other passages where the word is translated, describe how you picture the people of Susa reacting to the edict.

The commoners of Susa were appalled. Suddenly their neighbors with whom they had presumably enjoyed peace, if not friendship, were under the sentence of death. The crown had issued commands for a bloodbath.

Imagine the prospect of city streets strewn with the bodies of people they'd passed countless times. Even those who were aware and disapproving of their neighbors' ethnicity were surely a long way from wishing them (and their small children!) dead.

We've discussed a number of times how the Book of Esther paints a portrait of the Jews so well assimilated in Persian culture that many were virtually indistinguishable. Jews and non-Jews had businesses next to one another. Their children probably played together. They called one another by name.

The contrast between the palace and the populace in verse 15 "undoubtedly implies empathy with the situation of the Jewish community on the part of the inhabitants of Susa."[16]

One commentator reminds us of a very important element in the public crisis. The palace inflicted a prejudice on the population that most didn't originally—or perhaps *ever*—share. The enemies of the Jews in Esther were a small group in leadership. The Book of Esther does not present Gentiles as generally anti-Jewish or the Jews as inherently set against the populace of the host culture.[17]

What does the transfer of prejudice say to both leaders and followers?

Leaders:

Followers:

These elements considered, absorb the scene again. Spurred on by the king's command, the couriers went out, and the edict was issued in the citadel of Susa. The king and Haman sat down to drink but the city of Susa was bewildered.

The scene in Esther 3:15 isn't the only split-screen in Scripture capturing an astonishing contrast. Please read Genesis 37:12-25, focusing particularly on the final verse.

Genesis 42:21 recalls the incident and helps fill in the picture. We can draw a comparison between the scene at the cistern and Esther 3:15.

What did Haman and Xerxes have in common with Joseph's brothers?

What stark difference do you see between them?

How people can have an appetite to eat and drink when they've imposed such peril on others is completely bewildering. You and I have certainly hurt people, but if we were aware of it, our stomachs probably felt sick and our souls felt disturbed until it was settled. If we don't feel that way, we've got a much bigger problem.

What was just another day to Xerxes was a very bad day to Susa. As for Haman, one commentator says, "he already tasted the sweetness of revenge."[18] A clueless king and a cunning killer make a frightful combination.

One has the power; the other has the passion.

One has the voice; the other has the vendetta.

God alone knows what drives a person like Haman to hate and entitlement, but to be sure, Xerxes was not absolved. With flabbergasting carelessness, he approved a human slaughter without ever bothering to seek counsel or double-check the threat.

Based on these discussions and what you've gathered so far, how would you characterize each man?

King Xerxes

Haman

We've each been hurt by someone, but no one on earth has hurt us more than those who seem callous to it. We're acquainted with trying to deal with the wrongdoing of others while they go on with life, oblivious to our pain. We fight an urge to corner them in a public place and scream, "Don't you get it?" If they won't judge themselves, the fleshly part of us would gladly enlist a group to help us judge them.

esther

The situation becomes even more complicated when you sense that the very person who helped your life to fall apart wonders why you can't get it together. There's nothing quite like someone who hurt you judging you for being hurt.

Can you relate to the complexity I'm describing? If so, and without using any names, how?

Now take the scenario I just described a step further. Imagine how we'd feel about the person appearing more than unconcerned. What if the person were smug or insidious enough to celebrate our harm? One of the hardest facts of life to accept is that some people are not sorry for the anguish they've caused. The most twisted among them might even be glad.

Perhaps we've all watched a television interview of a convicted killer or abuser who seemed maddeningly void of remorse. As if the crime weren't bad enough, he or she had the gall not even to be sorry. Like the "hypocritical liars" described in 1 Timothy 4:2, some people's "consciences have been seared as with a hot iron." The heart can grow so hard that it no longer feels. It becomes callous. *Seared.*

Let's learn to be thankful every time we feel sorry for even our smallest offense toward someone. God designed conviction to be uncomfortable so that we'd hurry to repentance and find relief in restoration. Feeling is a good thing, Beloved. Nothing is more frightening than a seared conscience. No doubt, Haman owned one.

I don't know if this is our first Bible study together or if you and I have taken several journeys through God's Word. God has used each study intensely to work on my own broken mind and heart, to equip me, and to lead me on my way. These haven't just been curriculum to me. They've been relationship. Dialogue. Pilgrimage. Transformation. Exhilaration. And healing pain.

If you named any of 12 titles of previous studies, I could tell you off the top of my head a dozen enormous truths God sowed into my personal life amid those pages. Today's lesson stirs up images in my mind of God's role that became most precious to me in the study of Daniel.

Nothing is more frightening than a seared conscience.

What title for God appears in Daniel 7:9-10?

"The _____ of _____."

Consider the context closely. Where does He appear to be? Circle one.

A courtroom   A dining room   A work room

Daniel 7:9-10 depicts God as Judge on a throne flaming with fire. For every time an earthly judge misjudges, a guilty person goes unpunished, or a sentence woefully insults the victim, there is the Ancient of Days. For every time a Hitler starves millions of people to death and then takes the easy way out, there is the Ancient of Days.

The last thing I have in mind is to encourage vindictiveness or discourage mercy. I believe to the marrow of my bones, however, that a soul has a health-need to know that justice will be served. Thankfully, by an all-knowing, all-wise God, we have just such assurance. His name, "the Ancient of Days," implies that the same judge who sat on the bench the day the wrong was committed will be sitting on the bench the day of sentencing.

Write your own paraphrase of Hebrews 4:13.

> The same judge who sat on the bench the day the wrong was committed will be sitting on the bench the day of sentencing.

Even if every Haman succeeded in his evil plan, he will not succeed in missing his court date. No one who refuses the payment of the cross will jump bail in heaven even if he or she got away with murder on earth. I need to know that. I think perhaps you do too. I can think of no better way to wrap up our third week of study than with these words:

"So the 'problem,' to whose resolution the rest of the story will be dedicated … is before us. Haman son of Hammedatha, the Agagite, the enemy of the Jews, has written into Persian law the edict that all the peoples of the empire are to be ready to destroy, slay, and annihilate all the Jews, young and old, women and children, and to seize their goods as plunder, on one day, the thirteenth of the twelfth month, the month of Adar. Public violence, murder, and pillage are to be unleashed to provide vengeance for Haman's wounded pride. Given the power of Haman's position and the irrevocability of Persian law, the doom of the Jews seems sealed. Or is it? One of the major characters of our story has not appeared in this tragic act by even the most veiled or subtle allusion. Yet, unbeknownst to Haman or the king (but well-known to us!), a member of this seemingly doomed race, now occupies, incognito, the chair of the Queen of Persia. But what can one woman do, however highly placed, in the face of such odds?"[19]

What can one woman do? Perhaps you've been asking that same question over your own life.

Stick around and find out.

The Human Dilemma of Destiny

Many of the biblical figures who fulfilled their God-appointed destinies shared some of Esther's basic inner conflicts.

Consider the dilemma of destiny from a human perspective:

1. The _____ _____. Reflect on Esther 4:11b.

2. The _____ _____.

Scenario #4

It's tough being a woman _____ ___

_____-_____ _____.

3. The _____ _____.

• Remember, destiny appoints _____ but affects _____.

• The _____ of a person's destiny always demands

a revelation of the _____. Consider the wording "if you

remain silent at this time." The Hebrew word translated *silent* in this

verse can also be translated _____.

4. The _____ _____.

(See verse 14.)

"The sentence contains a figure of speech known as *aposiopesis*—a

sudden _____ _____ of what was being said or written

so that the mind is more impressed by what is _____ _____,

it being too wonderful, solemn or awful to verbalize. In English

this figure is sometimes called the 'sudden _____.' "[8]

week four
If You Remain Silent

You and I are about to have the opportunity to test how much

we believe God about who we are and the positions we hold.

Principal Questions

1. Was Mordecai the only one in such a grief-stricken condition? If not, who were the others and exactly what did they do?
2. Why do you think Mordecai refused the change of clothes?
3. Why did Esther think Mordecai was asking too much?
4. What were the consequences of not approaching the king? What were the consequences of approaching the king? Which side seems to offer the greatest risk?
5. What special significance did the fast have that you might not have thought about?

Day One
Sackcloth and Ashes

TODAY'S TREASURE

"When Mordecai learned of all that had been done, he tore his clothes, put on sackcloth and ashes, and went out into the city, wailing loudly and bitterly." Esther 4:1

No chapter holds greater significance to Esther than the one we're unfolding now. Because the events in Esther 4 provoke such crisis and catharsis, we are devoting two sessions and five days of study to it. I so hope you were able to participate in session 3 where we looked ahead to Mordecai's powerful message in Esther 4:12-14. We will revisit those passages again later in the week. Today we rewind to the beginning of the chapter and fasten our gaze on the king's gate. Please read Esther 4:1-3.

Recall the God-ordained timing. Mordecai probably woke that morning thinking of Passover, only to discover that "he and all his Jewish friends had been sentenced to die. The rope of bondage of the exile with which he had become so comfortable had now become a noose around his neck."[1]

Reflect on Esther 4:1-3. Write two headlines that might have appeared in the next morning's newspaper, one on the front page and the other on the second, had a newspaper existed in Persia in the day of Esther.

Front Page Headline:

Second Page Headline:

Thus far the Book of Esther has showcased Mordecai as a very proud and capable man. Suddenly we see him wailing loudly on the public streets of Susa and tearing at his clothing.

Think of the last time you saw someone "wailing loudly and bitterly." How did you react inside and why?

I once sat behind a well-dressed man on an airplane who wailed until all of us around him could hardly pull ourselves together. Even if we don't know the person or share the grief, we feel an urgency to quell the demonstration—for the sufferer, but also for ourselves. Such unbridled grief reminds us of our own fragility. We see someone who has lost control and fear doing the same.

If Haman wanted a reaction from Mordecai the Jew, he certainly got one. The man's heart hemorrhaged with emotion until his skin scratched with sackcloth and his hands reddened from the rips in his garments.

Principal Question

Was Mordecai the only one in such a grief-stricken condition? _____ If not, who were the others and exactly what did they do?

The ancients did not hide their grief. Mordecai, however, did more than stand in the streets and wail. He marched his grief straight to the king's gate so that he could be seen and heard by those with political power. In effect, he intended to make the news so that people—including the queen—would awaken to the horror of the king's edict. The place Mordecai demonstrated his mourning has an added layer of significance to him personally.

Glance back at Esther 2:19, 21. Where did Mordecai work? Check one.

　At the king's gate 　At the king's gallows 　At Susa's city hall

Some crises are too important for saving face. Saving lives is worth losing face every time.

Don't miss the fact that Mordecai took his demonstration of grief all the way to the place where he drew his paycheck. The men with whom he worked saw him at his worst and most vulnerable. Some crises are too important for saving face. Saving lives is worth losing face every time. When was the last time you had to risk losing face to try to save something more precious than pride?

In God's economy saving is always worth losing. Now widen the lens on the city of Susa and see again the ironies that run like rivers through the Book of Esther. Within the space of two verses, Haman and King Headache enjoyed happy hour on one side of the gate while Mordecai wailed in sackcloth and ashes on the other. While Mordecai became the face on this picture of woe, throngs of voices joined him (see Esth. 4:3).

Lean in more closely to the Scriptures and you'll discover something even more significant about the Jews' demonstration of grief. Though the individual words appear many places in the Old Testament, the exact Hebrew phrase "with fasting, weeping and wailing" in Esther 4:3 appears only in Joel 2:12. Though Joel falls after Esther in our Bible, it was undoubtedly written prior to it. Many scholars believe the reference was intentional and assumed that the readers of the Book of Esther would also be familiar with the Book of Joel. I'll show you why the connection is so significant.

Please read Joel 2:12 and fill in the space accordingly. "Even now," declares the Lord, "_____ _____ _____ with all your heart, with fasting and weeping and mourning."

"Mourning" is exactly the same Hebrew word translated "wailing" in Esther 4:3. The blanks you just filled in offer excellent insight into the actions of Mordecai and the Jews that day in Susa. They weren't just grieving. They were demonstrating their desire to do something far more proactive.

What did Mordecai and other Jews intend to do? (Review your previous fill-in-the-blank response.)

Hopefully I framed the question well enough for you to see their mourning as a covenant people returning to their God. This insight could hardly be more important. From the beginning of our journey through Esther, we established that God's name may not be in the book, but it is on it. The entire theology of the book erupts from the peculiar doctrine of divine hiddenness.

One of our goals is to search for clues of God and godly activity within this most unique of sacred scrolls. You've just stumbled onto a wonderful revelation of relationship between the Jews of Susa and their God.

The reaction showed the Jews of Persia understood their peril to be associated with their wanderings from God. They had become so worldly and so thoroughly assimilated into Persian culture that they'd lost their protective shield. God had told His people from the time of Moses that He'd protect them and fight their battles for them as long as they worshiped Him only. If they forgot Him, He would still love them but He would not shield them. Instead, He'd use their enemies to turn His people back to Him.

As prophesied, God's people disobeyed Him and eventually both the Northern and Southern Kingdoms of Israel fell into captivity. Babylonian captivity ended with the decree of Cyrus, the first ruler of the Persian Empire, but the Jews in Susa and many of Persia's provinces neither regathered nor returned to Jerusalem. They remained in the comforts of a very pagan world.

When word of the edict announcing their upcoming demise hit the streets, they suddenly realized they had sinned against God and took on the actions of repentant people wishing to return. Can you grasp the great significance?

See some associations for yourself. Read Joel 2:12-17 and in the margin record every way the segment could have applied and spoken to Mordecai and the Jews strewn throughout the Persian Empire:

What do you think the phrase "rend your heart" means?

Let's target another especially rich association between the two segments. What two words are used both in Esther 4:14 (recalling session 3) and Joel 2:14? _____ _____.

The choice of words is no accident. Remember, all Scripture is God-breathed! When Mordecai framed his question to Esther with the wording "who knows," he most certainly had the words of Joel on his mind, suggesting that Esther's royal position was the means God might use to save them from calamity.

I learned something else very intriguing about sackcloth and ashes. Ripping off his clothes and putting on sackcloth and ashes represented a kind of public undressing and then redressing in the clothing of death to demonstrate "a change in status and state." Mordecai humbled himself "by voluntarily wearing the clothing of the poor," and "dramatically presenting himself as a dead person." The act was not only a ritual identification with the dead, but "a means of deliberately lowering one's status in the eyes of the community."[2]

Sackcloth and ashes symbolized not only the Jews' poverty of spirit before the Lord but their complete deadness without Him. Their actions cried out, "We are dead without You, Lord! Stripped of everything! You alone can resurrect this lifeless people. Have mercy on us, Lord. We desire to return to You."

Haman succeeded in driving Mordecai to his knees after all but not in worship of a man. Instead, he drove him to return to the Lord. That, Beloved, is precisely why God allowed it. Praise Him for His infinite wisdom!

Personal Question

Has God ever allowed threat of trouble in your life to drive you to your knees? If so, what did you learn through the experience?

"He is gracious and compassionate, slow to anger and abounding in love, and he relents from sending calamity."

JOEL 2:13

Of all rights bestowed on us as the children of God, perhaps none exceeds the right to repent and turn back to the Lord. I do not know where I'd be without the God-given right to repent and run back, beaten and bruised, to my God. I cannot count the times I've in effect said to Him, "I am dead without you. Destitute. Come and resurrect this lifeless woman from the grave." And He has never failed to do it. As Joel 2:13 so beautifully portrays, God is "gracious and compassionate, slow to anger and abounding in love, and he relents from sending calamity."

Today's lesson is not meant to teach us to wear sackcloth and ashes and take to the public streets with our repentance; however, if that were necessary for our land's safety, many of us would humble ourselves and do it. Today's lesson is meant to teach us, in the words of the prophet Joel, to "rend [our] heart and not [our] garments" and "even now … return to [the Lord] with all [our] heart."

Bask in the New Testament answer to the two-word question proposed in Joel 2:14. "Who knows?" Beloved, because of the cross of Christ Jesus, *we* can know. Conclude today's lesson by writing Acts 3:19-20 on a note card or piece of paper you can carry with you. Then act on it and celebrate it.

Repentance is not your punishment. It's your glorious right of daughtership. Your invitation to restoration.

Day Two
Deeper Than Appearances

TODAY'S TREASURE

"When Esther's maids and eunuchs came and told her about Mordecai, she was in great distress. She sent clothes for him to put on instead of his sackcloth, but he would not accept them." Esther 4:4

Even though I knew the story line of Esther before I ever began studying for this series, I find myself thoroughly caught up in the plot, waiting to see—and somehow even feel—what's going to happen next. An in-depth approach to Scripture changes so much. The Holy Spirit ends up unearthing hidden treasures and shedding light on details that make a narrative spring to life in a way that casual reading can't. I just love it. I also love you.

Today's Scripture segment must be painted into the same landscape as yesterday's to get the full picture. For this reason, let's begin by placing Mordecai and the Jews in the scene first, describing their appearance and actions based on Esther 4:1-3 and yesterday's lesson.

In the margin try to describe the scene strictly from memory; then check the text to be thorough.

As levity and aloofness twirled like ghostly dance mates on palace floors, the streets of Persia were packed with wailing Jews lying in the dirt. A pall of sackcloth blanketed the cities with such darkness that no commoner could conduct business as usual. The royals alone could exempt themselves from care.

None was more heartbroken and afraid than the one left to wonder if the lives of his people should have been worth the bending of his proud knees to Haman. "Had I only known!" Guilt is a relentless mocker even if it's misplaced. Tearing his robes and wailing bitterly, Mordecai's grief pounded on the king's gate like a battering ram. With this backdrop vividly painted, please review Esther 4:1-3; then read verses 4-8.

Describe everything you can possibly decipher about Esther's environment based on all eight verses.

Who was the obvious "go between"? _____

Why was he necessary?

How did Esther react when she heard about Mordecai?

Why do you think Mordecai refused the change of clothes?

Our inspired narrator intended for us to feel the distance between Esther and Mordecai. Physically the two were only a gate and a walkway apart. Socially they were on different planets. We're meant to squirm under the awkwardness of Hathach's mediation and the bureaucracy that necessitated it.

The delay and relay between Esther and Mordecai doubles the drama. Together they place the scene in slow motion until we can hear the sandals of Hathach clattering down the royal halls and see the last of his robe slip through the king's gate.

We picture the eunuch trying to have a private conversation with Mordecai while thoroughly exposed in Susa's open square. Perhaps Hathach tugged on the Jew's sleeve and urged him to whisper so they would not be greatly noticed—no small feat with his charge wailing in sackcloth as he was.

Imagine what was going on in Hathach's mind as he returned to his queen with Mordecai's refusal of clothing and rebuttal of bad news. What did the eunuch have to do to memorize word-for-word the messages volleyed between them? No run-of-the-mill "he said/she said"; these were matters of state. Issues of life and death.

Picture Hathach's puzzled expressions and tense posture as he traipsed back and forth between Esther and Mordecai. Feel his rapid pulse as he pondered the prospect of relaying such highly sensitive answers. While you're at it, consider that the drama of this peculiar *tête-à-tête* had only just begun. It hits fever pitch tomorrow.

Glance again at verse 4. What two groups of people told Esther about Mordecai?

  Eunuchs   Officials   Maids   Stewards   Jews

No doubt the narrator also intended to conjure a mental picture of the busy queen's quarters. We're meant to feel the frustration and irony that the one who raised Esther can hardly reach Esther. The aides buzzed around her like bees swarming their queen and probably ended up aiding her isolation more than her person. Not everyone who protects us and works hard to please helps us. Esther had become a dangerously buffered and pampered queen.

Feel the frustration and irony that the one who raised Esther can hardly reach Esther.

We're left to assume Esther and Mordecai rarely got to be face-to-face, and although they were clearly close to one another's hearts, for five years they had been reduced primarily to secondhand correspondence. One of the intriguing elements of the scene is how Esther—genuinely distressed—responded to the report of Mordecai's public displays of grief. Consider two ways her reactions missed the mark of Mordecai's needs and how we can relate:

Attention to appearances: Esther made no inquiry into what was wrong with Mordecai until he refused the clothes. To be fair, she may have offered him the wardrobe so he could pass through the gate and speak with her. Recall that according to 4:2, "no one clothed in sackcloth was allowed to enter" the king's gate. Then again, several clues infer something different. We have to wonder why a change of clothes would have given Mordecai access he rarely had anyway. And if a simple switch in wardrobe would have enabled him to an audience with Esther, why on earth wouldn't he have accepted it?

Mordecai may have refused the clothes because he resented the trivial treatment for his condition. At our times of greatest crisis and chaos, who wants to be told that we'd feel better if we looked better? While we easily recognize the role of appearance in Esther's rise to position; we'd still be wise to meditate on the emotional trap she was in, especially in a culture where we are trained to share it. Changing her appearance had seemingly changed everything for Esther. Forget that she was already "lovely in form and features" (2:7). In her experience, beauty treatments led to royal treatment.

Don't we tend to exercise the same rationale? The thought seems reasonable that our way of getting ahead should work for anyone. Esther's deep concern for Mordecai was real, but her remedy was wrong. He needed more than a change of clothes.

A change of appearance may get us through the gate, but it can't sustain us there. Sometimes we think a relationship would improve or an opportunity would arise if the person of our concern would do something about his or her lacking appearance. While a fresh haircut, neat clothes, and smaller waist may help temporarily, if the injured heart that covered itself in a sackcloth isn't treated, it will manifest its pain elsewhere. Most of our problems are a world deeper than our appearances.

Think of another way we can try to help someone in crisis by, figuratively speaking, handing him or her something else to put on. Share it here.

Personal Question

In reality, you and I know that the favor and sovereign plan of God changed everything for Esther. Not appearances. The harem was filled with beautiful women who went through months of beauty treatments. God alone chose a Jewish orphan girl.

We've touched on Esther's attention to appearances. Now let's consider a second way she missed the mark of Mordecai's needs.

She attempted a fast fix: Esther seemed to want to fix the problem before she even heard about it. I know the feeling. Offering a quick fix to a hurting person often can be more appealing than listening at length to the depth of his or her despair.

Simply put, sometimes we'd simply rather fix it than hear it. Why might this be true?

Our human nature not only sets us up for selfishness but to feel uncomfortable and incompetent when faced with someone who needs more than we have. Esther's situation provided the biggest set-up of all. When we consider how pampered and isolated she'd been, we may see why she prescribed a superficial dressing to a mortal wound.

If people around us helped us avoid every possible unpleasantry, fixed every hangnail, and anesthetized every headache for us, we'd quit learning how to deal with difficulty. We'd forget how to cope and we'd crush under the least inconvenience. In daily living, Beloved, strength comes from muscle, and muscle develops with a workout. This is as true spiritually as physically. What we don't use, we lose. I'd like to propose that Esther may have had "rank without substance" until now, but her life was about to change … and not because of her appearance.

Reread verse 8 carefully. List everything Mordecai told Hathach to do regarding Esther.

> Strength comes from muscle, and muscle develops with a workout. This is as true spiritually as physically.

Notice Hathach was to do more than show the edict to Esther. He was told to *explain* it to her. Read her the fine print. Make sure she didn't blanket the impact with denial. Get it through her darling, crowned head. With every footfall of the eunuch to the queen's chambers, the luxury of ignorance was fleeting. Esther's superficial life was about to be shattered, and a woman much deeper than her skin was about to be unearthed. If we're blessed, the same will happen to each of us.

As painful as the process may be, that which shatters our superficiality also shatters the fetters of our fragility and frees us to walk with dignity and might to our destinies. We are not the fragile flowers we've considered ourselves to be. We, like Esther, are the warrior princesses of God.

Day Three
Without Being Summoned

TODAY'S TREASURE

"For any man or woman who approaches the king in the inner court without being summoned the king has but one law: that he be put to death." Esther 4:11

I'm too caught up in our story line to chitchat. Let's get straight to it. Our text for today is Esther 4:9-11, but rewind to verse 6 for our reading so that we can recapture the tone. Go ahead and read the portion now. Esther 4:9 tells us that "Hathach went back and reported to Esther what Mordecai had said."

What do you think his report entailed?

Picture Esther's face while Hathach brought the news. The moment he walked into her presence, she probably pressed anxiously, "Did you see him? Did you find out what is wrong? What is it? Tell me!" Recall that Mordecai stressed the importance to Hathach that he *explain* the decree to her and then express what she urgently needed to do.

Place yourself in the scene. Ask yourself some questions to experience the unfolding drama. Do you think Hathach looked the queen in the eye or looked down at the floor? What reaction do you think Esther had when Hathach mentioned Haman? Had she been suspicious of him all along? Had something about him bothered her that she couldn't put her finger on? Had she chalked it up to jealousy because he had access to the king and she didn't? Or had Haman always treated her with syrupy charm? Was she shocked by his involvement? Or did she think to herself, *I knew it! I knew he was evil!*

How do you imagine the scene?

How do you think Esther reacted when she learned her husband flippantly agreed to have an entire people annihilated? Think through these questions, keeping in mind that Hathach and Esther were flesh and blood. They shared our same complex emotions. A wave of fear brought swarms of butterflies to their stomachs too. Human souls are all sewn from the same fabric.

Definitive moments dot Esther. Her collision with the truth in these verses was one of them. Suddenly her crown gave her a splitting headache. As we reflected on this segment together, Melissa reminded me of a haunting similarity in *Schindler's List,* one of the most disturbing movies I've ever seen.

The film tells of German businessman Oskar Schindler, who, despite many flaws, emerged as a hero by saving the lives of over one thousand Polish Jews during the Holocaust. The villain in the movie is a Haman-figure if we'll ever see one. One of the most unsettling elements of the story was the shift back and forth between revelry and agony. One review describes how the Nazi commander had an opulent chateau looming above the labor camp. He staged parties where revelers could look down on the prisoners and watch as "the commandant randomly shoots helpless inmates as if taking target practice."[3]

Not unlike our narrative, a gate was all that stood between the sufferers and the partiers, between those in chaos and those in comfort. The movie transitions from the alarmingly detached to a man—as flawed and selfish as the rest—who could no longer resist his conscience. The obvious difference is that Esther's detachment wasn't a matter of conscience because she didn't know the travesty was underway. Her detachment came with her crown, but she'd unfortunately pulled it down around her eyes.

I wonder if, as a means of emotional survival, Esther convinced herself that what the king found valuable about her was most valuable indeed. Esther placed a high premium on appearances because they comprised her worth. She had to prioritize the superficial because it seemed to be all she had.

> We are wise to force ourselves to keep differentiating between simple inconveniences and authentic tribulations.

When our old priorities don't go with our new life, we either return to our old life or adopt new priorities. Have you discovered this dilemma for yourself? If so, what were the circumstances?

Most critical to today's lesson, Esther had also detached from the common man's need. We tend to detach from sights and situations that make us feel badly about ourselves—especially when we feel powerless. If we think we can't do anything about a bad situation, we'd just as soon not have to see it.

Here's the trap, however: If we distance ourselves long enough from real needs, we replace them with those that aren't. Pretense becomes the new real and suddenly a delay in the delivery of our new couch becomes a terrible upset. We are wise to force ourselves to keep differentiating between simple inconveniences and authentic tribulations. The more detached and self-absorbed we become, the more we mistake annoyances for agonies. It happens to all of us.

Personal Question   What recent inconveniences have you been tempted to treat as if they're true tribulations?

I often have to tell myself to get a grip and downsize how I've blown up a comparatively small problem. Until now Esther's daily challenges were probably proper table settings for dignitaries and finding maids who really understood her needs. With the crisis of the Jews, however, Esther had a crisis of her own ... and it was real. Through Hathach, their mediator, Mordecai had urged Esther "to go into the king's presence to beg for mercy and plead with him for her people" (v. 8).

Principal Question

Why did Esther think Mordecai was asking too much (v. 11)?

Note the hint of personal insult and injury as Esther reminded Mordecai that "all the king's officials and all the people of the royal provinces know." In other words, "Everybody with a brain wave knows what happens if you approach the king without summons! How could you suggest such a thing?"

Mordecai had asked Esther to walk through the valley of the shadow of death. If Xerxes was tired of her and ready for a new queen, he could have used her unsolicited approach as an opportunity to take her head. No one would have questioned it. Like Vashti, the masses would have agreed that disobedient Queen Esther got what she deserved.

Esther's final statement in verse 11 is very telling. How much time had passed since Xerxes had summoned her last? _____

What might this time gap have implied to you if you were Esther?

There's trouble in paradise. Apparently Esther did have a worry greater than the snag in the upholstery. Maybe five years into her marriage she feared the king's desire for her had cooled. "Whatever her fears, it seems likely that the ruthless King Xerxes will not extend the golden scepter if the queen's death would be somehow expedient to his other interests."[4]

Can you imagine having to wait to be summoned by your husband? For those of us who are married, what if, when your husband finally calls, you are commanded to drop everything and go regardless of how you feel or what you're doing? This was Esther's life. Why hadn't Xerxes called for her? Had he called for someone else instead? The Bible withholds certain answers, but we have to ask them if we're to wrestle effectively with the text.

J. G. McConville adds background to the reasons for Esther's hesitation. He explains that Persian authority demanded the inaccessibility of the king to any except those he chose to call. To infringe this etiquette was viewed as an act of treason. "To enforce the ban upon the over-bold, a squad of men armed with axes stood about the throne ready to hack them down—unless the king in his mercy extended his golden scepter to restrain them."[5]

> To stand by and do nothing out of self-preservation is to be dead already.

The queen had spoken. The case was presumably closed. Hathach, surely emotionally disheveled by now, nodded his head, turned on his heels, and left the queen's quarters, bound for the wailing man in the public square.

No doubt Esther assumed that Mordecai would accept her explanation and understand the impossibility of his request. He couldn't possibly expect his beloved little Hadassah to take such a chance with her life. Or could he?

Sometimes we fear that fighting for what is right will kill us. Then again, it occurs to us that to stand by and do nothing out of self-preservation is to be dead already.

Day Four
For Such a Time as This

TODAY'S TREASURE

"And who knows but that you have come to royal position for such a time as this?" Esther 4:14

Today we arrive at the most famous portion of the Book of Esther. If you knew only one segment of the narrative before this study, Mordecai's eloquent appeal to Esther "for such a time as this" was probably it. The segment is so vital to the narrative that we gave all of session 3 to an advanced look at it.

Now we view it in context and see what other riches God has hidden there for us. Please read Esther 4:12-14. Now that we've studied the preceding verses, we've developed a more accurate picture of the awkward mediation stringing together the two-cord dialogue between Esther and Mordecai.

Name their go-between from memory, if at all possible: _____.

When he delivered the queen's reply to Mordecai, in all likelihood both he and Esther assumed that Mordecai would concur that the risk of his request was too high. He'd see clearly that Esther could not approach the king and beg for mercy. The probability of her losing her life was too great.

To what was surely her surprise, Esther instead received such a strong and pointed response from Mordecai that we have to respect Hathach for having the courage to deliver it. Since Mordecai could not see Esther face-to-face, he intended his words to be like firm hands on her shoulders shaking the passivity out of her.

Mordecai delivered two strong points of persuasion in verses 12-14. We'll picture them as a hand on each shoulder. In the margin identify both.

Mordecai's points:

1.

2.

Let's concentrate both on what Mordecai said and implied. Notice he stated the negative implication of *inaction* followed by the positive implication of *action*. Look first at the negative implication. In Esther 4:13 Mordecai shook her with the risk she hadn't considered. "In case you've forgotten, *you* are Jewish too. If you do nothing, you and your father's family will perish."

Clines says this was not so much a threat as the other pan of the balance in which Esther's fate was being weighed. Ironically staying out of the king's presence was no less dangerous than entering it—an irony Vashti had already encountered. "One queen stays out when bidden, the other will enter when unbidden; but whereas Vashti risked only the wrath of the king, Esther risks the king's sentence of death or else a divine punishment on her and her family."[6]

Circle the phrase "the other pan of the balance."

Here's a graphic of the implied scale. I've purposely displayed it in perfect balance. Here's how I'd like you to view it: Up until verse 13, Esther had only weighed the consequences of approaching the king. She'd not considered the consequences of refusing.

Please "weigh" both risks by describing them on each side of the scale.

APPROACHING   REFUSING

Now that you see the risks on both sides, which seems weightier? On the side of the risk that weighs most, draw an arrow down. On the side of the risk that weighs less, draw an arrow up.

After Mordecai shook Esther by one shoulder, he grabbed her by the other. This time he stressed the positive implication of action: "Esther, what if you were born for this very moment? Think how unlikely your position is! What about all the events that led to your queenship! Why on earth did we stay here and not go to Jerusalem when we could? Why was Vashti deposed? Why were you the exact right age at the exact right time to be chosen for the harem?

"Why, amid so many girls, were the eunuchs so partial to you? Why did they go out of their way to help you? More astonishingly, why did the king have such favor on you? Why didn't he just make you one of his concubines? What in the world made him marry you and set the crown on your head? Hadassah! Open your eyes! Why is a Jewish woman the Queen of Persia at such a time as this? Must it not be providence? Must it not be *God?*"

We see God's providence in Esther's life because her position held such importance, but perhaps you're having trouble relating this to your life. At first, I did too. We may think Mordecai's exhortation to Esther has little relevance to us. How much do we really have in common? For starters, we're not queens, nor do many of us hold the kinds of high positions that invite an obvious parallel. Furthermore, we can't imagine the fulfillment of one comparatively insignificant destiny affecting so much or so many.

You and I are about to have the opportunity to test how much we believe God about who we are and the positions we hold.

Personal Question

Look up the following Scriptures and record what they say about you and your position if you are a follower of Jesus Christ. With each then candidly circle how you tend to apply each segment by choosing one of the four descriptions: Figuratively, spiritually, literally or I don't apply it at all. (By "spiritually" I mean the tendency to limit the application to a spiritualization that is somehow true in God-terms but not in "real" terms. The exercise will be most helpful if you're painfully honest.)

Matthew 11:11 _____
I tend to apply this Scripture ...

| Figuratively | Spiritually | Literally | Not at all |

Matthew 13:11-12 _____
I tend to apply this Scripture ...

| Figuratively | Spiritually | Literally | Not at all |

Luke 17:20-21 _____
I tend to apply this Scripture ...

| Figuratively | Spiritually | Literally | Not at all |

1 Corinthians 4:20 _____
I tend to apply this Scripture ...

| Figuratively | Spiritually | Literally | Not at all |

1 Peter 2:9 _____

I tend to apply this Scripture …

_____

Figuratively   *Spiritually*   *Literally*   *Not at all*

Revelation 1:6 _____

I tend to apply this Scripture …

_____

Figuratively   *Spiritually*   *Literally*   *Not at all*

Revelation 5:9-10 _____

I tend to apply this Scripture …

_____

Figuratively   *Spiritually*   *Literally*   *Not at all*

Beloved, absorb this with your whole heart: You are royalty. Not figurative royalty. Not just spiritual royalty. You are in the most literal sense possible the daughter of the universe's King. You have royal blood in a way that even Esther did not. The crimson bloodline of Christ flows through your veins.

For now the kingdom of God on this earth resides within you, but one day your eyes will spring open to the most brilliant reality sight can behold. The kingdom of God will surround you, complete with palace, mansions, streets, and horses. In ways incomprehensible now, you will reign there with Him. All that we now call "reality" will be a mere shadow of the vivid world we have coming. Right now you are representing the King on official business in another land, but you are no less royal than the Queen of England would be if she visited the White House. Or the Bronx. She is queen regardless of where she is and how she is treated. Her status is secure. So is yours. When she's cut, she bleeds royal blood. So do you.

Not only are you royalty but you also have been placed in your sphere of influence, regardless of the size you perceive it to be, "for such a time as this." Ecclesiastes 3:2 tells us there is "a time to be born and a time to die." God cut out those exact perimeters for you and me on the kingdom calendar so that we would be positioned on earth right now. Likewise, Acts 17:26 tells us unflinchingly that God "determined the times set for [us] and the exact places that [we] should live." You see, even your current location is part of the set-up for your kingdom destiny. As we learned in one of our earliest verses on providence in this series, in Christ "we were also chosen, having been predestined according to the plan of Him who works everything in conformity with the purpose of His will" (Eph. 1:11). These realizations should be stunning and marvelous to us, exploding our lives with significance.

The hard truth of Mordecai's exhortation to Esther also applies to us. We can refuse to walk in obedience to God or cower in fear from our calling and He will undoubtedly still accomplish His agenda. As for us, however, we will

You have royal blood in a way that even Esther did not. The crimson bloodline of Christ flows through your veins.

pass up the fulfillment of our own entire life-purpose and we—and perhaps even "our father's family"—will miss a mighty work. Frighteningly, perhaps even a mighty deliverance. One of our biggest obstacles in our most important moments "for such a time as this" is the difficulty of the destiny-serving task.

Glance back at session 3 and record scenario 4 here:

Know the feeling? So do I. Every giant-size weight drops into our laps right on schedule. None of our purposes will be fulfilled easily. All of them will require the most difficult decisions we think we can make. Decisions that we may feel will practically kill us. Then God does something miraculous and we become something we're not. That's when "who knows?" becomes "I know."

At some of the hardest times in my life, I have been able to make the more difficult choice out of pure blind-eyed, bent-kneed acceptance that it was somehow part of a greater plan. I was beaten by a conviction that throbbed relentlessly against my strong self-centeredness. As much as my flesh wanted relief, I knew that when all was said and done, I'd sit on that side of glory having much rather fulfilled my calling than served myself all the way to meaninglessness. I had to accept that I was not called to an easy life. I was called to a purposeful life.

Are you coming to some of the same conclusions? If so, what circumstances have helped you?

At strategic times of internal war I stop and ask myself, "What if this is a critical moment? What if this very thing, this very decision, is the most important piece of the puzzle comprising my purpose?"

God has profoundly used the conviction that those heightened times of decision in my toughest trials could be "make it or break it" moments in my destiny. Much like Mordecai suggested, I always knew God would accomplish His will and do what He intended, but if I made a man-ward (vs. Godward) decision, I'd be left out of a divine loop that would eventually mean everything to me.

Beloved, in the times of greatest struggle when you make the Godward decision over convenience, earthly comfort, or carnal pleasure, you too have come to a critical moment in the fulfillment of your destiny. A *defining* moment. A war is being waged over your head in the unseen realm, and a great cloud of witnesses is cheering you on. You have no idea what's at stake.

Day Five
Fast for Me

TODAY'S TREASURE

"Fast for me. Do not eat or drink for three days, night or day. I and my maids will fast as you do." Esther 4:16

Recently I've felt drawn once again to the long-winded acrostic sprawled across the pages of Psalm 119. I love its unbridled celebration of the Word. Verses 92 and 93 are among my favorites: "If your law had not been my delight, I would have perished in my affliction. I will never forget your precepts, for by them you have preserved my life."

In Melissa's old vernacular of "Amen," *true that*. Without the Word of God as my daily bread, I would honestly be buried in a pit so deep that I wouldn't recognize daylight.

I also love verse 37. "Turn my eyes away from worthless things; preserve my life according to your word." God has used the fascination He's placed in my heart for Scripture to turn my eyes from so many worthless things. The store shelves are filled with books, magazines, and movies that reinforce a warped worldview. They make you unhappy with monogamy and even unhappier with yourself in ways you cannot fix.

Many people who know how neck-deep you and I are in Bible study don't understand our affinity for it. They still picture Scripture reading like taking a beating or like swallowing a dose of terrible-tasting medicine to get over a virus. They have no idea that it just may give you one instead.

Until they get into Bible study for themselves, they can't imagine how thrilling it can be and how healthy and free their minds can feel. Think about this for a moment: Many of the women in our small-group Bible studies today tried a taste of it because they saw your joy and the impact it had on you. Praise God, a voracious love for His Word is gloriously contagious! Agree with me in prayer this moment that more and more women will catch this holy virus and never get over it.

Today we set our sights on the last three verses of Esther 4. Because this segment of Scripture has such high priority in the narrative, it will also be the focus of our next session. I hope so much you won't miss it. I've saved some of our most personal applications from these verses for the time we get to spend together in class. Until then, we have plenty to keep us occupied as we draw this week's homework to a close. Please read Esther 4:15-17.

Praise God, a voracious love for His Word is gloriously contagious!

What exhortation had Mordecai sent through Hathach to Esther in the previous verses (4:13-14)?

Based on the verses you've just read, how influential was his plea?

What had Esther decided to do?

Even though Esther would approach the king alone, she had no intention of preparing alone.

What did Esther call for? _____

What kind of fast was it? _____

What groups of people or individuals were told to participate in the fast?

The fast Esther commissioned holds chief significance for several reasons:

The contrast: The most pronounced motif in the entire Book of Esther is feasting. The chapters are practically tied together by tablecloths. Not coincidentally, this fast divides the feasts in the narrative in half, strongly implying that the remaining feasts only occur because this fast took place.

The timing: Remember, the news of the decree hit the provinces the very day the Passover celebration was intended to begin among the Jews. Feasting was the cornerstone of the entire remembrance. Only something monumental could have trumped the commanded ritual, turning its feasting into fasting. Perhaps we can best relate by imagining dreadful news on Christmas Day, calling for fasting while turkeys roast in the oven and pies cool on kitchen counters. The emotional whiplash would be brutal.

The severity: In the ancient world most fasts were either limited to daylight hours or certain foods and rarely included fasting from water. The risk of dehydration was too serious. Severe maladies often call for severe remedies, however. Perhaps most interesting is what this kind of fast would do to Esther's appearance. Remember, the harem girls were fattened up for the king, not starved into sticks.

The implication: A momentous element of the fast in Esther is the profound implication of prayer. In a book of the Bible with no mention of God, fasting indicates prayer. And prayer indicates God. After all, fasting for fasting's sake is futile. Our assumption is that Esther and the Jews of Susa went without

food so they could wholeheartedly focus their petitions before God. Their refusal to receive sustenance demonstrated their desperation to receive something much greater: deliverance.

Glance back at all four of the reasons why the fast held special significance. Name one among them that you might not have thought about and explain why.

On day 1 of this week's study we compared the scene of mourning, sackcloth, and ashes at the opening of chapter 4 with the words of Joel 2:12-17. Fill in the following blanks according to verses 15-16.

"Blow the _____ in Zion,
_____ a holy _____,
call a sacred assembly.
_____ the _____."

List every way these verses parallel Esther's actions in Esther 4:15-16.

In the whole of Israel's history, God's people were never called to fast for fasting's sake. They were called to forego food to deny all else but God. We must ask ourselves why this occasion would be any different. The following portion of Joel 2:17 describes a petition God's people were told to make as they gathered together for a holy fast: "Let them say, 'Spare your people, O LORD. Do not make your inheritance an object of scorn, a byword among the nations.' "

How closely would you say this petition echoes the one the Jews in Susa needed to make?

The parallels in Esther 4:15-17 could not be more remarkable. Perhaps they find the height of their significance in the way they etch "God" in the blanks of this unique book. Consider the words of Dr. Karen Jobes:

"Whether Esther was mindful of Joel's prophecy or not, she in effect 'blows the trumpet in Zion,' commanding Mordecai to call a fast for all the Jews of Susa, to see if the Lord may relent from sending this calamity on her people. For the first time in this story Esther identifies herself with God's people and responds to the prophetic call to repentance by joining with the Jews of Susa in this fast."[7]

God's people were never called to fast for fasting's sake. They were called to forego food to deny all else but God.

I love the imagery Dr. Jobes assigns to Esther as one blowing the trumpet. Who was less likely? We simply have no idea what God will do with even the most reluctant life. Some leap to their destinies. Others lag and loom, yet God persists, "for God's gifts and his call are irrevocable" (Rom. 11:29).

The very woman who had hidden her identity so she could live royally in Persia stood to her feet and blew the trumpet of regathering loudly for the scattered people of Zion. The shrill sound reverberated from palace walls to peasant homes until thousands of voices melded together in heavenly ascension: "Spare Your people, O LORD!" A splintered people became as one timber. She who had systematically reinvented herself returned to her roots … at the risk that she'd be buried by them.

Esther came to what many would call her "defining moment," a term purposely included in the final paragraph of your previous lesson for your meditation. Sometimes our most important moments come hand-in-hand with our willingness to reveal that we aren't really who we've seemed to be. Our protagonist was a double-minded woman who, interestingly enough, possessed a name for each side of herself. She was Hadassah, the Jewess, and Esther, the Persian. I can't imagine that any of us has persistently resisted the lure of double-mindedness.

What two names might represent your duplicity?

_____ the _____
_____ the _____

I struggled terribly in my adolescence and young adulthood with desires to be both smart and gullible. Both innocent (which I felt I'd never been) and alluring (which I felt was all I could hope to be). Both godly and deadly. Then God allowed hardship and consequence to press against me from both sides until a decision had to be made and part of me had to die. Consider these words describing Esther's dilemma and, in turn, our own: "In a crisis situation such as this, there was no neutral position. Failure to decide brings personal loss and misses the opportunity to fulfill God's purposes."[8]

Circle "failure to decide." What do those words convey to you personally?

At times nothing is more consequentially decisive than refusing to make a decision. At critical moments—even those unrecognizable at the time—failure to decide is to decide on failure. As a warring concoction of anxiety and hunger overtook her, Esther wrestled until one part of her, wounded and weary, won. She was a Jew and, ironically, her exposure would prove her a poor one. She'd mustered every ounce of her strength to side with her weakness. Though the

> Esther came to what many would call her "defining moment."

pious and pagan alike might think her a failure, she'd not be guilty of a failure to decide.

Esther would identify herself with her covenant people even if it killed her. If it didn't, life as she'd known it was dead anyway. There was no way back. She must step into the unknown known and into the hiddenness completely unhidden.

Fully exposed, only a providential force could protect her now. Xerxes' scepter was in the hand of God.

As you conclude this week's journey, let Steven Curtis Chapman's words from "Miracle of the Moment" resonate in your soul toward all you face.

There's only ONE who knows
What's really out there waiting

In all the moments yet to be
And all we need to know
Is HE'S OUT THERE WAITING

To Him the future's history
And He has given us a treasure called RIGHT NOW
And this is the only moment we can do anything about

And if it brings you tears
Then taste them as they fall
And let them soften your heart

And if it brings you laughter
Then throw your head back
And let it go, let it go

YOU GOTTA LET IT GO

Listen to your heartbeat

There's a wonder in the here and now
It's right there in front of you
And I don't want you to miss
THE MIRACLE OF THE MOMENT

Available on
Steve Curtis Chapman's
This Moment CD,
or on iTunes.com

esther 4:11-17

Part One

Our protagonist made three shifts that moved her from self-preservation to brave determination.

1. Esther had a _____.

"She [Esther] had to _____ _____ in order to do what God had created her and positioned her to do."[9]

2. Esther _____ _____ _____.

Consider general fears, then our context's specific fear:

• Facing any _____

And if _____, then _____.

Scenario #5

It's tough being a woman in the _____

_____ ____ _____.

    • Facing fear of _____

       Hebrews 2:14-15 from The Message: "By embracing death,

       taking it into himself, he destroyed the Devil's hold on death

       and freed all who _____ through life, _____ ____

       _____ ____ _____."

Recall a quote we discussed in week 3 of our homework:

    "Living perpetually in the shadow of immanent catastrophe,

    the Jew was threatened not only physically but psychologically.

    Walking in the _____ _____ _____

    was as _____ as _____."[10]

3. Esther _____ _____ _____
she was offered.

week five
A Table Set for Providence

As Haman smugly shared the king's table that night, adorned with

his royal signet ring, the Queen was conspiring against him with the

checkmate of his life. Haman had no idea that his nemesis sat across

from him at the king's table, wearing a petticoat and pouring his tea.

Principal Questions

1. With her three-day fast completed, how did Esther dress for her fateful appearance before King Xerxes?
2. Why on earth do you think Esther requested Haman's presence?
3. Why do you suppose Haman might have exercised restraint?
4. Why do you think Haman went home and threw another party?
5. Why couldn't Haman be satisfied just to have Mordecai poisoned?

Day One
The Gold Scepter

TODAY'S TREASURE

"When he saw Queen Esther standing in the court, he was pleased with her and held out to her the gold scepter that was in his hand. So Esther approached and touched the tip of the scepter." Esther 5:2

Chapter 5 rises off the page and onto the stage as Esther rises to her feet to approach the king. We will set our sights on Esther 5:1-2 in our present lesson, but let's step back several verses so we can feel the steep climb of the drama. Please read Esther 4:12–5:2.

Reflect on Esther's powerful words at the end of week 4 and complete the sentence: "And if I _____, I _____" (Esth. 4:16).

Session 4 challenged us to face our worst fears. We talked about how the enemy and our own self-destructive natures combine to taunt us with "what ifs." Once we are in Christ, Satan has no authority to destroy us, so he settles for the next best thing: *threatening* to destroy us. Based on our histories and behaviors he deduces what we ourselves are most convinced would raze us.

To the Devil, the irony is delicious: Our distrust of God tattles on us, telling our enemy exactly how to get to us. Many of us habitually rehearse, "If _____ ever happens, then I'll just _____." Our fears become like long, bony index fingers pointing at our vulnerabilities. Once Satan sees what we believe would be the end of us, he threatens and torments us with it.

Our natural human defense is to grovel before God and plead with Him not to let those things happen. Our conditional trust not only makes us an open target for enemy torment; it also positions us as negotiators and beggars before God instead of secure children who trust their lives to their faithful Father. Those times when our fears become reality we feel devastated. We think God is unfaithful, and Satan essentially gets what he wants—us to believe that life is over. Unless our belief system changes, for all practical earthly purposes, it is. After all, as a man thinks, so is he (Prov. 23:7).

Don't misunderstand. I'm a huge proponent of praying *against* what we fear and *for* the desires of our hearts. I also believe we're *free and safe* to voice our worst nightmares to God. In times of crisis and demonic attack, however, our vulnerable souls need something more. The most critical breakthrough of faith you and I could ever experience is to let God bring us to a place where

Our conditional trust positions us as negotiators and beggars before God instead of secure children.

"If _____,
then God will take care
of me."

"If _____,
then God has a plan."

"If _____,
then God desires to
accomplish something
monumental in me."

"If _____,
then God's going to
demonstrate His suffi-
ciency to me."

Personal Question

we trust Him—*period.* We don't just trust Him to let us avoid what we fear most. We determine to trust Him no matter what, even if our worst nightmare befalls us. We have no greater victory and can render Satan no harsher blow.

Remember, in the session, you filled in the "If ... then" blanks other ways. Let the statements in the margin jog your memory.

Each of those statements reverses the fiery darts of the Enemy and causes a ricochet back to his own inflated chest. Nothing about this approach is easy, and I have not begun to master it. I fear the same things you do: tragedy, loss of a loved one, debilitating disease, betrayal, and rejection.

No one welcomes suffering. Equally, no one can wholly avoid it. Though most of what we fear never happens, our lists roll out so long that some of it probably will. Our only steadfast defenses against life's certain uncertainty is unconditional trust in a Savior who loves us more than His own life.

Fill in the following "ifs" with several things you fear most and your "thens" with new conclusions reflecting the hope of Scripture:

"If _____

then _____."

"If _____

then _____."

"If I perish, then God _____."

May God plant these convictions deeper than the thorns of earthly pain can penetrate. As hard as trusting can be, living with constant fears is harder.

Principal Question

Now, let's fix the lens on Esther 5:1. With her three-day fast completed, how did Esther dress for her fateful appearance before King Xerxes?

Esther's actions were deliberate. The earthly plan that unfolds over the coming chapters will be hers. Mordecai told her what to do but not how to do it.

Fill in the concluding words of chapter 4 that are meant to wave like a flag for the changing of the guard:

"So Mordecai went away and _____ all of Esther's _____."

Esther was now in the driver's seat. She took responsibility, but she also took the reins. After three days of spiritual and mental preparation, she got prepared physically. Make no mistake. Esther's full intent was to dress for success. "Esther had no intention of being what Daisy Buchanan called 'a pretty little fool.'"[1]

Those royal robes were a power suit if you've ever seen one. Even though Mordecai told her to beg and plead with Xerxes, she did not approach the king as a beggar. Neither did she approach him as a wife alone. Clearly she appeared before Xerxes as none other than Queen of the vast Persian Empire.

Though rattled with fear and insecurity, Esther needed to be regal. Stately. Smart. She must be a force to be reckoned with. Sexy had better give way to savvy or her neck could give way to the noose. Quaking in her glass slippers, Scripture's Cinderella rose to the occasion. Based on bits and pieces of historical evidence, a handful of quotes, and blends of human nature, this is how I think the events may have then unfolded. Ready or not, the time had come:

Esther hoped the three-day fast would end with reprieve and she'd not have to approach the king, but no miracle occurred. No prophet spoke. No plague overtook the Persians.

Only time would tell if they were on their own. If they were, all the empire would know it, because God's exiting signature would be written in Jewish blood. Esther had never felt more alone. More forsaken. Ironically, a person is never less aware of divine intervention than when he or she has been chosen to render it. Sometimes God's hand is so close that it covers the eyes.

Esther's maidservants held out the pieces of her royal wardrobe. Each stared at the floor, trying to hide her fear. Before sliding the first layer over her head, Esther glanced at her frame in the mirror and marveled how quickly she'd withered with the fast. Her stomach screeched with such a war of hunger and nerves that she couldn't distinguish one from the other. For once, she was thankful for all the heavy layers of royal garb. They would muffle the sound of her stomach and amplify the size of her body.

Robes were draped delicately across her collar bone to frame a necklace of greater worth than a commoner could see in a lifetime. One of the maidservants stood atop a cushioned stool, combed and pinned Esther's raven hair until no contortion of terror could hide her beauty. Another maidservant handed the crown to the one standing on the stool. She placed it carefully on Esther's head.

Xerxes' bride looked to the mirror as the attendants stepped back. Had she not been so riddled with self-doubt, the vision would have taken her own breath away. Instead, she drew air into the deepest part of her lungs, exhaled, and nodded with intent toward the door. With every step toward the throne room, she gained a small measure of strength.

Esther paused at the entrance to the king's hall. In a few short footsteps, she'd be visible and there would be no turning back. She knew if she tarried an instant, she might run. Her attendants strode hastily to her side and fanned the train of her robes until the marble floor was blanketed with her splendor.

A hall of pillars stretched between Xerxes' throne and the entrance where Esther stood. Esther could see him now. She could also see the soldier standing guard over him holding a large sword for the rapid disposal of any unwelcome guests. Her heart pounded so furiously that her ears rang. A mixture of admiration and astonishment over her uninvited appearance caused a stir among observers. The king looked up from a document and then drew down his brow as if focus would help him fathom the sight. Only her beauty exceeded her audacity, and feeling the weight of the crowd's expectation, King Xerxes somehow found himself more intrigued than insulted.

"When he saw _____ _____ standing in the court" (5:2).

You see, the woman who stood at the opposite end of the king's hall was not just the fairest of the harem. She was the Queen of Persia … and never more fully than now. "[The king] was pleased with her" (5:2).

The Hebrew echoes the exact same phrase from 2:17 like reverberations down the airy halls. She'd done much more than receive Xerxes' favor. She'd *won* it. Crucially, the Scriptures will mark their move to the banquet, not the bedroom. Sexy had not won his favor here. God-given savvy had.

So Xerxes "held out to her the gold _____ that was in his hand. So Esther approached and _____ the tip of the scepter" (5:2).

Our scene freezes today with the tip of Esther's fingers touching the tip of Xerxes' scepter. The historical resonance of captive Israelites is riveting: "Like Moses, [Esther returned] to the court as deliverer—and during the specified time for Passover. After reclothing herself, she [took] her stand in the inner court of the palace, [faced] the king and [awaited] his response."[2]

How often does our own King hold out the scepter of His approval and though we inch forward in timid approach we choose not to reach out and touch it? Oh, that we'd receive such royal invitation even when our hearts pound within us until our ears ring! Who knows what a mighty deliverance is at hand?

How often do we choose not to reach out and touch our own King's scepter of approval?

" 'I am the Root and Offspring of David, and the bright Morning Star.' The Spirit and the bride say, 'Come!' " (Rev. 22:16-17).

Day Two
My Petition and My Request

TODAY'S TREASURE

"If it pleases the king to grant my petition and fulfill my request, let the king and Haman come tomorrow to the banquet I will prepare for them. Then I will answer the king's question." Esther 5:8

We concluded yesterday's lesson with the tip of Esther's trembling fingers on the tip of Xerxes' outstretched scepter. His guard was only a few feet from him and probably had his sword drawn, thirsty for a kill. After all, it was the highlight of a job that could otherwise tend toward monotony.

This particular day in Susa's palace, the drama was so thick the guard could have cut it with his knife. Remember, Esther's actions were illegal (4:16) and it was his job to know it. Her favor with the king by no means secured an extended scepter. In those few seconds, the king had to weigh Esther against his own ego. Could he take the chance of giving the officials grounds to conclude for a second time that the king couldn't control his wife? Intrigued and perhaps refreshed by her boldness in a world where grown men groveled to him, the King of Persia decided to risk it. Please read Esther 5:3-8.

What were Xerxes' first words to Esther after sparing her life?

I strongly suggest to you that Xerxes knew something was wrong based on her demeanor and not just her broken protocol. The Hebrew word (mah lak) translated "What is it?" is also used in the following two Scriptures.

Circle the obvious corresponding question in each reference:

"And the angel of God called to Hagar from heaven and said to her, 'What troubles you, Hagar?' " (Gen. 21:17, ESV).

"What ails you, O sea, that you flee? O Jordan, that you turn back?" (Ps. 114:5, ESV).

Both questions are translated from the same Hebrew wording in Xerxes' inquiry of Esther. We may conclude that the king asked his queen more than simply, "What is it?" He asked her what was *troubling* or *ailing* her. One scholar explains "the nuance of the idiom [is] more literally, 'What's with you?' "[3] In Hebrew, the question always implies the obvious agitation of the person asked.

Pause for a point that might encourage all of us. Esther did what she needed to do, clearly the will of God, but not as one perfectly collected and confident. In fact, if she hadn't been wearing so many layers, proper observers might have been aghast by circles of perspiration under her arms.

Beloved, do we believe that the only way to do something acceptably is to do it perfectly? Sometimes God is more aware than we of just how much He requires of us. He knows how hard it's going to be for us.

I could stop and sob with relief. I've told you before I've never conquered my nervousness over speaking or my self-doubt in writing. My heart pounds before I speak, and afterward I'm drenched to the bone with sweat. Every time I send in a manuscript, I wonder if a single word was worth hearing. Still, I persist because it appears to be God's will. Can you relate?

God has opened my eyes to the stronghold of perfectionism through loved ones who share their struggle. It's not only painful. It can be debilitating. After all, what would have happened if Esther had waited to go to the king until her hands stopped shaking and her heart stopped pounding?

Do you happen to struggle with perfectionism and perhaps could use a little ministry? Do you feel if you can't do something to perfection, you ought not bother? Do you frequently feel pressure to perform tasks that will result in applause? When you blow it, do you wait a long time before trying again? Do you feel the need to always make an "A"?

If you answered yes, why do you think this is a challenge for you?

Perfectionism is a disposition to regard anything short of perfection as being unacceptable.

Personal Question 👑 In the margin list ways a continued stronghold of perfectionism could be a severe detriment to your destiny.

I'm not suggesting we shouldn't do our best. I'm simply saying that sometimes just surviving certain tasks without falling apart *is* our best and in those times God is not ashamed of our performance. He's proud of us for fighting overwhelming human emotions to do His will. God isn't interested in our stellar performance but in our hearts. He loves our willingness and obedience despite our insecurities.

I know a dad who videos all his gifted son's athletic events and then hardly gets through the front door of their home before he sits the boy down—still covered in sweat—to view and critique his performance. The kid is in middle school, for crying out loud. Can't a touchdown still be a touchdown even if the boy tripped his way across the goal line?

Glance back at Esther 5:3-4. What did Esther request?

_____

Why on earth do you think she requested Haman's presence? Principal Question

_____

In ancient Persia, the king ordinarily dined in small gatherings like this only with his mother or queen. Haman, however, was second in power only to Xerxes and literally wore his signet ring, placing his inclusion within protocol. What makes the invitation suspect is the hidden hostility of the hostess.

I wish I could hear why you think Esther included Haman. Here are a few of my thoughts. As a woman, I believe Esther might have wanted to see and discern how unbreakable the bond was between Xerxes and Haman. She also might have wanted to look Haman in the eyes and see what they communicated. The saying "keep your friends close and your enemies closer" might also apply here. Esther also may have fully intended to expose the evil in Haman at the first banquet and never planned the second.

God chose not to give away exactly why Esther included Haman at the table. The exclusion makes the story even more intriguing.

Look at Esther 5:5-8 again. "As they were drinking wine" in verse 6 conveys more than meets the eye. The Hebrew literally means "at the banquet of wine,"[4] suggesting they were in the final course of this ancient Eastern meal. By this time, they'd fed their stomachs and the king's ego, and all the proper amenities had been observed. Only in this final course could a request properly be made to the king and, even then, only at his urging.

Think how eternally long this meal must have seemed to Esther. Imagine enduring multiple courses of an extensive meal before etiquette allowed you to ask an urgent question. Patience is not my strong suit, particularly when the matter feels pressing. I would have blurted out, "That idiot is trying to kill us!" over the first round of buffalo wings. Furthermore, after three days of fasting, my nervous stomach would have pitched a fit over rich food. Alas, perhaps that's why Esther was Esther and I was not.

During the wine course, how did Xerxes practically offer Esther carte blanche and for the second time (v. 6; compare v. 3)?

As we'll discuss in our upcoming session, the expression "up to half the kingdom" was rhetorical rather than literal, but the offer certainly conveyed the king's intention to bestow magnanimous blessing. Give careful thought to this strategic question: If the king made Esther such an extravagant offer, why didn't she take it? If he threw the door open so broadly, why didn't she walk through it? Why did Esther stall?

> Patience is not my strong suit, particularly when the matter feels pressing.

Theorize and in the margin write every reason that comes to your mind:

Some scholars think Esther was nothing less than brilliant and the evening was going exactly according to plan. Others think she retreated and thought better of the timing. Still others think she chickened out. Few scholars view the second banquet as the actual request. Almost all agree that Esther asked for a second banquet for the platform of her true petition.

One commentator explains Esther's response as an "anacoluthon,"[5] meaning a break in grammatical sequence. Here's an example "This situation is just so—I've never been angrier in all my life." The commentator concludes: "Esther began as if she were going to state her petition but then broke off and instead invited the king and Haman to another banquet … in my opinion, the clever way in which she induces the king virtually to grant her request before he knows what it is suggests that she knows full well what she is doing."[6]

He may be exactly right. On the other hand, most of the time when I break off in the middle of a sentence and abruptly start another, overexcitement has my mind ahead of my mouth. How about you? Might the anacoluthon suggest she became overanxious and redirected her initial intent?

That Scripture doesn't tell us the reason cancels out any certainty, but the possibilities are extremely intriguing, aren't they? We'll talk more about this subject in our next session. For now, however, we'll draw toward conclusion with an often-mentioned possibility that set my mind awhirl.

"Since early rabbinic times, Jewish commentators have often thought the idea is to make Ahasuerus jealous of Haman—Why should the queen be so eager to have him at her party?"[7] Fascinating theory, isn't it? And, since you and I are women, let's not be too quick to consider it far-fetched.

For what reasons might Esther want to make the king jealous?

Let's talk human nature for a moment. If I already feel threatened by someone and jealous of her, I'm going to be twice as likely to believe something negative about her and equally passionate to react. Wouldn't you? I think men would, too. That's why I'm so intrigued by this theory.

If Esther was truly in the driver's seat (and that's debatable), this may have been the very way she cleverly drove Haman to the edge of a cliff. According to Dr. Levenson, Esther "thus predisposed" the king to distrust and dislike Haman so that he'd "grant her request to do [Haman] and his hate-filled cohorts in."[8] The second banquet 24 hours later would provide just enough time for Xerxes to become suspicious and angry but not enough time for him to talk himself out of it. How's that for provocative? And we used to think Bible study was boring.

Day Three
The High and Low of Ego

TODAY'S TREASURE

"Haman went out that day happy and in high spirits. But when he saw Mordecai ..." Esther 5:9

One of the marvelous things about an in-depth study on a brief book is we get to take the time to explore more complex emotions and relationships. We also have the opportunity to search for any visible prints of God's invisible hand, a feat of no small significance in a book like Esther.

Savor the opportunity today to take the text nice and slow. Only two verses comprise our segment today. Please read Esther 5:9-10. Let's do something fun. Let's switch roles for a few minutes. You are writing today's lesson instead of me. Think about what you'd want to explore and which direction you'd take with these two verses.

What three points of application would you make for this lesson?

1.

2.

3.

What I'd give to see your three points! I so hope you did the exercise because it's meant to remind us how much the masterpiece of God's Word can say to us in a few words. Further, true engagement in Scripture necessitates you also think about a text and not just have thoughts placed in your head. When we exercise the glorious luxury of meditation, even the briefest portion can invite us to deepest thought. Sometimes *God* tells us something profound about Himself. Sometimes He tells us something profound about someone else, other times about ourselves ... like what a mess we'd be without Him.

Through years and much personal embarrassment, I've come to understand a little more about why Christ calls us to die to or deny self and follow Him. It is not because humanity is such a titanic disappointment and summarily unworthy of His love on our own. Amid all the depravity of this world, man is still God's prized creation and most valued treasure. Christ's purpose in calling us to deny ourselves is that we'd deny our selfishness, ambition, pasts, or any damaged emotions the right to cheat us of His far higher plans for us.

The masterpiece of God's Word can say much to us in a few words.

Read 2 Corinthians 4:10-11. Exactly why are we called to this thing the New Testament elsewhere calls the "crucified life"?

Any time God calls us to die, His purpose is to reveal larger life.

Listen, Beloved. God's forte is life. He's just not willing to leave things dead. A paramount theme in Esther is what God can do when we resolve to obey and "if I perish I perish." Any time He calls us to die, His purpose is to reveal larger life.

God designed the human psyche. He knows that nothing leaves us more hollow than being full of ourselves. We have no greater burden than our own egos. I'll add that we have nothing more breakable. Our present segment shows that the human ego is about as strong as a cheap balloon bouncing around in a room of sharp needles.

We, as human as Haman, can practically feel his plunge from "rapture to black anger."[9] When filled with ourselves, we are fragile people who never perch atop a mountain without our toes next to its crumbling edge. Let's go back to Esther 5:9-10 and start unpacking it piece by piece. Verse 9 begins with the time frame: "Haman went out that day."

Glance at the preceding verses. What had just happened "that day"?

What was Haman's mood as he departed the banquet?

Can you picture the full measure of Haman's ecstasy in verse 9? The words translated "happy" and "in high spirits" in the NIV are also used to describe the joy of the Israelites as they departed one of the most celebratory events in their history. After the dedication of Solomon's temple, when God filled the house with His glory, Solomon blessed the people and sent them home.

Read the account of their departure in 1 Kings 8:66. How is their mood described? _____

The Hebrew words translated "joyful and glad in heart" are the same ones translated "happy and in high spirits" in Esther 5:9. The commentary points out that, at the time of the temple dedication, truly "the Jews were at their greatest."[10] Ironically, in Esther 5:9 Haman saw himself at his greatest too. What is troublingly beyond coincidence is that the Jews were at their lowest.

Human character is never more flawed than when one person can reach his highest only when another is swept in the depths. Only the smallest person needs others flat on their backs to feel tall. Such is the driving force beneath all oppression.

As Haman smugly shared the king's table that night, adorned with his royal signet ring, the queen was conspiring against him with the checkmate of his life. God prepared a chess table before Esther in the presence of her enemy, and she'd gotten the gumption to play. The following is one of my favorite descriptions of what happened: "By seeming to honor Haman, [Esther] fattens him for the kill, for now he goes out elated at being invited to sup with the royal couple, full of his own—very transient!—importance."[11]

How had Haman been "fattened for the kill"?

Haman's spirits didn't get to enjoy the high altitude for long. What happened in verse 9 to instantly evaporate his wonderful mood?

The sight of Mordecai fully composed at the king's gate must have almost hurled Haman over the edge. We can be sure the enemy of the Jews relished the rumor that the source of his contempt was seen earlier in sackcloth and ashes, tearing his clothes, and overheard "wailing loudly and bitterly" (4:1).

The king's gate was Mordecai's workplace. Haman surely assumed the Jew had lost the esteem of his colleagues and would hardly be tolerated to return to such important employ. Yet there he was as plain as the red on Haman's face. No sight would have been less welcome than Mordecai back in one steely piece. What had changed? After all, the edict was immutable! But, you see, God's man never is. A frightening circumstance may remain exactly the same, but God's child need not.

A terrifying thing had happened while evil basked in its success: *prayer and fasting.* A godless man had no idea the well of divine power a person could access from praying knees. There abides the drink that can steady the legs of a lamb led to slaughter while a wolf howls proudly nearby.

When was the last time you should have been frightened beyond any outward composure but God stilled you and kept you from reacting?

A frightening circumstance may remain exactly the same, but God's child need not.

As one naturally given to fear, I rarely experience a more vivid manifestation of God's presence than when I ought to be quaking with terror but I'm not. Mordecai's unwillingness to bow in 5:9 recalls his refusal in 3:2, but with one huge difference. This time Mordecai not only refused to bow but even to stand. Furthermore, he also refused to show an ounce of respect or hint of fear.

Imagine Haman's astonishment that the Jew would not grovel in the wake of the death warrant he knew the vizier had signed. After all, the aroma of the king's food and the queen's fragrance still lingered on his robes! We're never more appalled that someone doesn't grasp our importance than when we ourselves are most convinced of it. Haman's "bliss is sullied by Mordecai's continued refusal to do him honour—an offence that seems all the greater to him in the light of his increased standing in his *own* eyes."[12] One reason we desperately need to know our standing in God's eyes is so we aren't consumed with high standing in our own eyes or the eyes of others.

In the margin note where, according to Ephesians 2:6, believers in Christ are positioned, and why God placed us there according to 2:7.

Our God is so wise. He honors His children but constantly determines to keep them humble. He doesn't hesitate to tell us that though this earth may scorn and mock us, we've been seated with Christ in the heavenly realms. Lest we take an ounce of credit for our lofty positions, however, He reminds us that we are there "to show the incomparable riches of his grace, expressed in his kindness to us in Christ Jesus" (Eph. 2:7). We can serve from our knees on this earth because we're seated with the King in heaven.

> We can serve from our knees on this earth because we're seated with the King in heaven.

The humble believer may feel that dwelling on our high position in the kingdom could cultivate a boastful spirit but, actually, the outcome is more likely the reverse. Knowing where we are positioned in Christ quells our deeply imbedded psychological need for self-exaltation.

Have you discovered this to be true? If so, how?

Haman was so high in his own eyes that Mordecai's unwillingness to rise was doubly appalling to him. Scripture tells us he was "filled with rage." That's one of the painful consequences of a suddenly popped ego. The balloon has been stretched and misshapen until the emptiness feels twice as cavernous.

The depleted ego looks anywhere for instant inflation. If it can't find pride, rage provides ample hot air. Interestingly, Haman somehow restrained himself from showing his anger or from taking any action at that time.

Principal Question

Can you speculate why Haman might have exercised restraint?

Don't think for a moment Haman didn't have a reaction. It will be the delectable fare of our study tomorrow. He simply managed to delay it until he walked through his front door. In all probability, he didn't want to give the officials who observed the dishonor the satisfaction of knowing he cared. Haman considered Mordecai his biggest problem but "how ironic that the queen's flattering invitation was in reality a greater threat than Mordecai's indifference."[13] Haman had no idea that his nemesis sat across from him at the king's table, wearing a petticoat and pouring his tea.

Day Four
No Satisfaction

TODAY'S TREASURE

"All this gives me no satisfaction as long as I see that Jew Mordecai sitting at the king's gate." Esther 5:13

God compiled the whole canon of Scripture to teach us about human nature as well as His nature. God's full intent is for us to view them side-by-side, but not just so we'll cower with humiliation in the light of His holiness. Our Creator unquestionably wants us to know He's God and we're not, but He also wants us to see who we were meant to be when He formed us in His image.

If we focus entirely on Scripture's disclosure of our feeble humanness, we'll either lose heart or close the book. But what would God's kingdom gain from a people who were only humiliated? What would be the reward of our existence if we were only repentant and never repaired?

Discontent with selfishness and weary of ego, we finally become willing to lose ourselves to something greater. In doing so, we find Christ as we've never known Him and, pooled in the reflection of His eyes, startle to discover that a part of ourselves resembles Him. With these thoughts in mind, let's season today's lesson from Esther with a little New Testament theology.

Before we stare in the face of a pathetic side of human nature, we need to savor God's way of ensuring that we'd not be left to our basest selves. Read 2 Peter 1:3-4 and meditate on it long enough to be astonished. Don't look up from the page until its revelation is profound to you.

In what do you and I get to participate? _____

As people in whom the Spirit of Christ dwells, we are not abandoned to our own self-consuming, self-destructing natures. We get to be different. In ways incomprehensible to us, we who have placed our trust in His Son actually participate in God's divine nature. Today we're going to cling to this truth as Scripture puts on display an uncomfortably convicting human propensity.

Let me go ahead and get this off my chest: Haman was a buffoon. He rises on the pages of Esther like a caricature of a lack of character. Today's segment paints his narcissism like a water-color cartoon strip. If you're like me, you might get a little confused over the identity of the distorted image: *Is it Haman or is it me?* Our reading today will overlap yesterday's to refresh our memory. Please read Esther 5:9-13. Had Haman's day not been long enough? He'd already been to a high-brow banquet.

Why do you think Haman went home and threw another party?

What do you imagine Zeresh was thinking as Haman threw his bizarre party?

Put yourself in the position of two different people attending Haman's spontaneous party. Set aside his wife, Zeresh, as one of them and a friend in attendance as the other. Since we're not given any information about the friends, draw up a fictitious profile of one based on what you'd assume about a person in close association to Haman. For instance, what do you imagine was his socioeconomic status? How well might this friend and Haman have known each other? Now, describe several things you picture Zeresh and this friend thinking as they listened to Haman carry on that night.

Complete the profiles in the margin.

As you imagine one of Haman's friends, how do you picture his socio-economic status?

You can count on one thing: It was a long night at Haman's house. He blew his boasts in his guests' faces like puffs of smoke from a stale cigar. Apparently the only people who got to talk were those who talked about him. The man bragged on his wealth, sons, high honors, opportunities, and the elite company he got to keep which, incidentally, his guests weren't privy to share. Haman was arrogant and indulgent enough to think his guests would enjoy a heaping helping of him. Sadly, maybe some of them did.

Then the mood of the evening changed. All of a sudden Haman's countenance dropped to the floor and his fragile mask shattered into a thousand pieces. Anyone remotely attentive could have instantly deduced why he'd thrown a party. His well-earned ego was bruised.

Haman had everything a worldly man could want but one. What was it?

What do you imagine the friend thinking while he listened to Haman?

We've arrived at the spot where I was most tempted to confuse Haman with myself. I have been in this spot, letting my preoccupation with one solitary person steal the joy that countless others brought me.

 Have you? If so, how?

One of the most eye-opening things God has shown me about bondage is that we can become addicted to a person. Haman was addicted to Mordecai. He couldn't quit thinking about him. Haman's hatred of Mordecai became a mental preoccupation and so caused the most outrageous irony of all: Haman bowed down to Mordecai. Make no mistake, we serve whatever masters us, and nothing masters us more completely than the person who refuses to bow to our rights, desires, or demands. We become fixated on the one from whom we cannot get what we want.

We tend to picture bondage in terms of an addictive substance, a compulsive behavior, or looming feeling like unforgiveness. I don't think we realize our stronghold can be a person until it *is* one. A person becomes a snare to us any time he or she consumes an excessive and unhealthy space in our thoughts, whether negative or positive. The individual may be someone …

- We are attracted to *or* feel threatened or defeated by.

    Which case is illustrated by Ecclesiastes 7:26?

    Which case is illustrated in Exodus 10:7? (Check the context.)

- Whose approval eludes us or whose happiness consumes us.

    What insight does Galatians 1:10 lend us?

- Whom we adore, despise, or, far more complexly, both. Our problem people often are those we "love" one moment and "hate" the next.

    Why do you think such a fine line can exist between adoring and despising someone?

We form mental strongholds toward those who won't give us what we want or need. Sometimes they quit giving us something they once supplied and we want it back. Perhaps they broke the rules of our relationship. Very often our people-snares are those who make us feel out of control with our emotions. They are the ones around whom we are most compelled to perform or, worse yet, make fools of ourselves. We see both of these subtle elements in Haman. The people who have become the biggest snares to us are the ones about whom we're most prone to say, "I never act this way with anyone else!"

Can you relate to what I'm describing? If so, how?

We could list many examples of mental fixation on a person, but let's round out the picture with some that invite us to relate whether we're 18 or 80.

- We go to a great party but we can't have a good time because our "person" either didn't show up or didn't pay attention to us. Mind you, this could be someone we hate but we still want to control.

• God is putting our lives back together after a terrible betrayal. Ample time has passed and God has gifted us with a wonderful person. We can't be happy with the terrific person who has accepted us, however, because we're still fixated on the person who rejected us.

Now that you have the idea, offer another example:

Whether or not our people-snares preoccupied us (and often they didn't), somewhere along the way we felt emotionally mastered by them. The truth is, however, the person did not emotionally master us. Our *thoughts* about the person emotionally mastered us.

We need God's healing in our minds even more than our relationships. Unfortunately, I can speak from experience on this subject. I've let people become inordinate mental preoccupations. One I adored. The other I hated. My experience makes me deeply compassionate toward someone going through the same misery.

Today's lesson offers practical helps. First, we need to let Haman's stronghold make us aware of our own. Realize our preoccupation with that person is probably painfully obvious to the people around us just as Haman's was to Zeresh and Haman's friends. Embarrassment is our friend when we let it motivate us to change. Let's decide today that we no longer want to be mentally snared by that person and agree with Christ to do what is necessary to bring our thoughts captive to the knowledge of God (2 Cor. 10:5).

If this is what you desire, articulate your agreement with God. Rehearse in His ear what we thought we needed from the person who has preoccupied us and kept us from enjoying what so many others offered.

Lord, I wanted (or felt I needed) the person to …

Complete the prayer in the margin.

Now, let's ask ourselves an honest question. If we got what we needed or wanted from the person of our preoccupation, would it "fix" us? In the best-case scenario, perhaps something they could do or say might help, but could they truly fix what was broken enough to cause the preoccupation?

Why or why not?

Finally, what do you think has been the root of your preoccupation with this person?

God is the only One who can tend to the secret places where pain calls to bondage. Would you let Him minister to you there and begin the healing process? Admitting we have an area of brokenness is a huge step toward wholeness. Remember the questions that began our lesson? Perhaps God will add new meaning to them now as we allow our first thoughts today to pose our last.

What would God's kingdom gain from a people who were only humiliated? What would be the reward of our existence if we were only repentant and never repaired? Discontent with selfishness and weary of ego, we finally become willing to lose ourselves to something greater. In doing so, we find Christ as we've never known Him and, there, pooled in the reflection of His eyes, startle to discover that a part of ourselves resembles Him.

That, Beloved One, is what happens when human flesh and blood—with all its frailty—participates in the divine nature.

Day Five
Then Go ... and Be Happy

TODAY'S TREASURE

"Then go with the king to the dinner and be happy." Esther 5:14

I am extremely intrigued by what makes people tick. I love human interest stories. Better yet, I love human exhibits like airports and shopping malls. They leave some room for the imagination so a curious soul like me can take a few clues and try to fill in some blanks. To me, *why* people do what they do is the texture of the human fabric. Nothing tells me more about how people tick than how they relate to others, particularly if their nonverbal communication is shouting louder than their words.

Go ahead and call me nosey. I'll probably overhear you. That I have great hearing and can usually make out what the couple is saying three tables over in a restaurant hasn't helped me break the habit.

Our text today from Esther is comprised of one verse, but the discussion it could initiate would last for hours if we'd let it. This solitary verse will offer us an invitation through the front door of Haman's house and into his marriage. Let's take a look at what made this couple tick.

Our focal Scripture today is the final verse of Esther 5, but let's glance back to the beginning of the scene so we can recall the details leading up to this moment. Please read Esther 5:11-14.

> Nothing tells me more about how people tick than how they relate to others.

What was Haman's issue (v. 13)?

Exactly what did Zeresh and all of Haman's friends advise him to do?

Here's an important piece of information if we want to brush our hands over the texture of human fabric at Haman's house. "Absorbed in his prideful obsession with his enemy, Haman is obviously utterly at a loss to know what to do. So it is his wife Zeresh (and his friends, though the Hebrew order of 5:14 makes her the primary spokesperson) who dictates his course of action."[14]

They couldn't have all naturally arrived at the same solution. Probably Zeresh offered the drastic remedy, and then his friends jumped in with happy assent. After all, somebody needed to think of something. Otherwise they were going to have a mess on their hands. Haman had been drinking virtually all day. If they couldn't come up with answers after he exposed the chink in his armor, things were liable to get ugly fast.

Haman was that unsettling and irregular kind of person who was harder to bear with his mask off than on. He was the sort who'd whine and snivel to you and then get mad at you later because you saw him like that.

I can think of several times individuals have disclosed something to me that I knew they were going to regret later. My stomach turned with dread, knowing that after they had invited me into such close proximity, they would probably end up getting mad at me in order to reinstate comfortable distance. Several times I've even interrupted with the question, "Are you sure you want to tell me this?"

 Have you ever experienced an uncomfortable disclosure that you feared would have negative repercussions? If so, describe the last time without using names or the kinds of details that might dishonor someone.

That day in Haman's home, he slid from wine to whine. One minute he was blowing his own horn. The next minute he was blowing his nose. Surely most of his guests squirmed with discomfort and shifted their eyes to one another, wondering what would—or *should*—happen next.

If someone in the group had enough guts, you might picture him offering this kind of reasoning to Haman: "Don't worry about one guy. After all, he'll be dead with the rest of the Jews by next Adar. You are second in command. You wear the king's signet. All of Persia bows down to you. He's trying to get a rise out of you. Ignore him. Or get someone to poison his lunch for crying out loud. He's a flea." Or, if the adviser was fearless of reprisal, he might have said, "Grow up and get over yourself. It's not all about you."

Here's what Haman got instead: "Have a gallows built, seventy-five feet high, and ask the king in the morning to have Mordecai hanged on it" (5:14) To give you a little perspective, that height is the equivalent of a seven-story building. The kind of gallows inferred in the Hebrew context and from Persian historical records was probably not for hanging by a noose or for crucifixion. The gallows inferred in this context was far more likely for impaling the body on the tip of a large stake for the precise purpose of displaying the victim.

"The point of impalement is not punishment, but exposure to disgrace. Simply killing Mordecai would not assuage what feels like enormous injury to Haman, with his fragile ego. Only an enormous, visible disgrace of Mordecai will bring him satisfaction."[15]

Why couldn't Haman be satisfied to just have Mordecai poisoned?

In ancient Persia impalement was reserved for those the victor intended to mock. It was a dead giveaway to any perceptive person that the victim had been a thorn in the victor's flesh and a wound to his ego.

According to Herodotus, Haman's own king offers a perfect illustration. A Spartan warrior by the name of Leonidas insulted King Xerxes, refusing to fear him. The Spartan's courage was all the more impressive because he knew his small army of 300 had no chance against Xerxes' hundreds of thousands. Destined to lose, they fought to make a point more than a victory. After Leonidas and his small band stunned the Persians by slaughtering about 30,000 of their soldiers, the hero did indeed meet a violent end at Thermopylae. He died with his dignity, however, refusing to hand it over to a king he reviled.[16]

When the Persian king came upon Leonidas's body, he ordered it beheaded, stuck on a pole and carried before his forces. "King Xerxes had hated Leonidas more than any other living man. Otherwise he would never have violated the corpse in this way, since the Persians, more than any people I know, honor men who are brave in battle."[17]

This kind of impalement is what Zeresh suggested, but in Esther 5:14, the "pole" was prescribed to be 75 feet! Ironically, those who demanded this disgrace for their enemy rarely failed to have been disgraced by them first. Both Haman and Xerxes were perceived to have been made a laughingstock by those whose heads they sought to display.

Interesting, isn't it? But what does this peculiar piece of antiquity have to do with you and me? Thankfully, impaling somebody's head on a stick is not exactly the solution that comes to us when someone in our family asks how to deal with an offense. The question is: *What does?*

Look carefully at the wording primarily attributed to Zeresh after she advised Haman to build a gallows. "Have Mordecai hanged on it. Then go with the king to the dinner and _____ _____."

Do you sense any hint that Zeresh was willing for Haman to do something outrageous if he'd hush then and get happy? One reason I'm tempted to think so is because I've felt that way at times. Granted, less radical solutions entered my mind, but the irritation with someone who could never seem to get happy is similar. Haven't you ever been so tired of hearing a loved one complain about someone that you wanted to say, "Go do something about it and get on with it!" Dr. Karen Jobes points out that "Zeresh counsels him simply to eliminate immediately the cause of his dissatisfaction."[17]

What kinds of risks are we taking when we pursue the immediate elimination of dissatisfaction? Often our advice for our loved ones is pure and selfless, but other times we want our family member to get some resolution because she's about to drive us over the emotional edge. If a fly buzzing around his head is what's causing him to whine and moan, we'll finally offer to swat it with a sledgehammer to get some relief.

If Zeresh is Scripture's *Exhibit A* for swatting a fly with a sledge hammer for her husband, we'll find *Exhibit B* in 1 Kings 21:1-16. Read these very intriguing verses and complete the following:

What did King Ahab want?

How did he act when he didn't get it? (List every description in v. 4.)

Have you ever had a family member react similarly to not getting what he or she wanted? _____ Without giving names, when was the last time the sulking or anger was so interruptive or interminable that you were tempted to do something uncharacteristic just to stop it?

What did Jezebel do for Ahab? _____

Do you think her actions reflected selfless marital devotion? Why?

Because so much evil resided in members of these two households, we should be slow to picture Zeresh and Jezebel as devoted wives who simply wanted what was best for their husbands. I'm not suggesting that no part of them meant to defend their spouses. I'm simply offering that they also might have been willing to do something outrageous to put an end to their husbands' foul moods. After all, an unhappy person isn't happy until everyone's unhappy.

As I reflected on Zeresh and Jezebel, a couple of thoughts surfaced in reference to womanhood. First, I considered afresh how much power of persuasion—both positive and negative—the woman of the house can have.

> The woman of the house can have much power of persuasion— both positive and negative.

Second, I reflected on how much women need and crave peace. The ability to persuade and the desire for peace can be wonderful elements in a woman and a blessing to her home when she's operating in the power of the Holy Spirit. If she's not, they could be dangerous. Sometimes I may want peace badly enough to advise my loved one to do something swift … but not necessarily something wise. Can you relate in any way?

Several months ago Melissa and I struck up a conversation with a young woman who said, "Remember the infamous cheerleader—mom trial? I was on that squad." Of course, we remembered. The whole sordid story monopolized the headlines for months. A mom who wanted to further her daughter's ambitions as a junior high cheerleader decided that the archrival and star of the squad posed the problem. Her solution was to make financial arrangements, complete with a diamond-earring down payment, to dispose of the child's mother. Did you catch the fact that these girls were in junior high? Thankfully, the mom was unsuccessful, but her absurd plan caused every thinking mother in metropolitan Houston to give second thought to the lengths we were willing to go for our children.

The vast majority of us could accurately say, "But I'd never do anything like that!" As foolish as I've been, I can't imagine going to those extremes either, but lessons can be learned nonetheless. Outlandish cases like the ones we've studied today can cause us to take stock of a few things in ourselves.

Use the following questions to take stock in your life:

_____ Do I have a low tolerance for the discomforts and upsets of those around me?

_____ Do I feel pressured to come up with solutions to a loved one's persisting problems?

_____ Do I ever grow weary enough of my loved one's problem that I could be tempted to give advice normally uncharacteristic of me?

_____ Do I tend to get inordinately wrapped up in my loved one's conflicts with people and develop strong feelings like jealousy, resentment, or hatred toward their opponent?

_____ Do I tend to take a quick trip from passionate to irrational?

If you answered any of the above questions with *yes*, what is your alternative?

Today's lesson is a wake-up call. Let's ask God to strengthen and fortify us to love fully but wisely. May He guard our hearts and minds from such a low tolerance for someone else's turmoil that we could end up advising or acquiescing to something that simply is wrong.

What is the moral of today's story? Keep your head on your shoulders and his head off the stake.

> The ability to persuade and the desire for peace can be wonderful elements in a woman and a blessing to her home when she's operating in the power of the Holy Spirit.

Sometimes God _____ the issue of _____.
Amazingly, other times He seems to _____ it.

Reflect on the importance of knowing ...

1. When it's _____.

See verse 1. Compare Hosea 6:2.

2. When it's _____ ____ _____.

Ecclesiastes 3:1,7 say, "There is a time for everything, and a season for every activity under heaven ... a time to be _____ and a time to _____."

• Sometimes we need to be _____ even when man invites us to _____.

Consider the idiom, "Even up to half the kingdom."

(Compare Mark 6:17-28.)

• Sometimes the _____ _____ _____, but they don't _____ _____. See Job 34:2-4. (Compare 2 Cor. 6:1-2.)

3. When it's time to _____ for _____

_____ time.

- The time wasn't _____ _____ _____.

  (Recall Mark 6:23.)

- The time wasn't _____ _____ _____.

  Commentator Adele Berlin suggests the delay is "a clever move on Esther's part to disarm Haman and make him think he was the center of attention. This plays to Haman's _____ _____."[11] Similarly, J. Gordon McConville explains that the delay allowed time "for Haman's misguided _____ _____ _____."[12]

4. When the _____ is _____.

  (See Isa. 40:31, KJV.)

Scenario #6

It's tough being a woman who can balance

_____ with _____.

What Goes Around

Just to know we are significant to God and He's willing to

orchestrate a holy set-up to speak to us is monumental to every

woman who ever feared she was invisible or unremarkable.

Principal Questions

1. Why this night of all nights was Xerxes' memory jarred?
2. Why had Haman come to the king's court?
3. What suggestions did Haman present to King Xerxes?
4. What phrases out of the king's mouth included the word "you" in reference to Haman (6:10-11)?
5. What reason did Zeresh and Haman's friends/advisers give for his certain demise (v. 13)?

Day One
Sleepless in Susa

TODAY'S TREASURE

"The king could not sleep; so he ordered the book of the chronicles, the record of his reign, to be brought in and read to him." Esther 6:1

A story on our local Christian radio station amused me. The topic was choosing the ringtone for your cell phone that best expresses you. Listeners chimed in with everything from TV theme songs to recordings of their mothers nagging, "Pick up this phone!" One woman called with a story about her good friend, a prayer warrior, whose ring was the "Hallelujah Chorus." After an intense and victorious time of prayer with fellow intercessors one day, one of the women said, "I sensed God's presence so strongly today. I even felt like I could hear the angels singing!" The friend didn't have the heart to tell her she'd forgotten to silence her ringer and the "Hallelujah Chorus" was playing in her purse.

All sorts of things are happening in the heavenlies around us. If our ears were opened to hear them, the sounds of angelic activity would be deafening. God invited the prophet Ezekiel to both see and hear events in the immortal realm. He described the sounds: "When the creatures moved, I heard the sound of their wings, like the roar of rushing waters, like the voice of the Almighty, like the tumult of an army" (Ezek. 1:24).

Believe me, when our ears are finally opened, we won't mistake what we hear for the muffled sound of the "Hallelujah Chorus" coming from our handbags. We'll more likely have to cover our ears and steady our feet to bear the sound of angels singing.

As our sixth chapter of Esther unfolds, the Jews in Susa, terrified and far from the temple, had no idea how close God was. In fact, you might say He was right there in the king's quarters, just where a king should be. Since one King neither slumbered nor slept (Ps. 121:4), perhaps He wanted to make sure the lesser didn't either. Please read today's text: Esther 6:1-3.

Verse 1 begins with the words, "That night." Glance at the previous chapter. What night was it?

What did the king request since he couldn't sleep?
- Warm milk   A platter of food
- Harp music   The book chronicling his reign

All sorts of things are happening in the heavenlies around us.

When my girls were little, I often rocked them to sleep with a bedtime story. The stories in highest demand were about them. I'd recount all sorts of feats they'd accomplished like climbing the ladder of the slide without my help. Children love to hear about themselves. Apparently, so do juvenile kings. After all, what could be a better sleep aid than hearing about ourselves? Instead of lulling the king to sleep, the chronicles reminded Xerxes of an oversight.

What was it? _____

Sometimes Christ walks through our crisis dressed in the best disguise of all: ordinary events. He tucks a miracle in the fold of His robe and sweeps in and out unnoticed. Only in retrospect do we realize that a divine visitation graced our cold, crude winter and the resurrection of spring is on its way.

Sometimes we grab the hem of Christ's garment for dear life and are healed. Other times it brushes past us and we never recognize that the turn-around marking the months to come began with a single touch. We've come to call events like these *providence*. Today's event commands attention precisely because it is so forgettably ordinary. Consider three elements captured in Esther 6:1-6 that together are too uncanny to call coincidence. First, *the timing*: About five years passed since Mordecai had foiled the assassins.

Why do you think this night of all nights Xerxes' memory was jarred?

I often think of the words of Jeannette Clift George: "God is never late, but He misses a few good opportunities to be early." Amen to that! But, oh, the wisdom of God to know that if the answer comes too early, we'd miss His greatest act. Second, notice *the circumstance*: The king couldn't sleep. Goodness knows he'd had enough wine that day, but when God has a mind to keep a man awake, no sedative on earth can stop Him. The Septuagint makes the point explicitly: "The Lord took sleep from the king that night."[1]

Sometimes sleep escapes me because my mind won't rest, I had that last cappuccino a tad too late, or my hormones are fighting over which side of the bed they want to sleep on: the sweet side or the mean side. Other times sleep escapes me because the Lord took it. He intended to keep me awake to attend to something I keep overlooking in the relentless demands of daylight.

In those times He not infrequently reminds me that I didn't give proper notice to someone who did something for me. My mama didn't raise her babies without manners. When I miss something out of nothing but the pitiful tyranny of self-importance, I'm sick at heart. Relief doesn't come until proper recognition has been served with a heaping side order of apology.

How about you? When was the last time the Lord took sleep from you?

> Sometimes the Lord keeps me awake to attend to something I keep overlooking in the relentless demands of daylight.

In those times when God Himself takes our sleep, His reason isn't always a reminder or a reprimand. Sometimes He simply has something to say. I love the story of the boy Samuel. God also kept him awake one night, but with a decidedly different agenda than he served with King Xerxes.

In the margin briefly describe what happened in 1 Samuel 3:1-10.

I can't describe how I long to hear the audible sound of God's voice. Never once have I heard with my physical ears God's voice calling, "Beth! Beth!" but I've heard a summons many times in my heart. Until I see Him face-to-face, few things are dearer to me than the invisible but unmistakable tug on my heartstrings to awaken and come meet with Him.

I'm still profoundly moved at the thought that God desires my company. Just as surely He desires yours, Beloved. Sometimes when we're awakened for no other apparent reason and we sense God is near, what could be more precious to Him than our saying, "Speak, for Your servant is listening"?

Fascinatingly, Scripture proves over and over that a person doesn't have to be a child of God to inadvertently be a servant of God. The Lord employed a number of unsuspecting kings and cohorts to do His bidding in the Old Testament and can use a pagan as surely as a progeny. That night in the citadel of Susa, Xerxes was about to serve God—whether he wanted to or not.

Third, note *the subject matter:* Chronicles of ancient kings were copious, detailed descriptions of coronations, conquests, queens, and coups. Mind you, Xerxes' reign was around the 13th year by this time so what the reading material lacked in valor, it made up for in volume. Furthermore, if Xerxes was like most ancient kings, he called for his chronicles often. As Dr. Breneman puts it, "The kings of the great ancient empires always kept annals of their reigns. Apparently the king delighted in hearing the records of his own reign."[2]

The suspiciously providential part of the account is that the reader of Xerxes' chronicles just happened to earmark the portion about Bigthana and Teresh. I'm reminded of another time when God had the perfect part of a scroll earmarked for public reading. Please savor every word of Luke 4:14-21.

Who was the reader, what was the reading, and why was it significant?

The mention of Christ's public reading in the same lesson with the reading of Xerxes' comparatively ridiculous chronicles seems insulting until we make one connection. If the Jews had been annihilated, the promised Savior could not have come from its bloodline. Don't think for a moment Satan wasn't trying to slip Xerxes' signet ring on his invisible finger. Well versed in Scripture, Satan was aware from the first prophecy that the Messiah would come from Judah. Why do we think he tried so often to destroy the Jews? Opportunist that he is, Satan probably thought he had a fighting chance this time. He banked on Israel's rebellion ripping a hole in God's protective covering, leaving them defenseless. Satan surely pictured their graveyards strewn with the dry bones of forfeited promises. If that's what he thought, he woefully mistook man's unfaithfulness for God's.

What does 2 Timothy 2:13 assure us? _____

God cannot break His promises. His Word is not only His bond but it is also His very breath. Yes, God disciplines His children—but so they can live and not die. Much was at stake for God's nation in the timing and subject matter of Xerxes' reading material. Incomparably and eternally more was at stake in the timing and subject matter of Christ's public reading in Luke 4.

> God cannot break His promises. His Word is His bond and His very breath.

Even you and I experience times when we know God has deliberately caused us to read or hear a strategically timed message. If we've walked with God for long, we've experienced moments when we were so amazed or alarmed over something said to us at a specific time that we felt as if He'd either been reading our e-mails or our minds. He was reading both.

In such times doesn't your face flush with wonder over whether people around you know God pegged you? Don't you sometimes think they must be staring at you? If the word you received from God was an encouragement or affirmation, couldn't you almost jump to your feet and give a shout of praise?

Personal Question

☙ Describe such a moment when you knew God strategically timed something you read or heard.

I love moments like these even if God has something hard to say to me. Just to know we are significant to Him and He's willing to orchestrate a holy set-up to speak to us is monumental to every woman who ever feared she was invisible or unremarkable. Don't we all feel that way at one time or another? Experiences like these are wide-eyed reminders that God is deeply attentive to our most secret hurts, concerns, and hopes.

Perhaps most astounding today is not that God would time the reading of a Persian king but that He'd time the reading of common people like you and me—people simply trying to live the life of faith on the sliver of light we have, sometimes wondering if we're even on the radar screen of heaven.

Every now and again Christ seems to stand to His feet and read His Word over us like we're the only ones in the room. He then seems to take a seat authoritatively and sum it all up: "Today this is fulfilled in your hearing." Translation? "You heard me. This one's accomplished." And, wonder of wonders, we did! He who is both universally and internationally providential is also personally providential.

When the God of all creation reserves a remark for you, Beloved, that's all you need to be remarkable.

Day Two
Who More Than Me?

TODAY'S TREASURE

"Now Haman thought to himself, 'Who is there that the king would rather honor than me?' " Esther 6:6

I start every Bible study with a plan and proposed theme, but never once has a series gone exactly where I expected or entailed precisely what I assumed. Esther is no exception. Among many surprises, the thought never once occurred to me that we would end up relating with Haman as much as with Esther. Though we can't imagine our lives ever bearing the poisonous fruit of Haman's, we've recognized small seeds buried deeply in the soil of our human hearts that, if watered by enough pride, ambition, and prejudice, could grow into something appalling.

Perhaps the most frightening thought of all is that we, like Haman, might be too self-absorbed and self-convinced to realize that we've become someone we can't stand. Don't brace yourself for a downer. If we have a heart for Christ and an authentic desire to pursue godliness, lessons like these become protection as much as conviction. Today's segment is intriguing to me, and I hope you are as quickly captivated by its prospects. We begin our reading from the top of chapter six, adding on three new verses. Please read Esther 6:1-6.

What on the king's mind caused him to summon someone for advice?

Watch providence at work again. Who just happened to be in the court?
   Haman   Esther   Mordecai   Jesus

Take a moment to understand the reference to the court. This area was the closest proximity anyone had to the king without a summons. Not coincidentally, at the time of Xerxes' inquiry, Haman had just arrived.

Why had Haman come?

Please stop long enough to absorb the time element. All the events we've studied in Esther 5 have occurred within the last day and evening. Esther 6 opens with the words "that night" referring to the night following Esther's dinner for Xerxes and Haman as well as the gathering at Haman's house a little later.

The events described in Esther 6:1-3 occurred during Xerxes' sleepless night. When the king inquired who, obviously among his advisors, happened to be in the court and learned that Haman was present, some commentators are not even sure the sun had come up.

Obviously Xerxes wasn't the only one wide awake all night. The gallows were clearly under construction. Haman did not wait until morning as Zeresh and his friends advised him but hopped right to it. Don't be hasty to picture him with hammer and nail. Esther 5:14 assures us that he *had* the gallows built. Haman shook the royal builders out of their slumber and put them to work. Sawing logs took on a whole different meaning that night.

What did the king ask Haman (v. 6)?

Write the exact words Haman "thought to himself":

"Haman, unable to imagine that the king would consider anyone other than (literally, "more" than) himself, responded in terms of his own fantasies. Had not the line between his own wishes and the king's command become quite permeable in chapter 3? Wasn't the king, of late, quite magnanimous when the queen had approached unbidden? Didn't the exclusive guest list for the queen's banquets suggest a shared admiration for him by the royal couple? And now he finds the king waiting for him early in the morning with what appears to be a blank check! Haman has arrived at the crack of dawn eager for revenge, but he is also obviously eager (as always) for his own honor."[3]

Now, Haman thought to himself, *Who is there that the king would rather honor than me?* Take it out of the palace and into the workplace: Who deserves more credit for _____ than I do? To whom is recognition longer overdue than me? Think wider than the workplace. How about the home? Our church?

Are you cringing like I am? Wouldn't you hate to have anything in common with the foolish behavior depicted in Esther 6:6? What on earth possessed him? Maybe two of the same things that possess us at times. Let's find a new way to give them names. Take a quick trip with me in your imagination to the set of the game show "Wheel of Fortune." You are the winning contestant in the category of history's villains. The tension is building. Your heart is racing. You now must solve a three-word puzzle for the grand prize. You brace yourself as the bonus category is announced: *Among the things that made Haman mistake himself for the person King Xerxes wanted to honor.*

The clock is ticking. You now must solve the puzzle.

PRE___U___PTI___N   ___ ___D E___TIT___E___E___T

If this just isn't your day for word puzzles, glance at the last paragraph of today's lesson for the answers.

In the space below, write the two words from the puzzle and describe their connection to Haman in Esther 6:6.

_____ : _____

_____ : _____

We risk Haman's wrong notion at least two ways: We can think about ourselves so much that we assume others are too. Circumstances can prompt our version of Haman's embarrassing presumption. Riding the fickle waves of opinion, we can be full of ourselves one week and down on ourselves the next.

I must have been having one of those full-of-myself weeks when, in a crowded elevator a few years ago a woman said, "I love what you have on. You really look good." I'd already gushed with gratitude and prepared to tell her where I'd purchased it when I realized to my humiliation that she was talking to the woman behind me. It was the longest elevator ride of my life. She tried to soothe the awkwardness by saying, "But you do too!" It remained woefully unsoothed. By that time my antiperspirant was already having a code red.

Oh, please tell me you have an example of a time when you mistook somebody else's praise for your own! If so, share it here, and, as long as we're willing to learn a lesson, let's laugh at ourselves while we're at it!

We don't have to think highly of ourselves to think obsessively of ourselves. Perhaps you can't imagine a self-view lofty enough to assume you're being praised, but if it were criticism, would you jump to the conclusion in a second flat? In both cases, we base inappropriate presumptions primarily on self-consumed thoughts.

Continually thinking others are talking about us—whether positively *or* negatively—is an unhealthy self-preoccupation. Even when we've given people plenty to talk about (been there!), becoming self-consumed and chronically self-conscious only traps us deeper in the prison of presumption.

What advice can we receive from the following Scriptures:

Romans 12:3

Philippians 2:3-4

> We don't have to think highly to think obsessively of ourselves.

The second way we risk Haman's wrong conclusion is this: We can develop a ravenous appetite for honor—even if we try to keep it hidden. I have a good friend who received more awards from elementary school through college than her bedroom shelves could bear. Her trophies spilled downstairs and into the den until they nearly took over the entire house. Understandably, her parents received as many accolades from them as she did. When she got out of college and entered the "real world," she humbly confided to me the struggle she'd had breaking her addiction to honor.

I was fascinated by the thought of a very different kind of stronghold most people probably wouldn't recognize. We don't have to receive honor to crave honor. All we have to do is give over to our insatiable human natures.

> How can each of the following Scriptures act as appetite suppressants in our bouts of craving honor? Please be specific.

Matthew 23:6

John 4:44

John 7:18

Romans 12:10

Write Psalm 62:7 in the margin.

One of the bad things about an insatiable desire for honor is that sooner or later it's going to make a fool of us, robbing us of the very thing we intended to receive. Haman made sure he was first in line to see the king early that morning. After all, he had important business. God forbid that daylight should burn when a man needed to hang for the Grand Vizier's honor.

I love what one commentator said about the inspired writer's "gift of irony" in verse 4. Though unbeknownst to Haman at the time, "here the early bird is gotten by the worm."[4] And he never saw it coming.

I don't know how you feel about today's lesson, but the message has been loud and clear to me. Two of the last words I'd want in a word puzzle depicting my life would be "presumption and entitlement." At those miserable, self-consumed times when the double-headed monster cranes its neck in my life, may I be transferred instantaneously in my imagination to one more round of "Wheel of Fortune."

I'd peer at a word on the puzzle board, and buy a vowel: R _ P _ N T!

We don't have to receive honor to crave honor.

Personal Question

Day Three
A Would-Be King

TODAY'S TREASURE

"Have them bring a royal robe the king has worn and a horse the king has ridden, one with a royal crest placed on its head." Esther 6:8

Yesterday I met Shirley across the checkout counter in the shoe department. Beckoned by that marvelous word *clearance*, we'd both been so busy trying on shoes and studying our feet that we hadn't looked up to realize we'd studied Scripture together. We finally made the connection at which point the sweet cashier was caught in the crossfire of sudden joy. She seemed mystified that two seemingly normal women could derive that much excitement from studying something like the Bible. But, oh, if she could only study today's lesson with us, she might throw off every heel that hinders, the sling-back that so easily entangles, and run with perseverance to the class marked out for her!

Let's begin with a recap of yesterday's segment. Remember what Haman assumed Xerxes meant about someone the king wanted to honor? In our previous lesson we fastened our attentions solely on Haman's thought process: He *thought* Xerxes was talking about him. Today we're going to hop on a train and take the scenic route from Haman's brainstem to his tongue, fastening our attentions on what he then said. Please read Esther 6:6-9.

List in the margin every suggestion Haman presented to King Xerxes.

How do you think he was able to answer so quickly and elaborately?

Haman sounds to me like a man who had daydreamed a similar scene before, casting himself in the starring role. We've arrived at one of those moments in Scripture when reading Hebrew would add considerable dimension to our lesson, but that's where good commentators come in particularly handy. On week 5, day 2, we talked about a break in sentence structure called an "anacoluthon." Allow me to refresh your memory. An anacoluthon occurs when the person conversing breaks off one sentence abruptly and starts another. For example, when I met Shirley at the counter yesterday, I may have said something like, "I've seen you at—are you coming on Tuesday nights right now?"

In my example circle the moment when the anacoluthon occurred.

An anacoluthon occurs when the person conversing breaks off one sentence abruptly and starts another.

The Hebrew syntax in verse 7 suggests that Haman did something similar, though most English translations don't reflect it. Haman began a sentence but broke it off. However, this anacoluthon conveys not hesitation but eagerness.

Haman was "fascinated by the phrase, 'the man whom the king desires to honor.' The break in the syntax suggests that Haman is pausing to savor the phrase, which he applies to himself. In his eagerness, he begins his reply with this phrase rather than with a courtesy formula such as 'if it please the king.' Haman rolls the phrase 'the man whom the king desires to honor' around in his mouth four times, beginning and ending his little speech with it."[5]

In his "overanxiousness to promote himself,"[6] Haman tossed propriety ("if it pleases the king") for opportunity (take it and run!). After all, the most adept opportunists have no greater expertise than exploitation. Their first thought in every new development is how to work it to their favor.

Dr. Levenson suggests that, with the words "the man whom the king desires to honor" echoing in Haman's head, "his narcissism is momentarily preventing him from formulating an effective reply to the king's question."[7] He was so astonished that someone finally thought as much of him as he thought of himself that he couldn't think straight. Bent minds never do.

Read Haman's suggestions in verses 8-9 again. Exactly how many times did he use the words "king" and "royal"? _____

We've come to the part of the lesson I find most fascinating. I hope to be able to prove to you that nothing about Haman's list was random. He was far too calculating for that. Let's see from several other Scriptures if we can determine what he had up his shrewd sleeve. We start with a portion of Genesis where we'll find Joseph, the beloved son of Jacob, in a prison cell in Egypt.

Set the stage by reading Genesis 41:14-16. Pharaoh summoned Joseph ...
   So he could testify on behalf of the chief cupbearer.
   So he could overturn his prison sentence.
   So he could tell him his brothers had arrived.
   So he could interpret his dream.

In succinct terms, how did Joseph respond to the request (Gen. 41:16)?

Now pick up the storyline with Genesis 41:33 where Joseph offered Pharaoh counsel based on the dream's interpretation and read through verse 42.

In what ways do Joseph and Haman appear to share rank?

Read Genesis 41:42-45, overlapping one verse from the previous segment.

In the margin record every similarity and difference between Joseph's celebrated exaltation and Haman's proposed exaltation in Esther 6:8-9.

I'm sure you noted both Joseph and Haman were second in command to their respective kings. Both were entrusted with the royal signet ring, and both scenes are tied together by parades—Joseph's in reality and Haman's in fantasy.

Contrasts seem subtle on the page but were enormous on the ancient pavement. I'll ask you to recount some of them for dramatic effect. Pharaoh dressed Joseph in robes of fine linen and had him ride in a chariot.

Exactly how did Haman want to be dressed? _____

How did Haman want to ride? _____ _____

Let's make another stop in Scripture to see if we can put the pieces of Haman's puzzling mind together. What does 1 Kings 1:28-35 involve?

How was Solomon transported (v. 33)? _____

Are you getting the picture? Some scholars wonder whether Haman not only desired to be *like* the king but also to *be* king.

This also shows why Christ requested a colt "which no one has ever ridden" for His triumphal entry (Luke 19:30). In one of the most significant prophecies ever fulfilled, throngs of joyful followers cried out, "Blessed is the king who comes in the name of the Lord!" (v. 38). This proclamation foretold by Zechariah concerned a kingship conferred by God alone. No man has ever worn the crown Christ's Father reserved for Him. In fact, ultimately all other diadems are cast at His feet and at His glorious revelation, "on his head [will be] many crowns" (Rev. 19:12). Until then, many a mortal will think himself—or herself—more worthy of the crown than the one who wears it.

Haman not only wanted to ride one of the king's horses but to wear one of his robes. The robes of ancient Persian kings, described as "purple with gold embroidery" were seldom touched by nonroyals, let alone shared.[8] Adele Berlin explains, "This is a very serious request, tantamount to asking for the kingship. A person's garment is considered a part of his body, or a part of his being."[9] Adding to the intrigue, the Persian royal robe was thought to possess a magical power, in some way conferring royalty on its wearers.[10]

Haman could not make royal blood flow through his veins, so he had little hope for succession in the natural realm. He may have surmised that if he managed to get one of the king's robes on his shoulders, he could conjure magical powers that would confer kingship. Belief in magic was tremendously widespread in ancient kingdoms. Little did Xerxes know that his closest associate would like to use a little hocus pocus to snag his throne.

To make such audacious requests in Esther 6:8-9, Haman's lustful gaze appears fastened to the one thing that eluded him. He'd ascended as high as a man could reach, standing on the tiptoes of average feet. What remained was in view, but he needed to step on the footstool of a throne to grab it.

When Xerxes asked his advice, Haman's mouth watered with the metallic taste of royal blood. No wonder he could never bring himself to say, "If it pleases the king." Consider a question carefully and answer only after taking a quick plunge into the turbulent waters of the human psyche. We've all heard that man wants what he can't have, but I'd like to ask why.

Personal Question   What do you believe causes the human mind to carry this urge?

We trace this tendency all the way back to the tree of the knowledge of good and evil. In the garden of Eden the serpent convinced Adam and Eve that God was holding out on them. Mind you, they'd been told they could eat the fruit from every other tree (Gen. 2:9). Unimaginable variety! Not just apples and oranges but papayas, mangoes, pomegranates, and all kinds of delicacies you and I have never imagined, but they became fixated on the one thing they couldn't have, ironically cheating themselves of the goodness and creativity God offered.

Tragically, we've done the same thing at times. Something in the corner of our eye catches our attention—and captures our desire. It may have seemed distant or even distasteful before, but now it seems within our reach and, for crying out loud, within our rights! We're human, after all.

The forbiddenness of it tantalizes our nerve endings. We feel alive again. Young. Daring. Unwelcome conviction wells up in our souls that we must redefine to resist. The moment we rename caution *prohibition,* our flesh throws a fit. We protest, "God is trying to take away my fun, my freedom. It's my life! My choice."

The inevitable end turns into the ultimate irony. In our pursuit of freedom, we end up forsaking all else and developing an obsession toward one thing. Cornered like a caged animal against a barbed-wire fence, flesh torn and bleeding, we gaze over our broken backs, behold the expanse of God's happy will, and howl. The serpent promised life and delivered death. The Creator promised death and delivered life.

Describe the significance of Romans 8:32 in view of the above.

Let's cast our Haman-gaze away from that thing that will destroy us. The only thing God wants to withhold from us is havoc.

Day Four
Just As You Have Suggested

TODAY'S TREASURE

"Get the robe and the horse and do just as you have suggested for Mordecai the Jew, who sits at the king's gate." Esther 6:10

I like my coffee strong and my Bible study stronger. I've got a fresh cup, so dark and thick that even a dousing with cream hardly turned the color. My Bible is open beside me where I can turn the page or simply brush my palm across it. To my soul's touch it has the warmth and life of my grandson's plump, busy hands but with power beyond the strongest human bond.

In my Bible the pages of Esther look pretty ragged by now. The edges are curling, and my notes are smudging, but the pursuit of God in Scripture and its connection to the human experience, are life to me. Yesterday I read words that pierced my heart with pangs of fresh affection for the Word.

Author Patricia Raybon described a time when she sought the presence of God in a hospital chapel while her husband underwent life-and-death surgery. "I picked up a Bible. I waited for that nice rush that comes from holding a worn, loved copy of the Scriptures. Bibles like that have their own heat. They've been prayed over, cried on, sung with, stroked and gripped and loved so hard they just emote— just by being touched—that human loam and steam and hope that faith gives off."[11]

Don't miss the point by looking for the doctrine in it. Steep yourself in the emotion. *Glance* over at your Bible. Think what you've been through with God in those pages, even if this is your first study. Think of the hope, guidance, assurance, and affection you've sought. Think how thankful you are that God wrote something you can hold to your chest, rocking back and forth, when your heart is shattered and your sight too blurred to read. Every Bible is the Word of God, but with no ears to hear it, hearts to love it, or hands to warm themselves by the fire of it, man is tragically lost to it.

Truly, Christ has spoken words to us that "are spirit and they are life" (John 6:63). Even discomforting words about a dead soul like Haman have life for the willing hearer. We learn as much from Scripture about what we don't want to be as what we do. We also have the benefit of knowing something Haman didn't know when he bounded into his bold list of ways to show a man (himself) honor. Haman was suffering from a chronic case of mistaken identity—a malady about to cause the embarrassment of his life. Before we read the next segment in Esther, please read Proverbs 18:6-7.

We learn as much from Scripture about what we don't want to be as what we do.

How might those verses suggest trouble was brewing for Haman?

Psalm 59:12 echoes the sentiment. Pride is a state of the heart that, sooner or later, is betrayed by the mouth. Matthew 12:34 tells us why: "For out of the overflow of the heart the mouth speaks." God created man with an undeniable heart-mouth connection. As our previous lesson illustrated, what's in the heart will inevitably come out of the mouth.

The heart-mouth connection is our glorious outlet when we not only *want* to praise God but must or a stone will cry out. It compels us to whisper "Mommy loves you so much" to a sleeping child, but this heart-mouth connection also serves a purpose in hidden sins such as pride. When we tumble (and we will), our words help us clearly identify what caused us to trip.

You see, we may not always remember the pride we felt, but we'll rarely forget the words we said because of it. Few things echo in my mind like proud words that I know led to the most humbling experiences of my life.

In His grace, however, God always provides a way of escape. At any moment we can make the choice to humble ourselves. Proverbs 16:18 assures us that pride comes before a fall, but if we're willing and genuine, we could decide to fall straight to our knees.

Haman didn't want to fall to his knees, however. He wanted others to fall to theirs—at his feet. Biblically speaking, he could have done nothing to more thoroughly cinch his own destruction. We now pick up our story line with Xerxes' enthusiastic response to Haman's audacious suggestions. Note the turn of events in Esther 6:10-11.

Principal Question

Record every phrase out of the king's mouth that included the word "you" in reference to Haman.

Several elements of Xerxes' instructions added gall to the turn of events. First note how the king identified the man he wanted to honor:

"Mordecai _____, who _____."

No two words were more acrid to Haman than: "the Jew." To him these two words shouldn't be said. They should be spit. The fact that Xerxes sought to honor a man he clearly knew was a Jew must have caused Haman's eyes to bulge from his head. However, this moment says as much about Xerxes as Haman. Had the king not put two and two together? Did he not realize that the man he sought to honor now was the same one he'd sentenced to death next Adar? Behold once again the obliviousness of Persia's king, an element that lends his character a nearly comical mystique.

"He does not connect Mordecai's Jewishness with the decree of destruction he authorized. The king had not bothered to find out which people he was consigning to destruction, and in any case he does not seem to recall the incident, as 7:5 implies. His memory is short, as his failure to remember Mordecai's service has already shown."[12]

King Xerxes' crown was simply too big for him. It kept falling down over his eyes. Had he possessed the least measure of discernment, he would have noticed the blood draining from his associate's face. In Nehemiah Xerxes' son and successor, Artaxerxes, would note the sadness of his cupbearer's face and inquire what was wrong (Neh. 2:2). Asking Haman if something troubled him wouldn't have been out of place—except for a king who was out of touch. Xerxes' identification of the Jew as the one "who sits at the king's gate" surely had to pour another bucket of gall on Haman's head.

Can you think of any reason why the reminder of this particular location would have been like salt poured in Haman's wounded pride? Explain.

To top it off, the instruction that drowned Haman in gall was the reminder that he himself "suggested" and "recommended" it. As the events of the day unfolded, he'd never once be allowed to forget that every detail was his idea.

According to Esther 6:11, what happened next?

If you're like me, you almost can't help but feel sorry for Haman, and the part of you that feels sorriest for him is the part that most fears humiliation—because you're scared you earned it. I don't like to see anyone humiliated, even someone who deserves it. Even someone I despise.

One thing harder to watch than arrogance is a person's profound embarrassment when it ricochets. One reason I shudder to see it is because I so desperately don't want to experience it. I'm well acquainted with the times I nursed foolish pride, and although profound embarrassment followed on numerous occasions, I've not received nearly the humiliation due me. Maybe I'm in this alone, but the part of my heart that most resembles Haman's is the part most reluctant to revel in Esther 6:11. I've grown enough to learn from it but not conquered enough to laugh at it.

In the margin list four words you could use to complete the sentence: "I'd much rather endure _____ than humiliation."

Personal Question

The irony is that pride is the very reason we'd rather endure almost anything other than humiliation, thereby parading us right down main street into the middle of it. Lord, help us. Lord, help *me*.

Esther 6:11 is as significant for what it doesn't say as what it does. Only one verse tells an entire royal event and the longest day of Haman's life. After all, he'd been up mighty early. Glance at Esther 6:11 again.

What are several major things the verse leaves unsaid?

I'd love to see your answers because you'd broaden my thinking. Perhaps we both noted one missing element. Esther 6:11 records nothing about the dynamics between Haman and Mordecai throughout the entire celebratory ordeal. Any looks, statements, or reactions between them are conspicuous in their absence. The only words out of Haman's mouth are ironically those that slid off his tongue when he thought they were intended for him: "This is what is done for the man the king delights to honor!" All else is muted.

Not having something spelled out can be an invitation to exercise some imagination. How do you picture the dynamics between the two archrivals that day as Haman escorted Mordecai through the city? I'll guide you into developing your own theory through the following activities:

Use one word to describe the atmosphere you imagine in the room when Haman took Mordecai the robe and horse: _____

Offer three words you believe describe Haman during the parade:
_____, _____, _____

Offer three words you believe describe Mordecai during the parade:
_____, _____, _____

Write one sentence you believe Haman might have said to Mordecai at any point that day:

Write one sentence you believe Mordecai might have said to Haman at any point that day:

We've been careful not to elevate Mordecai or Esther to places they might not have earned. At the same time we have witnessed impressive strength and courage in both as well as a willingness to do what was right at great personal risk. Let's give Mordecai credit where credit is due in this chapter. Please glance ahead with me to the very first sentence in Esther 6:12.

Where did Mordecai go after the parade in his honor?

Mordecai returned to the place he was ignored after he uncovered the assassination plot five years earlier. He went back to work. He didn't demand a higher position or higher pay. He simply went back to his job.

From the scene where he put on sackcloth and wailed, we've come to know Mordecai as a man unashamed to show his feelings. Yet here we see and hear nothing of his reaction. Missing is a single spark of evidence to suggest that he pumped his fists like the heavyweight champion of the world. We have no idea what Mordecai thought about the day.

We might glean several things from Mordecai's example. If we get overlooked for affirmation or promotion, so be it. Let's just do our jobs. If we get elevated and celebrated, so be it. Let's just do our jobs. Let's pursue a walk with God so close that the spotlights of this world—be they for us or against us—are eclipsed by His enormous shadow cast on our path.

There in the shelter of the Most High we find our significance and the only satisfaction of our insatiable need to be noticed. There and there alone we are free to be neither depressed nor impressed with the capricious reactions of this carnal world.

> We can find our significance and satisfaction in the shelter of the Most High.

Day Five
Sudden Sages

TODAY'S TREASURE

"His advisers and his wife Zeresh said to him, 'Since Mordecai, before whom your downfall has started, is of Jewish origin, you cannot stand against him—you will surely come to ruin!' " Esther 6:13

I've just returned from Nashville where I joined a group of loved ones at the funeral of someone very dear to us. Actually, you have more of a connection to him than you know because you hold this workbook in your hands. His name was Lee Sizemore and God entrusted the vision for beautifully crafted, warm and inviting video-driven Bible study to him.

When Lee contacted me on behalf of LifeWay 16 years ago and shared his vision, I honestly couldn't imagine how the concept would work. Picturing God pouring His Spirit out on a group of women through a television screen was a reach, but Lee seemed to know what he was talking about. We agreed to one. Then two. Then five. Then ten. Every series God entrusted to me, including this one—the 13th, was dreamed first with Lee on a long-distance call where we prayed together, often with tears, dedicating it to the Lord Jesus.

Lee produced over 100 series and with numerous authors. Without exaggeration, God used one individual to alter the entire landscape of Christian discipleship as we know it. And here's the catch: He did it all from a wheelchair. He'd been all over the world in that crazy chair to tape Bible studies.

His video-crew members, each like family to me, comprised the circle of pallbearers. As we stood at his open casket, one of them said to me, "We've carried him all over the world. We may as well carry him home."

Yes. It was an appropriate wrap. Lee and I often mused that God had rarely paired two more handicapped people for His kingdom: one physically, the other emotionally. When no other excuse remains except the mercy and power of God, however, He gets more glory. May it ever be.

As I begin this final lesson of week 6 and reflect again with you over the foolish pride and ambition of Haman, I can't help but think about my friend Lee. Crouched in a wheelchair, he stood head and shoulders above the most successful Fortune 500 men this world can boast because he invested his life in the only thing that lasts. He poured himself out like a drink offering, often amid physical discomfort and pain, so that people—especially hurting people—could learn how to know Christ through God's Word.

From a wheelchair, Lee made the Scriptures handicap accessible to those crippled by life and lost loves. In stark contrast, Haman spent his life sculpting a monument to himself, and it was starting to teeter. No matter how successful the Hamans of this world momentarily seem, they ultimately and tragically prove to be failures. Worse yet, *fools*.

Read Esther 6:12-14. Recall we glanced ahead to verse 12 toward the end of our previous lesson to reflect on Mordecai returning to the king's gate.

Why was this piece of information significant to us?

In contrast, where did Haman go? _____

Compare the terms in verses 12 and 14:
    Haman _____ home (v. 12).
    The king's eunuchs arrived and _____ Haman away (v. 14).

Suddenly everything in the narrative is on fast forward. We feel the rush and hurry of events almost as if they're getting away from us. Sometimes we wait and wait for God to move, then when He does, we protest that He's moving too fast. Our cries, "Lord, why do You wait?" turn into "Lord, wait!"

Esther 6:13 records the second time Haman rushed to his wife and friends for an ego infusion. In fact, the two scenes in Haman's home are bookends of sorts for the verses recording his tortured peak and astonishing plunge.

Turning to family and friends at times of need or celebration is appropriate, but I have a feeling that Haman nearly drained his support group dry. Insecure people with big positions and bigger egos are exhausting. They seldom rally from their self-absorption long enough to reciprocate, and when they do something is usually in it for them. We know from experience that lending emotional support to someone doesn't always flow from a pure motive.

How have you seen at least one way we can be self-serving in our shows of support for others?

If Haman ever acted as if he cared about anyone else, you can be fairly certain it flowed from something like you just described. He was the kind of person who convinced himself that others were privileged to get to live vicariously through him. He was mistaken.

Sooner or later people weary of an attention hog and no longer care to mask their true sentiments. I believe something similar happened at Haman's house that day. Note the boldness of Zeresh and his friends.

What was their bottom line (v. 13)? _____

I'm anxious for you to note a switch in terms. Read verse 13 carefully. The people gathered at Haman's house are called by two different terms.

Neighbors	Fellows	Counselors
Magicians	Friends	Advisers

The meaning of the Hebrew word translated "advisers" is "literally 'wise men.'"[13] According to several commentators, the term "wise men" may be "used here in a deliberately ironical sense, that is, they are wise *after the fact* (v. 14)."[14]

When was the last time you wanted to scream, "Now you tell me"? Nothing makes me want a handful of someone's hair like making a mistake in judgment and having the person who never offered to stop me say, "I had a bad feeling that might happen." Everybody's wise after the fact. Incredulously, we ask, "Why in the world didn't you tell me that?" Let's pause for just a moment and discuss possible answers to that question.

1.

2.

In the margin list three reasons why a person may not tell us what he or she really thinks about a situation.

3.

Sometimes I think my enthusiasm, determination, or even desperation may be so pronounced that someone might feel reluctant to tell me the truth. I seem too headstrong to stop. Help me, Jesus. I want to be willing to receive good advice even when it shatters my great idea. Don't you? Other times the person may be in denial just like I am, repressing her misgivings. Then, when the worst case scenario occurs, the thought catapults from the back of her mind to the front and, suddenly, she knew all along that it was going to happen.

One commentary explains the change of heart among Zeresh and Haman's friends like this: "Difficult situations shed the veneer of superficial character traits. Haman's wife and friends surround him with encouraging advice when he is at the peak of his power (5:9-14). When he is disgraced, however, they offer him only negative words that neither comfort nor guide (6:13). The friendship they show him quickly vanishes in chapter 6 when he experiences a setback."[15]

Have you experienced a difficult time when your friends distanced themselves emotionally? If so, what do you believe was at the root of it?

Sometimes I think people superstitiously fear trouble rubbing off on them. Or they simply run out of emotional energy to continue supporting us. Praise God, He's never afraid of us or worn out by us.

What reason did Zeresh and Haman's friends/advisers give for his certain demise (v. 13)?

Notice they did not say Haman *might not* or *would not* stand. They emphatically said he *could not* stand. Why would this be true?

"They see in these events an omen: 'Since Mordecai, before whom your downfall has started, is of Jewish origin, you cannot stand against him—you will surely come to ruin!' (v. 13). There is little doubt that an ethnic rivalry was at the root of Haman's enmity with Mordecai; now it is clear to those closest to Haman that the Jewish side will win.

"What capricious superstition had once supported (with the casting of the *pur*), it now denies. Zeresh speaks with the wisdom perceived by Gentiles when God is present among his people (Num. 22–24; Dan. 2:46-47; 3:28-29). Haman's friends are referred to ironically as 'wise men' (NIV *advisers*). They offer no hope to a man who is marked by fate to fall. Like Balaam, they recognize the futility of trying to curse God's chosen people and bless Israel's enemies—especially when they are Amalekites (Num. 24:20; Judg. 5:21)."[16]

This was a terrible forecast for those who didn't belong to God. For those of us who are in covenant with God through Christ, however, what kinds of encouragement can we take from this concept?

Before we conclude, I want you to draw your attention to a play on words. Less obvious in English, the masterful writer of Esther weaves the Hebrew verb translated "to fall" like a prophetic tapestry throughout the narrative.

As I offer examples, circle every use and tense of the word "fall" the following paragraph.

> We're told in 3:7 that the lot "fell" on the month of Adar. In 6:10, Xerxes told Haman to do everything he suggested for Mordecai and "literally, not to let anything he had prescribed 'fall.'" (NIV translates the Hebrew verb as "do not neglect.") "Zeresh consequently uses the verb three times in her prediction: literally, 'Since Mordecai, before whom you have begun to "fall" before him, is of the seed of the Jews, you will not prevail over him but will "surely fall" before him.' (The Hebrew construction uses the verb in two different forms to provide emphasis in the phrase 'surely fall.') Haman's fate is complete in the next chapter once he 'falls' on the couch before Esther (7:8). From that point on, it is fear that 'falls' on those who oppose the Jews (8:17; 9:2-3)."[17]

In less academic terms, no one has further to fall than the one who set himself up. The humble, on the other hand, who spend their ailing strength on the weak will be lifted up in due time.

Remember my friend Lee? His health took a downward spiral after he fell from his chair. I've never been able to bear the thought of him, all alone in a hotel room, trying breathlessly to pull himself up by his wilting hands. A few days ago God raised him from that chair and caused his first steps in 20-something years to be on streets of gold, sprinting like a handsome youth toward the throne. At the thought, I recalled an e-mail I received from him a few years ago. He and his wonderful wife, Myrna, were going through the Daniel series and were perched in front of session 7. Lee wrote, "You just read Daniel 7:9." Allow me to interrupt his e-mail to share it with you.

"As I looked, 'thrones were set in place, and the Ancient of Days took his seat. His clothing was as white as snow; the hair of his head was white like wool. His throne was flaming with fire and its wheels were all ablaze."

You might want to read those last five words again. Captivated by them, my friend, Lee, continued, "I had no idea God's throne is the holiest of wheelchairs!"

All will fall before God's throne. Blessed is he—and blessed is she—who doesn't have far to go.

All will fall before

God's throne.

esther 6:6-11

The sixth chapter is "the hinge of the story of Esther."[13]
*God appoints or allows circumstances (often crises) in our lives
to redirect our paths. Today we explore the unexpected pivot
point of Esther by giving a name to an important concept in
the book:* _____ _____ ___ _____ *also
called* _____ _____ ___ _____. *Review Esther 6:6-11.*

**These reversals are part of a literary tapestry
that will open our eyes to see ...**

1. The beauty of the book's _____.

Am I willing to do the _____ to see the _____?

Two literary devices are employed magnificently in the Book of
Esther. The first is called "_____ _____."

What in the world is it? In its tightest form, chiastic structure is
_____ _____. In other words, it is a
_____ of structures to emphasize an _____
_____.

What's the best way to picture it?

• The "_____" that begins the word *chiastic* is the 22nd
letter of the _____ _____.

It is written like this: _____. The letter itself represents the

_____ literary structure of a chiasm (literally in Greek,

a crossing).

What's the best example of it in the Book of Esther? Chiastic

structure is deliciously illustrated in the repeated occurrences of

_____ _____ _____.

2. *The beauty of the book's* _____.

Esther's best theology is in its _____. To offer a

perfect example, we'll consider a second literary device called

"_____."

What in the world is it?

- "Peripety: a _____ _____ of events

  that _____ the expected or intended outcome"

  particularly in a literary work.[14]

Scenario #7

It's tough being a woman _____ _____

responsible ____ _____ "_____."

"A peripeteia swiftly turns a routine sequence of events into a _____

_____ _____."[15]

EDITOR'S NOTE: GP stands for God's Property, a gospel choir who sings with Kirk Franklin and other recording artists.

week seven

Where Is the Man?

Jesus came for people just like us. All saved by grace.

Freed by grace. Oh, for grace to love Him more!

Principal Questions

1. Why do you think Esther added the disclaimer that if they were only being sold as slaves, she wouldn't have disturbed Xerxes?
2. What similarities can you draw between Haman's actions and what you know about Satan in the rest of Scripture?
3. Exactly why did Haman stay behind when Xerxes left the room?
4. What did Haman do the moment the king left the room? When the king returned, what assumption did he make?
5. What was the king's state of mind after Haman's execution?

Day One
I Would Have Kept Quiet

TODAY'S TREASURE

"If we had merely been sold as male and female slaves, I would have kept quiet." Esther 7:4

I love women. Every time I pass a woman on the street, I want to stop the car and invite her to Bible study. The less she looks like the type, the more I want to ask her. I want her to know how much God loves her and what an awesome plan He has for her life and how He still reveals it through the Bible.

Hair salons are some of my favorite potential places for divine encounters. Just today I had my neck craned back and my head in the shampoo bowl while two hairdressers I've come to love began chatting in Spanish. I was an idiot not to take Spanish in school since most Houstonians speak the language, but this time I didn't need it. These two darling women spoke a language I clearly understood. The one looked at the other with a big smile, patted her tummy with one hand, and held up five fingers with the other. At that point, the one washing my hair answered in English, "I'm starting today!"

We both know what they were talking about, don't we? Women and dieting: Is there any pair that seems more destined to spend life together? Deliver us, Lord! A few minutes later one of the hairdressers started telling me in English what they were talking about. We all had such a great laugh when I interrupted her with, "Allow me to interpret. You've lost five pounds!" Bingo. Our encounter reminded me of one of the chiastic structure examples:

Eat to live.

Don't live to eat.

We learned that a chiastic structure is a reversal of wording to emphasize an overarching point. It's also called "inverted parallelism." I gave you several examples in the session and reminded you of one in the last paragraph.

Make up one of your own and write it in the margin.

I'm so thankful for your study-stamina. I feared some might resist braving the waters of linguistics. I want us to heighten our appreciation of Scripture and marvel not only over *what* God inspired but *how* He inspired it. The artistry of biblical Hebrew is at times stunningly beautiful. We caught a glimpse of God's artistic side in our session through the illustration of eight dinner plates representing eight of the banquets in this unique book. We learned that the

Book of Esther is a canvas of brilliantly colored chiastic paint strokes that find many of their intersecting points in the sixth chapter. Indeed, Esther 6 is the reversal point for the entire book.

Open the seventh chapter where we begin to encounter the dramatic results of those subtle reversals. Our focus is Esther 7:1-4, but we'll back up to refresh our memories concerning recent events. Please read Esther 6:12–7:4.

What dinner course were the king, Haman, and Esther observing when the pertinent conversation took place?

the wine course   the dessert course   the entrée

The wine course was the final course of a long Persian meal. Imagine the anxiety churning in Esther's stomach. Finally Xerxes posed the question, offering the same rhetorical gesture of "up to half the kingdom."

If these chapters were a movie, by this time we'd throw our popcorn at the screen and yell, "Tell him! Tell him!" Have you ever watched one of those flicks where a crisis could be averted by the truth but the character, for whatever reason, was reluctant to tell it? When the question finally came, Esther didn't blurt out the answer. Rather, she framed it very carefully.

At first glance, her ceremonial introduction ("If I have found favor with you, O king") sounds identical to the one she used at the banquet the evening before. But she made one slight change that hosted a world of difference. This time she did not address him in the more distant third-person form: "If I have won the King's favor." She spoke directly to him in a far more intimate tone: "If I have won *your* favor." In our immodest, say-whatever-you-think culture, we may not fully appreciate the difference, but in an ancient society it spoke volumes. If someone had wronged me and I wanted Keith to take it personally, I'd probably say: "Would you like to know what someone did to *your wife?*"

Personal Question If you were trying to get a heightened reaction out of your parent, how would you frame it?

Esther played the wife-card and wisely so. After all, she was about to tell him something about his wife that he could find most disconcerting.

With thoughtfulness and proper appreciation for her plight, fill in the following blanks from verse 4: "For _____ have been sold for destruction and slaughter and annihilation."

There you have it, Sister. The proverbial cat was out of the bag. King Xerxes had married a Jew and crowned her queen of the vast Persian Empire. He didn't just arrive at the conclusion gently. She shot him there like a rocket. By using the words "I and my people," she conveyed that they were one. Their

destiny was her destiny. The wise queen knew that Xerxes' willingness to protect his queen via his own dignity could well be his sole motivation for sparing a people he'd already sentenced. Again, Esther chose her words carefully as she voiced her request.

Look at Esther 3:13. What three actions were commanded by royal edict to be carried out upon all Jews, young and old, women and little children?

In 7:4 Esther repeated forms of those exact three words. You'll find them in the verse you filled in just moment ago. Find the verse near the bottom of page 156, and circle the three words. Offer a reason why she might have framed her description of the edict exactly that way.

Esther probably repeated the same terms—destruction, slaughter, and annihilation—to jar the king's memory and to emphasize the horror. Meanwhile, the mastermind behind the plan drank wine at their very table. I love the insight of one commentator on the fine line Esther had to avoid crossing:

"She understands full well the delicate and precarious nature of her position. The threat against her and her people has two perpetrators, Haman and the king, and both are present with her. She must somehow fully expose the culpability of Haman, while at the same time never appearing in any way to be bringing any charges against the king. Hence, her response is extremely well thought out and presented with the utmost tact."[1]

Making the king defensive would have been a grievous mistake. One of the most eye-opening elements of Esther's well-planned exposure to Xerxes is recorded in the second half of verse 4.

What condition did she claim wouldn't have warranted his involvement?

Why do you think she added the disclaimer?

Clearly both Esther and Haman recognized that the king had little interest in anything that wasn't centered on him. Xerxes was all about Xerxes. His self-centeredness was his weak spot and the quickest way to get close to him.

Esther may well qualify as one of the master politicians of all time. She approached the negotiating table with little or no experience, yet "she accomplishes the seemingly impossible, that is, the sidestepping of an irreversible law."[2] Of course, you and I know that the providence of a sovereign God was the overarching reason for her success, but few of us would deny that He used her approach: mannerly, feminine, sweet, smart, and shrewd.

God used Esther's approach: mannerly, feminine, sweet, smart, and shrewd.

The apostle Paul viewed success with words from a different perspective. What point did he make in 1 Corinthians 2:4-5?

The Holy Spirit's power was as surely at work in Persia that night. Esther just didn't realize it. A lover of words and language, I find the dialogue in the Esther narrative extremely interesting. I hope you do too.

A few days ago at a conference in a northern city I ran into a woman who told me about the desk clerk at their motel. The clerk was curious why so many women were descending on the city. When the woman told her about the conference, the clerk's face became radiant and she clutched her heart. She explained that she'd taken one of the Bible studies in prison and had received Jesus as her personal Savior as a result. The story nearly moved me to tears. Although we continued talking, I could hardly concentrate on anything else. I hopped in the car and asked the friend driving me to take me to that motel. To my disappointment, the clerk wasn't at work but her supervisor expected her about the time the conference began.

I left her a note telling how touched I was by our connection and how I'd love for her to be my guest at the event if she could attend any of it. I left a phone number so she could let us know. The next morning I learned that the clerk had indeed called and was coming. She explained that she'd be late because she wore an ankle bracelet for her parole and couldn't leave before a certain time. I could have bawled. During praise and worship a friend on my event team whispered in my ear, "She's here and she brought a friend. Is this a good time for you to meet them?" The clerk and I hugged like old friends who hadn't seen each other in way too long. She and I were two captives set free and not one more than the other.

I could see her face the entire time I taught and, in doing so, strangely saw my own. I loved her so much. In fact, more than is possible for strangers. I knew it was the love of Jesus using my simple frame as a momentary conduit. As I felt the smallest hint of His love for her, I also got the oddest feeling that He loved me too. After all, He came for people just like us. All saved by grace. Freed by grace. Oh, for grace to love Him more!

I kept thinking how right Jesus was when He said that we who would be willing to know the truth would be set free by it (John 8:32). He meant His truth, of course, but I started thinking how imprisoned we are by our unwillingness to tell the truth about ourselves. To just be honest. Authentic. I'm not talking about making shocking confessions that make us feel better but devastate someone else. I'm talking about simply being truthful about where we've come from … and where we hope we're going.

Why can't we be truthful? The answer may be what it could cost us. That's why Esther hesitated—why she had to fast, pray, and plan. For hosts of people to be delivered, she had to tell the truth about herself. And it could be deadly. Sometimes you simply decide that people are worth telling on yourself.

Jesus came for people just like us. All saved by grace. Freed by grace. Oh, for grace to love Him more!

Day Two
An Adversary and an Enemy

TODAY'S TREASURE

"Esther said, 'The adversary and enemy is this vile Haman.'" Esther 7:6

My man amuses himself by pausing a television show with the character or newscaster frozen in the most awkward facial expression possible. He then leaves the person captured on screen in his or her indignity for a good half hour while he casually spreads himself a ham sandwich. I don't think it's funny, a fact that makes it all the more amusing to Keith. I try to remind him that someone could do that very thing to *his wife*. Goodness knows I offer plenty of weird expressions to freeze into indignities. *How would he like that?* I asked him. He claims he'd be appalled, but with a man like Keith, you never know.

We concluded yesterday's lesson at a highly charged moment. To say we left the characters hanging would be an understatement and a prophetic word for one of them. We begin today's lesson by applying Keith's technique to the scene. Reread Esther 7:1-4. Imagine that you pushed "pause" on the remote control and froze the scene at the very end of Esther's sentence in verse 4.

Describe the expressions and postures you picture on each character:

Xerxes:

Haman:

Esther: 1.

Now read Esther 7:5-6. Finally, she said the scoundrel's name. What a relief! And what a risk! We'll discuss Esther's finger-pointing later, but we need to peel away several layers of the scene first. Note Xerxes' immediate reaction.

List in the margin the two questions he asked.   2.

I'd suggest that Esther purposely didn't identify Haman when she stated her crisis in verse 4. She waited until Xerxes asked the identity of the villain to point out their dinner guest. The Bible records a similar approach to identifying wrongdoing to a reluctant confessor in 2 Samuel. Glance at the subject matter of 2 Samuel 11 to remember the circumstance, and read 2 Samuel 12:1-7a.

What metaphor did Nathan the prophet use to confront King David?

Describe David's reaction in verses 5 and 6. _____

What four words did Nathan say to David in verse 7b? _____ _____ _____ _____!

Talk about a frozen-on-screen moment! Imagine David's expression. As reality sank into King Headache's skull he probably made a similar face.

Toward the end of our previous lesson we talked about a very fine line Esther had to avoid crossing in her request to the king. Remember, Xerxes' passivity was as much to blame for the death sentence on the Jews as Haman's activity. Xerxes was also the only person on earth who could save them. If Esther made him defensive, she'd lose her case and probably her head.

Brilliantly, she left out Haman's identity in verse 3 so she could put a bow and arrow in Xerxes' hands before she pointed him toward the target. Had he known from the beginning that the culprit was his own right hand man, the king might have protected him. Instead, he'd virtually indicted him by the time he identified him. What could he do but follow through? And by the time she'd raised his ire through the palace roof, why wouldn't he want to?

Let's lower the stakes and relate. If Sabrina, my ministry director, told me someone on our staff was goofing off at work after repeated warnings, I might rush to advise the employee's dismissal. If I then learned it was Amanda or Melissa, I'd feel caught by my own words and obliged to follow through. If Sabrina began instead, by saying, "I need to talk to you about your daughter," I'd probably feel defensive and react differently. Make sense?

👑 Can you think of a time you spoke too soon but didn't know how to renege? If so, in the margin describe the experience.

In Esther 7:5 did you note Xerxes' wording? "Where is the man who has *dared* to do such a thing?" How do you discern the difference between the questions, "How could you?" and "How dare you?" Do they hit you differently?

To me "How dare you?" voices offense above injury. It is a question posed by someone who is appalled with insult. This one tiny word may suggest to us that "Xerxes' concern is not for the endangered people, and not even primarily for Esther's safety, but for the royal honor. This has somehow (it does not matter exactly how) been offended, and he wants to know who is to blame."[3]

If the English translation of the dialogue between Esther and Xerxes in verses 5 and 6 is dramatic, the Hebrew is lightning-bolt electric. "Although lost in English translation, the king's fury is effectively communicated in the Hebrew words, which sound like machine-gun fire when pronounced aloud."[4] In my own paraphrase, "Who is he? Where is he? How dare he!"

"The emotion and anger of Esther's reply are also lost in the bland English translation. In the Hebrew, her words ring out with staccato cadence."[5] Stay with this thought so you can hear its punchy alliteration in your heart like the drum in a marching band. Esther's "accusation [of Haman] is built of two phrases of three beats each, with the second phrase punctuated by identical opening syllables. Each word is a blow."[6]

So, picture it: Xerxes and Esther paired on the dance floor of splendid drama, their words tap-dancing back and forth but not with the light foot of the carefree. Each syllable was like a steely stomp on a marble floor, echoing accusation so high pitched it could have shattered the wine glass in Haman's trembling hand. Of premier priority, by the end of this rumba, both Esther and Xerxes were on the same side of the dance floor.

In the margin write the first thought you think Haman had the moment Esther identified him. Keep in mind he likely had no idea she was a Jew.

Lock your eyes on Esther's identification of Haman in verse 6. What two names did she call the vile man Haman?

Adversary   Blasphemer   Betrayer   Murderer   Enemy

Those two identities ring with haunting familiarity. First Peter 5:8 warns us our "*enemy* the devil prowls around like a roaring lion looking for someone to devour." The name *Satan* means *adversary*. In the most monumental terms, you and I have a far more dangerous adversary and enemy than Haman. So did Esther. Reflect on chapters 3 through 6 of the Esther narrative and think about ways Haman's actions echo what you know about Satan.

In the margin note all the similarities you can draw between the two.

Principal Question

Since I knew the question was coming, I already had some answers ready and our comparisons are probably similar. Satan is an arrogant (Ezek. 28:17), ambitious (Isa. 14:13-14), deceiving and manipulating (John 8:44) opportunist (Luke 4:13) who has been a "murderer from the beginning" (John 8:44). Over and over I am astonished at the effectiveness of our enemy to deceive people into thinking that Christianity is bondage, but his path (disguised as human independence, Matt. 16:23) is freedom.

How does Psalm 18:3-6,16-19 contrast God's care to the enemy's attack?

161

Satan, our adversary, promises freedom but, after gaining trust, delivers such destructive entanglement that his victim feels life being squeezed out of him. God, on the other hand, delivers us to "a spacious place" where He rescues us because He delights in us (Ps.18:19).

Be onto the schemes of the Enemy. He knows you've been chosen by God for such a time as this. As surely as Esther exposed Haman to Xerxes, expose your enemy to Christ. Unlike Esther's king, yours already knows the identity and tactics of your adversary and enemy, but your victory begins the moment you take your stand along His scarred side.

Day Three
Begging for Life

TODAY'S TREASURE

"But Haman, realizing that the king had already decided his fate, stayed behind to beg Queen Esther for his life." Esther 7:7

I know a man reaping the whirlwind of a two-year bout of destructive choices. He doesn't understand why his wife won't believe he's a changed man. To his credit, he has been on a great track for the last two weeks, but before that he broke promises just like the ones he's making now. His stance: It's real this time. Her stance: Why should this time be different from the rest?

I watched someone very dear to me spend himself blind both financially and emotionally on 15 rounds of rehab for his wife, only to have her drink on the way home *every single time*. When he laid down a boundary, she morphed into the victim, guilt-shaming him and telling how mean he was.

What does mercy mean? Does it mean giving someone what he or she wants? Do we trust the untrustworthy? Where's the balance between pardon and prudence? Try as we may we cannot read another person's mind, look in his heart, nor be certain of her motive. God alone possesses the power. He knew no one else could handle it. We often battle deep conflicts of soul over whether or not to trust a person.

Personal Question

Without mentioning names, in the margin describe the general circumstances of your last time to battle over trusting.

Are you thankful for your decision now or do you regret it?

These are hard issues, aren't they? Esther has introduced discussions we didn't expect. Undoubtedly we're about to have one of those days. The second half of today's lesson will raise a difficult question, but not because it's rarely asked.

By the way, have I told you lately how much I love you and appreciate the privilege to study God's Word with you? Had I simply studied by myself, I'd never have taken the time to grapple with certain questions. You have dramatically intensified my walk with Christ. That means everything to me.

Read Esther 7:6-7 and try not to look ahead. Let's look at several elements captured in this segment before we tackle the bigger issue.

First, what was Haman's reaction when Esther pointed him out?
_____terror _____shame _____fury _____anxiety

Note who his reaction was toward. Two little words have enormous implications. "Haman was terrified before the king _____ _____."

Suddenly Esther was a force all her own. No one comes into the full-throttle power of their destiny all at once. Almost invariably we discover that kind of enabling in a time of desperation when we can no longer depend on ourselves. It then grows in private places of prayer. Something else strikes me with significance in the wording of 7:6. This is the first reference specifically to "the king and queen." We've met them in the same scenes but they were not two people sharing life together as one. Up to now they have not once been showcased in print as a pair standing side-by-side on level ground as an actual couple.

Don't get me wrong. They are still light years from normal. If we're looking for a study on healthy marriage, we're barking up the wrong tree with Xerxes and Esther; however, something worthy of mention is inferred here.

A husband and wife can bond when a threat arises. We can be two people living very separate lives when, all at once, crisis shoves us onto common ground. In Satan's vicious attacks against our marriages and families, he remains unmoved until we decide, as different as we are and as much conflict as we've had, to stand together. Then, Beloved, he is terrified.

What did Christ say about this in Matthew 12:25?

Praise His merciful name, the reverse is also true. A united kingdom stands, but no more strongly than a united household. Now let's concentrate on Xerxes' reaction to the news that Haman had prepared the destruction of his queen.

What did Xerxes do (v. 7)? _____

Why in the world do you think he charged out of the room?

If a tidal wave of crisis threatened my family and my foolish actions had been complicit in it, I'd need a time-out! Xerxes' situation was even more complicated. He had to weigh the value of a good wife versus a good right-hand man. Hadn't they both betrayed him in a way? Had either been completely honest? His mind, which had yet to prove to be brilliant, was spinning like a top.

One honest emotion kept the king of the vast Persian Empire tied by a thin heartstring to the rest of humanity—he was angry. A man had tried, however inadvertently, to take his wife. Everything we know about Xerxes suggests that his primary interest was always himself, but I wonder if something foreign to him, something he could neither understand nor define, fanned the flames of his rage. The Hebrew word *rage* in 7:7 is used one other time for him.

What were the circumstances in Esther 1:12? _____

This time Xerxes wasn't infuriated *at* his queen. Perhaps the solitary unselfish sliver of him was infuriated *for* his queen. Maybe, if only for a moment, Esther wasn't just Xerxes' queen. She was also his wife. With a man like Xerxes, attraction comes and goes. Attachment was the question now. Was he more attached to a woman or to his right-hand man? Vashti had been instantly replaceable. Was Esther? Ironically Haman knew the answer to the question perhaps more rapidly than Xerxes.

What did Haman realize (v. 7)? _____

Principal Question We've now arrived at the issue introduced at the beginning of today's lesson. Exactly why did Haman stay behind?

Let's emphasize the fact again: Haman begged Esther for his life. In the margin write several sentences he might have used in his plea:

Verse 8 suggests that Haman was probably down on his knees as he begged Queen Esther for his life. She did not give it to him. Scholars through the centuries have grappled with whether or not she did the right thing. The more aware of our own need for mercy, the more prone we are to extend it.

Couldn't God have worked Israel's deliverance through a repentant Haman? Would God not have received even greater glory? God said of Himself in Ezekiel 33:11, "As surely as I live, declares the Sovereign LORD, I take no pleasure in the death of the wicked, but rather that they turn from their ways and live. Turn! Turn from your evil ways!"

I don't think Esther should have spared Haman, and I'll tell you a few reasons why. I don't think she could take the chance that he or the situation would change. Furthermore, does begging for one's life equal repentance? Is anything more natural or instinctive than pleading for your own skin when it's in jeopardy? One commentator spoke most rationally to me: "So long as

an enemy as powerful and shrewd as Haman lived, he was a threat to Esther, Mordecai, and the Jewish community. To say here that Esther was merciless and unfeeling is to misinterpret the entire situation. Thus, while her heart might have prompted her to be merciful, logic and prudence restrained her."[7]

I think Esther did the only thing she could wisely do, but maybe not without wrestling. Perhaps the only solid ground beneath these murky waters is Haman's ancestry. If King Saul had done his job generations earlier and annihilated the Agagites like God told him to do, Esther and the Jews wouldn't have been faced with this vicious murderer.

Keith's dearest friend of 25 years sits on the bench of a Houston court. Those on trial in his courtroom are blessed to have him for a judge. I've never known a man and his wife to seek the wisdom and discernment of God more passionately. Can you imagine having the responsibility of overseeing who gets leniency and who needs severity? Who gets a life sentence? Who gets death?

I'd like to think that most judges take their positions seriously and reverently, but here's what I know for certain: Whether in a courtroom or in one of our kitchens, if man refuses mercy to someone who should have received it, God will never refuse it. The reverse is equally true. If man showers mercy on someone who squanders it, the Ancient of Days will always have the final say. The last face Haman saw in his earthly life was Esther's. The first face he saw in eternity was God's. Woe unto the one whose regret did not turn to repentance.

I can't think of a better way to end than asking you to write Proverbs 26:27 in the margin. Thank you for your vulnerability, Dear Sister.

Day Four
Will He Even?

TODAY'S TREASURE

"Just as the king returned from the palace garden to the banquet hall, Haman was falling on the couch where Esther was reclining." Esther 7:8

Sometimes God allows the unjust to get a taste of their own medicine through injustice. With deep sobriety, this week reminds me that people really don't get away with murder or even its premeditation. Our scene today is the superlative Old Testament illustration of a passage from Proverbs.

"The one who digs a pit will fall into it, and whoever rolls a stone—
        it will come back on him." Proverbs 26:27

Write the same proverb in your own words:

Haman accused and condemned an entire people for a crime of insubordination they did not commit. Ironically, the crowning blow that condemns him to death will be a crime he did not commit. Knowingly or not, Haman had placed himself in Satan's hands only to be betrayed by him. It happens every time. First Satan lies to us. Then Satan lies for us. Then Satan lies about us. Please read Esther 7:6-9, allowing the segment to overlap previous readings so we can experience the full effect.

Principal Question   What did Haman do the moment the king left the room?

When the king returned, what assumption did he make?

As readers we know that nothing could have been further from Haman's mind than sexual advances toward the queen. He was a bit preoccupied with begging for his life. Xerxes had no such knowledge nor might he have cared. A preconceived notion may have caused him to jump from suspicion to conviction in the blink of a green eye.

Think back to our discussions on chapter 5. Remember several scholars think Haman's inclusion in the dinner parties may have aroused the king's jealousy. To be sure, Esther was dressed to absolute perfection, perhaps even lovelier than the king recalled. He, on the other hand, had been preoccupied and hadn't bothered to call for her in 30 days. The men who worked nearest to him may have been loyal, but they weren't blind. Let's face it. Sometimes we take for granted what we have until we see that someone else admires it. When we've grown sadly accustomed to a beautiful sight, nothing jars a fresh vision quite like seeing it through somebody else's astonished eyes.

Esther possessed the kind of aura that robbed the room of all other attentions. Don't be quick to picture her less exquisite than she'd been five years earlier when she first appeared before the king. In my opinion a woman only grows lovelier the first four decades of her life. Then, as they say, she grows wise. (Wise enough to pick the right hair color, I hope.)

Esther invited no one but Haman to dine with the royal couple, a fact that might have seemed reasonable for one intimate dinner gathering, *but two?* Perhaps Xerxes dismissed the notion at first—too egotistical to imagine that Esther could have any other interest. When Xerxes stormed back into the room and found Haman on Esther's couch, he put two and two together and got six. Even the geniuses among us can have a little trouble calculating a simple equation when their minds are spinning. I have a feeling most of us have learned the hard way that suspicion can wildly impair summation.

166

When was the last time you put two and two together and got six?

A few years ago someone felt "protective" enough of me to let me know that they'd seen my husband at a Chinese restaurant with a woman and that they seemed familiar with one another. Don't think for a moment that I can't jump to conclusions, but I couldn't help but think Keith would have lost his ever-loving mind to carry on with another woman in public. I know women from Bible study who would have accosted him right in the restaurant and beaten him bloody with their workbooks. Wontons would have been flying.

My marriage is far from invulnerable, but the numbers just didn't add up on this one. Sure enough, the other woman turned out to be Tina, my beloved sister-in-law, and, yes, the two of them are pretty familiar with one another.

Hopefully in those times you and I put two and two together and got six, we didn't sentence someone to irreversible consequences over our miscalculations. Strong visceral feelings like jealousy are extremely untrustworthy sources for reading a situation and even worse for inviting appropriate responses. Jealousy is a notorious misperceiver.

If you agree, why do you think this is true?

Personal Question

Read the Scriptures in the margin and list specific impacts of jealousy.

Proverbs 6:34-35

Haman got the right sentence even if for the wrong reason. We've just had another run-in with providence. God could use even a clueless king's misperceptions to exact His judgment. Haman didn't stand a chance when Xerxes walked back in the room. The king couldn't blame himself, so somebody else's head was going to have to roll. One of them—Haman or Esther—had to go.

Proverbs 27:4

Keep in mind that by the time Xerxes found Haman collapsed on Esther's couch, the pump of the king's anger had been primed by the humiliating predicament he found himself in, thanks to his right-hand man. Xerxes had signed off thoughtlessly on an immutable sentence of death that included his very own queen who, incidentally, would be recognized as a Jew before the snap of a noose. The circumstances etched a *fait accompli* for Haman and the king hastened to sign his name to it.

Song of Songs 8:6

One commentary explains that, "Harem protocol dictated that no one but the king could be left alone with a woman of the harem. Haman should have left Esther's presence when the king retreated to the garden, but where could he have gone? His choice was either to follow the king, who had bolted in anger from his presence, or to flee the room, suggesting guilt and inviting pursuit. Haman is trapped. Even in the presence of others, a man was not to approach a woman of the king's harem within seven steps. That Haman should actually fall on the couch where Esther is reclining is unthinkable!

Haman's untoward behavior is so unimaginable that in the Aramaic *Targum of Esther* he falls on the queen's couch only because the angel Gabriel has given him a firm shove, sealing his fate. It is Haman's final, fatal action."[8]

I doubt Gabriel got to give Haman a shove, but I don't doubt he was close by and willing. Did you catch the part of the quote concerning the required distance between a man and one of the king's women? Another commentary echoed the custom: "No men, other than assigned eunuchs and the king, were allowed within seven paces of harem women."[9] I don't know much about harems, but I know about homes. As the mother of two daughters, I rather like that approach. The young men who came calling on our teenage girls should have been well advised to keep a distance of seven paces from them or they'd find themselves half a pace from Mr. Moore.

Haman's desperation caused him a deadly lapse in decorum. Glance again at the king's accusation of Haman in Esther 7:8. "Xerxes's reaction is an exclamation, literally: 'Also to ravish the queen with me here in the house?'"[10] One commentator explains that our English translation comes from a sentence fragment in the Hebrew that indicates the king's agitated morale. He called Xerxes' state of mind "confused fury."[11] I've had some of that myself from time to time. How about you? Few things make us feel more out of control than being large on emotion and low on information. Thankfully for Xerxes, the king didn't have to think clearly about what to do next. He had someone to do that for him. Read Esther 7:9.

Who stepped in with a plan? _____

We've seen this character before. Read Esther 1:10-12. Who was he?

What had he experienced in this early segment of our narrative?

> To wrap up a life ready to meet our Maker is sublimely important.

Harbona was obviously among the assigned eunuchs who were allowed within seven paces of the king's wife. The narrative calls him by name twice and each in a context where one of Xerxes' queens, Vashti or Esther, was present. No surprise that Harbona was quick to suggest a sentence for Haman.

What did we learn about Esther at the very end of 2:15?

Harbona's position gave him a perch with a bird's-eye view to see both sides of center stage. Unlike Xerxes, he was large on information but perhaps not entirely low on emotion. He'd watched the power-hungry Haman weasel the signet ring right off Xerxes' finger. He'd also watched Mordecai's bravery overlooked and Esther's royal position all but ignored. Somewhere along the way,

Harbona had discovered their relationship … and their nationality. Possibly, he'd even overseen infrequent secret meetings. One thing is clear: Harbona was favorable enough to both Esther and Mordecai to offer the king the quick convenience of a nearby gallows and to point out that it was prepared by Haman to kill the man who'd protected his highness.

We don't get to see the look on Haman's face when he realized that the fate he'd assigned Mordecai with such wicked satisfaction befell him instead. Remember, they'd covered his face. He could have guessed the route however. After all, without God on our side, where we're going is just the ugly side of where we've been.

Day Five
A Hung-Up Life

TODAY'S TREASURE

"So they hanged Haman on the gallows he had prepared for Mordecai. Then the king's fury subsided." Esther 7:10

Lately I've given some thought to good endings. Not the kind that close books, though I do dearly love a well-written finish. I'm talking about good endings to lives. Perhaps the subject is on my mind because the first anniversary of my dad's death just passed. Like many of us, my dad lived a measure of his life crippled by defeat. But during my young adult years his knees hit the ground in repentance and he surrendered himself to serve Christ for the rest of his days. Dad ended well. I'll be blessed to come close to finishing mine as well.

To say that "all's well that ends well" is simplistic and at times inaccurate, but to wrap up a life ready to meet our Maker is sublimely important. Today we conclude our seventh week of study. The story line will loop around the neck of Haman and hang him from the top of the ladder he spent his life climbing. His life ends here, poorly and embarrassingly. After such a jealous pursuit of greatness, his body will dangle like a tattered flag over Susa waving the words, "Failure! Infidel! Fraud! Fool!" Our text in Esther consists of one brief verse, but in the way only Scripture can, it packs a punch, providing a critical transition in our narrative. Please read Esther 7:10.

Record how Haman's life ended.

What was the king's state of mind after Haman's execution?

This small piece of information subtly underscores what we've come to expect of Xerxes. Nothing has changed for the Jews, yet the self-absorbed king was awash with relief and his anger assuaged. One commentary captured it especially well. "The shocking 'exposé' of Haman's dealings and plots were viewed through the half-light of Xerxes's ego ... All the events were reinterpreted as direct assaults on [him]. He had no vision for the effect on others and the greater catastrophe that still hung over the Jews."[13]

Why do you think our ego could cause us to see a situation in half-light?

Perhaps half-lit in more ways than one, Xerxes felt a world better with Haman dead. Meanwhile, the Jews remained sentenced to death by irrevocable law.

Esther still had to face the music Haman composed. An old Yugoslavian proverb says, "Tell the truth and run!" Unfortunately, Esther couldn't tell the truth and run, nor often can we. As we've discussed in the last several weeks, to expose Haman and fight for the lives of her people, she had to expose herself. Unlike the secular proverb, Esther had to tell the truth *and stay* ... long after Haman's evil body was impaled on a pole.

When was the last time you were tempted to tell the truth and run?

Perhaps like Esther, you discovered that telling the truth was only the battle cry. The war had just begun. I love how one commentary offers a familiar scene from a movie to capture the predicament. "From the beginning of Esther 7 to its end, the Jews go from the depths of despair to seeing the death of despair—Haman, their enemy, is dead! The Jews can celebrate! Yet, all is not as it should be. Just as in *The Wizard of Oz,* when the Munchkins sing 'Ding dong, the witch is dead,' the viewer soon realizes that the killing of the witch (or of Haman) does not resolve all of the problems presented in the story."[12]

Haman was dead, but ten thousands of Persians stood to carry out his bidding. Even those mystified by the royal edict lacked the courage to question it. What would Esther do now? The real enemy of the Jews had taken a hit with Haman's death, but the larger plan was still in motion. He may have whispered to Esther his own rendition of the famous line, "I'll get you, my pretty," but he'd be sadly mistaken. She was more than a pretty face.

The brevity of today's text offers us the space to veer a tad for the remainder of this lesson. I'm praying the detour is Spirit-led because God seems to be going out of His way to open my eyes to this theme. This morning as I sat at my back porch table and prayed for God to fill me and thrill me to

write today's lesson, I mused over all the royal adventures we've shared in this unique Bible narrative. The Book of Esther is a fast-moving, nail-biting mini-series where evil threatens to win and reversals whirl and spin, where orphans become queens and villains trick kings.

Drama doesn't get better than Esther. As I made my petition for God's help in wrapping up this chapter, my mind swam with thoughts of royal intrigue. For whatever reason, my eyes also cased the morning's entries in my prayer journal as if they were lessons in amusing contrast. This is no Queen Esther. This is a middle-aged woman who pulled a load of underwear out of the dryer this morning. As I stared at my handwritten requests scrawled across the page, I was suddenly stricken with the beauty of simplicity.

I'd written things like, "Lord, please keep Keith safe as he travels to south Texas. Thank You for helping my man and me move past that argument this week." And, "Lord, thank You for protecting Jackson when he tumbled down the playground stairs. Shield his little body from his adventurous spirit. Thank You for his parents. Help them to love each other well today." "Lord, thank You for Melissa. For the homemade cookies she sent me in the mail. For the brand-new Bible pens she couldn't resist sticking in the box with them. For laughter, Lord. For love. For plans." "Lord, please help me not be so sad today about Sunny."

This may seem small if you don't have pets, but a few days ago I said good-bye to my little dog, my constant shadow of 16 years. It didn't make the evening news but it nearly broke my heart. Perhaps you offered a few petitions to God recently that seemed equally unimpressive by global standards.

In the margin list a few every-day items from your recent prayer list.

This is the stuff of ordinary life. We have trash to take out. Bills to pay. Mortgages to meet. Make no mistake. Extraordinary things happen around us continually. We just don't always recognize them. The thought occurs to me afresh that great lives don't always seem great while we're living them. They may seem embarrassingly regular. Seeking to be extraordinary isn't the answer because great lives are never achieved by making greatness the goal.

Today we draw the last few strokes on the character sketch of Haman, a man poisoned by his own pursuit of greatness. Driven by selfish ambition, his life ended tragically, but had it begun innocuously? As a boy, might he have been what we call a born leader? As a mom squirming on the couch of psychiatry where parents get blamed for everything, I'm reluctant to add to the unfair press. But when Haman's life went so awry, shouldn't we wonder where it first went wrong? The generations pouring into his life were not innocent in at least one respect. Children aren't born prejudiced. They're taught it.

Did the same group of people also drive his narcissism? And, even if they did, did they mean well? Might they have believed he was special somehow and told him over and over how destined for greatness he was?

171

Here's one reason I'm asking. In a thought-provoking article entitled *My So-Called Genius* author Laura Fraser recounts her remarkable journey from being a whiz-kid to a fairly-ordinary adulthood of unmet expectations. By age five she was well acquainted with the word *precocious* and told repeatedly how special she was. The next years did not disappoint. She was brilliant and darling and surpassed her peers, drawing the attention of adults who said she was destined for greatness. Then came college where she entered an academic world of peers who had been told the same thing.

By her late forties, Fraser had accomplished many good things but the expectation of greatness and the sense that she'd never quite achieved it (despite a best seller) haunted her with feelings of failure. All the well-meaning forecasts had done nothing but cast a pall of perfectionism upon her and, as her consultant so aptly pointed out, "Perfectionists always lose."

Fraser writes, "If your identity is wrapped in the magnificent things you're destined to achieve—as a great writer, musician, scientist, politician, chef—the thought that you might produce something mediocre can be devastating."[15]

I'm not suggesting that this kind of mentality produces a "Haman," but I do wonder what happens when someone is raised with strong expectations of greatness but no respect for his fellow man. Wouldn't any means to fame suffice? Keep that question in mind when you walk into session 7.

Haman's pursuit of greatness made him a shameless opportunist. For others, the temptation is to become a perfectionist. When Fraser was struggling with her first book that "had to be great," a psychologist posed an intriguing question: "You can write a good book, can't you?" Paraphrased: Do you have to do something great? Can you be happy to do something really good?

Think about it, Sister. Couldn't the craving to do something great keep us from doing something good?

In week 5 we discussed how perfectionism would have paralyzed Esther if she'd given way to it, but today's lesson offers us a chance to broaden the spectrum. Let's spread around the responsibility for destructive expectations of greatness to the generations. As parents, teachers, relatives, leaders, or observers, we are wise to be careful about telling gifted children how great they are destined to be. It is a trap and a forecast Fraser claims rarely pans out. She points out the monumental difference between talent and having a clue what to do with it and how genius rarely exempts people from having to work hard just like everybody else who wants to make it.

Don't get me wrong. I'm a big believer in encouraging young people just as the apostle Paul encouraged Timothy.

List a few things Paul told his "dear son" in the faith in 1 Timothy 4:12-15.

> To live for the greatness of God is to live the great life.

Accolades like these are meant to be balanced with the teaching that every gift is a trust placed in human hands by a holy God. The blessed recipient is responsible for developing the integrity, humility, and work-ethic to know what to do with it. (See 2 Tim.1:6!) Gift without grit is a pitiful waste.

Fraser's article made me think how wise God's way is. If we're willing to follow His path on the winding road map of Scripture, we have the joy of side-stepping this ankle-breaking trap. So will a few children we're privileged to train. Living just to be great will prove at least empty and maybe even deadly. We'd ask Haman if he weren't busy dangling from the gallows.

Spending ourselves for something infinitely greater still fans our parched souls with the God-given need to matter, but relieves us of the relentless pain of being the "It" person at the center of it. Haman wanted to be the "It" person in the worst way. In doing so, his life turned out to be a humiliating disaster.

To live for the greatness of God is to live the great life. Oh, I know we've heard it before, but what if it finally clicked? What if we awakened to what a dream-killer perfectionism is? To how pitifully small and unworthy a goal personal greatness is? We were meant for so much more.

Every one of us who embraces the glory of God as our purpose will end up doing great things precisely because we do God-things. His holy hand resting on the least act renders the ordinary extraordinary. Spooning soup into the mouth of the weak or manning the nursery so a tired mom can go to church are acts of high worship when offered in the name of Christ. He beholds the sight like a breathtaking work of art, tilting His head to study each subtle detail. "She has done a beautiful thing to me" (Mark 14:6).

Christ, the very One who called us to abundant, effective life and commanded us to splash in the cool springs of joy while living it, announced the following secrets to the great life without a hint of contradiction.

Read each segment thoughtfully, then record the secrets.
Matthew 16:24-26

Mark 10:43-44

Christ summons the disillusioned to the paradoxical bliss of spilling life lavishly, sacrificially for the glory of God and the good of man. Those with presence of mind and semblance of health are called to pour out the drink offering of their lives until the cup is overturned and every drop of energy slips—perhaps unnoticed, uncelebrated—into the vast ocean of earthly need. The last imperceptible drop of your well-lived life will sound to the hosts of heaven like a tidal wave hitting the floor of the Grand Canyon.

In effect Christ says, "I'm already great enough for both of us," relieving the willing of their woeful burden. "Just follow Me."

viewer guide ⚜ session seven

Esther 7–8:2 shows the impact of the climactic events on all four major players.

Every _____-_____ starts with ____ _____.

1. Esther _____ _____.

(See Est. 7:3 and 8:1.)

"Literally, '_____ ____ _____ ____ _____.' The author probably intended to convey more than is being suggested by the translation 'that he was _____ to her.' "[16]

2. Haman _____ _____.

(See Esth. 7:10. Compare Ps. 7:15-16.)

3. Xerxes _____ _____.

(See Esth. 8:1. Compare 2 Cor. 8:9.)

4. Mordecai _____ ____.

(See Esth. 8:1-2.)

Now see the "Turn It Around!" page and fill in the appropriate blanks.*

Editor's Note: This form is available in the leader guide and online at www.lifeway.com/bethmoore.

Turn Around Scenario #7

It's tough being a woman who feels responsible for the "how."

"The _____ _____ _____ to rescue the godly from trials and to keep the unrighteous under punishment until the day of judgment." (2 Pet. 2:9, HCSB)

"For ____ _____ _____ we are formed, he remembers that we are dust." (Ps. 103:14)

Turn Around Scenario #6

It's tough being a woman who can balance passion with patience.

"Yet the LORD _____ to be gracious to you; he rises to show you compassion. For the LORD is a God of justice. Blessed are all who _____ for him." (Isa. 30:18)

"The Lord _____ ... blessed are all those who _____ for Him." (ESV)

"That same day," Esther 8:1

"Rather than love, than money, than _____ give me _____.

— Henry David Thoreau (*Walden*, 1854)

week eight
The Right to Be Ready

Often when we thrill to the realization of a call from God, we picture

going from our faces to our feet as He increasingly elevates our position.

The reverse, however, is often truer in the earthly realm.

Principal Questions

1. As far as Xerxes was concerned, he'd offered Esther the world, but from Esther's perspective he'd not yet given her what she was after. How is she pictured in Esther 8:3?
2. According to Esther 8:7-8, what did the king suggest Esther and Mordecai should do?
3. According to Esther 8:9-13, how do the Scriptures invite you to feel the urgency of Esther and Mordecai's response?
4. How did Mordecai leave the presence of the king as the couriers departed Susa (Esth. 8:14-15)?
5. What happened in Esther 8:15-17?

Day One
Falling at His Feet

TODAY'S TREASURE

"Esther again pleaded with the king, falling at his feet and weeping."

Esther 8:3

I'm writing you again from the seat of an airplane, fighting the temptation to ask myself for the millionth time how this many tons of steel suspends 25,000 feet above the ground. I couldn't help but overhear the chatter between several flight attendants. OK, the truth is, I could help it but I'm dreadfully nosy and shamelessly distracted by people dynamics.

The male flight attendant said, "I hear congratulations are in order!" The female flight attendant quipped dryly, "Yep. That's right. I got married. And I probably made the worst mistake of my life." Wide-eyed, my first thought was that I surely hoped not. My second thought was how thankful I am that the first few months of my marriage were poor indicators of what lay ahead.

When the reality of a distant, unfaithful marriage sunk into Esther's pretty head, she also may have wondered if she'd made the worst mistake of her life. For now, however, she could play no such game with herself. Mordecai was obviously right. She'd come to royal position "for such a time as this" (Esth. 4:14). Two dinner parties behind her, Haman was dead, but in a matter of months so were the Jews if the rest of her plan proved unsuccessful.

We have a very interesting week of study ahead. Please begin by reading Esther 8:1-6. Hopefully you participated in session 7 because we focused on the first several verses of this chapter at that time. Let's recap briefly.

In the margin list the monumental events recorded in 8:1-2.

To our knowledge Mordecai and the king had never been face-to-face until now. Don't you wonder if Mordecai was overwhelmed by the palace or if he was as unimpressed as he's seemed up to now? One of my favorite parts of session 7 was the alternate wording of verse 1. Esther told the king what Mordecai "was to her." The tone suggests far more than identifying him as her cousin. She told Xerxes how much her adopted father meant to her.

Luckily for them at this critical point in the drama, Xerxes was impetuously moved. Why wait to get to know Mordecai? Somebody needed Haman's job or Xerxes might have to do his own. The king's signet ring flew off his finger and onto Mordecai's before Haman's hand could chill.

> Esther had come to royal position for such a time as this.

What irony appears at the end of verse 2?

In many ancient kingdoms the crown could assume title over a traitor's property, no questions asked. Mordecai now oversaw Haman's entire estate and, in fact, could have pulled a moving van right up to his mansion if he wanted.

Do you think you'd feel satisfaction or revulsion if the state awarded you the property of your archenemy? As far as Xerxes was concerned, he'd offered Esther the world, but from Esther's perspective he'd not yet given her what she was after.

How is Esther pictured in verse 3?

In 5:2 Esther *stood* before the king. In 5:6 and 7:1, she *sat* before him at the banquet table, but here Esther *fell* before the king, weeping and begging.

Often when we thrill to the realization of a call from God, we picture going from our faces to our feet as He increasingly elevates our position. The reverse, however, is often truer in the earthly realm. To accomplish our call, we must be humbled far more than exalted, though God certainly lifts up His faithful servant in due time. Up to now we've seen Esther composed if nervous. Here, however, urgency replaces dignity and tears fall like rain.

Sometimes you just can't hold yourself together a second longer. You've stayed strong to be everybody's rock through a difficult situation. You couldn't afford to lose your head because too much was at stake. Amazingly, you held it together through the most threatening phase, wondering all along what alien person with composure had overtaken your body. Then just about the time the first ounce of pressure came off and you imagined feeling relief, here it comes: the ugly cry. You can't stop it. You can't hide it. You can't excuse it. It's been storing up inside of you for months and the pressure cooker begins to blow. The face contorts, the chest heaves, the nose snorts, and the flood falls.

Have you ever had an ugly cry in public? If so, share it in the margin.

Maybe something similar happened to Esther. Consider the range of emotions she experienced within hours: She'd exposed Haman and watched Xerxes storm out in a fury. Her evil foe begged for mercy. She'd watched them drag him away, and in the blink of an eye, her beloved Mordecai stood before the king and was rewarded with his signet ring. The swing of emotions from Haman's execution to Mordecai's promotion was too much to bear with composure.

When I was 23 and Amanda was 1, two young men hid in the backyard of our home and waited for me to come home. Keith was out of town and they must have known it. Strung out on amphetamines, they were not looking to rob our modest house. Many believe they intended more devious harm. In a move I still cannot explain apart from God, I decided on a whim not go home but to drive straight to my parents' house several hours away.

After lying in wait for two hours, the young men ransacked our home, but my next-door neighbor saw them and identified them to police. One was on probation and immediately went back to jail. As I sat in the courtroom with the other one, heard him sentenced, and watched his frightened young face, out of nowhere I descended into the ugly cry. I couldn't help myself. He put me in the position to send him to prison. Punishment is due a criminal, but the process is often double jeopardy to the victim.

I wonder if Esther felt something similar over Haman's violent execution. Then, before she could process a single emotion, Mordecai received the king's signet, bringing Esther the first wave of relief and maybe the first permission to exhale. Sometimes two emotions mix like vinegar and baking soda and the heart erupts like a volcano.

On the other hand, perhaps Esther's weeping and begging was not nearly so complex—even part of the plan. She just hadn't known exactly when she'd execute it. Glance back at the last few phrases of Esther 4:8.

What had Mordecai told Esther to "go into the king's presence" and do?

Interestingly, the same Hebrew word for Esther's pleas in 4:8 is used to describe the queen's actions in 8:3. Until now she'd made requests but not pleaded. Only now did she do what Mordecai advised.

Sometimes people advise us to do instantly what can only be accomplished gradually. An emotional reaction earlier might have been disastrous. Perhaps Mordecai's presence and unexpected promotion also stirred courage and sentiment in her.

What do you think? Does Esther 8:3 depict an emotional outburst or a vital part of the queen's plan? One way or the other, the clueless king got more from a woman than he'd bargained for. Study verse 5 very carefully.

What was the bottom line of Esther's request?

If it ...

What have we already learned about the law of the Medes and Persians?

And if he regards ...

This reminder helps us understand why Esther offered an awkward amount of deference to the king before stating her request in Esther 8:5. She petitioned Xerxes to do something Persians didn't do. Have you ever been so nervous about what you came to say to someone that you rambled? I have! Please don't miss Esther's four-part preamble to her request.

And thinks it ...

And if he ...

In the margin complete the four statements from Esther 8:5 according to the New International Version.

> Approving of someone doesn't always mean approving of their requests.

All right already! Surely he got the point! The last statement, however, held the strongest innuendo of the four. "She bundles two attitudes together: the king's love for her and his approval of her plan."[1] In other words, to be pleased with me is to be pleased with my plan, and to love me is to do what I ask. We naturally want the king's approval of her to equal his approval of her request, but approving of someone doesn't always mean approving of their requests.

Agreed? Offer an example to explain why.

Esther's intro may have been a tad redundant, but don't think for a moment she'd taken leave of her shrewdness. She knew a law couldn't be repealed, so she carefully avoided using the word *law*. Instead, she asked Xerxes to overrule Haman's *dispatches* or *letters*.[2] She downplayed Haman's authority, presenting his actions in less formal and binding terms as evil schemes that the king could simply overrule. Her long title for Haman ("son of Hammedatha, the Agagite") kept the focus on him alone, carefully exonerating Xerxes of blame.

Genius. The approach proved unsuccessful, but it was genius nonetheless. As we narrow down today's lesson, consider how Esther concluded her request with rare transparency of heart and plea in verse 6.

What final reasons did Esther give Xerxes for overruling the law (v. 6)?

Very simply: "Do it for *me*, I cannot bear to see this happen." Xerxes might decide to spare Esther, claiming her crown as an exemption from execution. He might say her Jewishness need never be publicly known, but all her people would still perish. Esther's final plea was that if she was spared but her people slaughtered, her life would not be worth living. "I cannot bear it."

Haven't we felt that way at times? That the loss or peril of a loved one threatened us as well? At times like those we realize remarkably that, opposed to our usual track record, somewhere deep inside our selfish selves we really don't believe that life is all about us. We are interconnected to a community of people whose lives are wrapped up in ours. Plead as we may, sometimes we have to go on living in the absence of someone dear and even find that hearts over time can actually heal.

We also find immeasurable comfort in knowing that our fellowship with those in Christ will resume one happy day and nothing will ever interrupt it again. Until then, however, sad is the soul that determines to exist as an emotional island. Disconnected people can never be whole. Vulnerable and painful though it may be, a community of people whose lives are tied together by the tender strings of the heart is life the way God meant it to be lived.

To lay everything on the line for her people would either kill Esther ... or heal her.

Day Two
Do What You Want

TODAY'S TREASURE

"Now go ahead and send a message to the Jews in the king's name, telling them whatever you want, and seal it with the king's signet ring. But remember that whatever has already been written in the king's name and sealed with his signet ring can never be revoked." Esther 8:8, NLT

I've been looking for the perfect person all my life. I'm not talking about a romantic interest. I'm talking about a real, live tenable hero. Someone who'll never let me down, whose love will never cool, whose dark side doesn't exist. Someone who will never lose my respect, whose passion for God only swells with time, hitting its highest pitch with the last breath. Someone perfect right here on earth where I could let my idealism bask in the sun of him.

The only place I haven't bothered to look for that person is in my bathroom mirror. The embarrassing irony is that the only time I've come close to finding a perfect human, I fought so much self-condemnation and failure around her, I eventually had to distance myself from her. I'm just offering a little transparency here. There's something I want that I can't find. And some-*one* I want that I can't be.

Maybe at times I've been like the Israelites in 1 Samuel 8:20, begging God for a human "king" who would lead me and go out before me and fight my battles. I didn't see my request as a replacement for God. I spiritualized my quest for an earthly hero by agreeing to see him as a gift from God.

Humans are adept at finding ways to make what we want seem all about God. At least this human is. Thank goodness, He not only sees the desires of our hearts, but He also looks straight into the heart of our desires and knows when we're asking—even accidentally—for a false Christ. God gave the Israelites what they demanded and the consequences that came with it. Dissimilarly, He's refused my request and at times to no small disappointment on my part.

Have you had the same kind of struggle? If so, write your explanation in the margin. If not, explain why you think you haven't.

Keep these thoughts swirling while we read today's segment and unravel its royal threads. First, a review. In yesterday's segment Esther fell at King Xerxes' feet and presented a very specific request to him with weeping and begging.

What was the request in Esther 8:5?

- Reinstate Mordecai as a royal guard
- Grant her half the kingdom
- Destroy Haman's family
- Overrule Haman's orders

Xerxes' response to Esther's tearful request is the focus of today's lesson. Please read Esther 8:7-8.

Principal Question · What did the king suggest they should do?

I'd like to take a few minutes and build a case suggesting that the king was annoyed by Esther's request. Maybe even hacked. Our modern English rhetoric makes it less clear, but we find a few clues in a careful look at verse 7.

What two actions did Xerxes remind them he'd already taken for them?

He might have meant: "For crying out loud, haven't I done enough? What do you want from me?" "Rather than responding with sympathy, the king seems to be somewhat perturbed with Esther's impassioned plea. ... As far as the king is concerned, he has done more than his share."[3]

Without defaming anyone, when was the last time you enlisted someone's help only to hear the equivalent of, "It's not my problem"?

Now go ahead and send a message to the Jews in the king's name, telling them ...

Perhaps the person had the gall to suggest he or she had done enough already. I'm not suggesting we can never ask too much of people or that some of them haven't done quite enough. What I'm suggesting is that Xerxes had given Esther virtually everything but what she really wanted. The queen probably wanted to scream something like this to her stubborn, detached husband-king: "But you haven't yet done what I asked! Did I ask you for half the kingdom? Did I ask you to give Mordecai your signet ring? We are asking for lives here! Not things!" Take a look at Today's Treasure. I used a different translation for Esther 8:8 so that you could sense the shrug of Xerxes' shoulders.

and seal it with the king's signet ring. But remember that whatever has already been written in the king's name and sealed with his signet ring ...

In the margin fill in the blanks according to Today's Treasure.

Can you hear a little attitude in Xerxes' words? Another commentary points to a hint of impatience that this is not enough to satisfy Esther. He seems to say "Do whatever you can, *legally*, to please yourselves" but he removes himself.[4]

The Moore translation? "Knock yourself out. Just keep in mind you can't change that law. Do whatever you want. I don't care that much." When Keith uses the words, "Do whatever you want," I know instantly that he's mad at me. He'd assume the same about me. Nothing gets under his skin like being

dismissed, which is why I only use the tactic when I want to hurt him the most. Few suggestions are more hurtful than "I don't care." If you're like me, you'd rather someone yell at you than act like you don't matter.

Of course, we've got to give credit where credit is due. Certainly Xerxes showed Esther favor, particularly when he placed her in charge of Haman's estate, but he hadn't given her what she'd been after all along. She wanted the king to exercise his sovereign right as ruler and overturn the law. He refused. Furthermore, the needle on his caring meter had been at an all-time high, and if she continued to push, it might just bottom out.

At times like these, individuals as self-centered as Xerxes say to themselves, "See, that's why I don't like to get involved. People keep asking you for more. Give 'em an inch, they take a mile!" Sound familiar?

We want something more from our heroes than this, don't we? We want them to champion our cause. We want them to gallop in on a white horse, sweep us up shamelessly, and carry us off. We want a rescue … and, if not for ourselves, for someone we love. Where are the ones who will love us enough to love someone we love? And someone they *don't?* Isn't the truest test of our devotion what we're willing to do for our loved one's needy loved one? You see, we're not just looking for help. We're looking for bonafide heroes.

What frustrates us most and even infuriates us at times is knowing someone had the power to give us what we asked … but wouldn't. That was Xerxes. Agreed, Esther probably hadn't had the luxury of considering the king her hero, but for just a fleeting moment he had a sparkling opportunity to emerge as one. Every one of us has had a Xerxes, and far more convicting, every one of us has probably been one.

Can you think of a time when someone else really needed you to be his or her hero but you couldn't? If so, explain why. Personal Question

I've had a painful number of opportunities to be somebody's hero and bowed out even at the risk of losing the relationship. Several factors contributed to my unwillingness to be in the position: my fear of an unhealthy attachment, my hunch that the requests would never end (Hello, Xerxes!), and my failure at the role the last time around. I agonize over disappointing people, but sometimes heroism is so expensive that it leads you into emotional bankruptcy.

Situations like these always have two sides. As we try to weigh them, I'd like to suggest two reasons God allows us to have—and to *be*—fallen heroes.

God is jealous for our true enduring hero to be His own Son. God wants Jesus to be our unrivaled champion. He answers my prayers to love Jesus above all else by allowing someone to disappoint me and prove insufficient for me. When I kick and scream about feeling let down, I simultaneously awaken to the miracle that I've come to appreciate Jesus more and more.

It's time for me to wake up to the connection. You too?

Exodus 20:3

Deuteronomy 4:35,39

Isaiah 44:8

Isaiah 45:5-6

Acts 4:12

Look up the Scriptures in the margin and record the bottom line of each:

What two words were repeated over and over?

Beloved, those two words may have unparalleled influence on our life experience. To our great relief and joy, however, the "no-other" clause guards our hearts as much as it protects God's glory. Countless people are worthy of our esteem, but none can take the pressure of our unrivaled champion.

Sometimes God wants to show us what we can do rather than let us find someone who can do it for us. Don't miss this inference in Esther 8:8! God allowed Xerxes to shirk the responsibility so Esther would have to take it.

Sister, sometimes you and I are looking for someone to stand up and do what God wants us to do. Case in point: Nearly 20 years ago I moaned and complained to God that I couldn't find a single woman's Bible study in the format and depth of Henry Blackaby's *Experiencing God.* It drove me crazy. Had God supplied what I wanted at that time, I never would have tried my hand at writing curriculum.

Humor me through one more example: I wanted somebody in my battered and bruised family of origin to stand up, be strong, and tell us everything could be OK. My family members wouldn't argue with my assertion that in childhood I was the weakest of character and constitution in our family. My big brother said that I looked like I was about to burst into tears at all times and was scared of my own shadow. I longed for someone to break the chain of bondage we were in. Instead, God started that process by breaking me. I hope one of these two examples resonates with you.

Can you think of a time when God wanted to show you what you could do rather than let you find someone to do it for you? Please share.

Shakespeare's pen spilled ink on the pages of *Romeo and Juliet* in the ebb and flow of these moving words:

> Come, gentle night,—come, loving black brow'd night,
> Give me my Romeo; and when he shall die,
> Take him and cut him out in little stars,
> And he will make the face of heaven so fine
> That all the world will be in love with night,
> And pay no worship to the garish sun.[5]

Robert Kennedy used those last four lines in reference to his assassinated brother at the 1964 Democratic Convention. Beloved Sister, one reason God dissuades us from making champions of humankind is to keep us from falling in love with the night and paying no worship to the glorious Son.

Day Three

At Once!

TODAY'S TREASURE

"The king's edict granted the Jews in every city the right to assemble and protect themselves." Esther 8:11

Esther may not have gotten exactly what she wanted from Xerxes, but she got something huge: permission to enact any edict to counteract the slaughter. The king refused to repeal the old law, but he gave permission to pass a new one. Their minds must have been spinning like tops. Let's get to our text so we can see what happened next. Read Esther 8:9-13.

In the margin list several clues to the urgency of their response.

Principal Question

Sometimes God calls us to wait. Other times He calls us to act n-o-w. Some matters must be handled "at once" (v. 9). I have a friend whose middle school-age son was molested as a young child by a neighbor. God help him. God help all of us. Just a few days ago she learned that he's acted inappropriately with several children. This mom doesn't have the luxury of waiting. She must lovingly and wisely act "at once," and in his behalf as well as the others.

Dear Sister, one reason a morning prayer time is so critical is because we never know when a matter is going to arise that needs attention "at once." We don't get to deliberate about it for several weeks and study our options. If we're not surrendered to God already that day with our hearts and minds guarded by Scripture, we'll more likely react by impulse than by the Holy Spirit.

Every morning God already knows each joy and concern our day holds. Some crises are so horrendous that we feel like nothing could have prepared us for them. Other times we can see that God strategically placed the truths on our minds that would become hope and assurance to us for months to come.

Can you think of a time God prepared you in advance to be victorious in a situation where you had to respond "at once"? If so, please share it.

Personal Question

Days of fasting and prayer placed Mordecai and Esther in a position where they could rise "at once" and start making decisions. Once Xerxes voiced permission to issue a new edict, the seconds until they were released to make arrangements must have dragged by like an eternity.

Picture the pair finally being excused from the king's presence and having to abide by interminable protocol just to get out of the room. Imagine them backing down the aisle bowing, so as not to turn their backs on the king but the moment they were out of royal eye-shot, picking up their robes and running like the wind! Picture the scene like a great movie. Decisions had to be made, papers drawn, and horsemen summoned.

Listen closely to verse 13 and you can hear the sound of hoof-beats as the couriers rode swiftly through Persia on the king's fastest horses. If a divine score was playing over these events—indeed a song of deliverance (Ps. 32:7)—this would be the part in the masterpiece marked by *"ffff."* *"Fortondoando!"* The Conductor bids His orchestra, "Hosts of heaven, lift lyre, trumpet, tabret and pipes and play with all your might! Raise the volume till no ear or emotion can withstand it! Pound the drums. Crash the cymbals. Flood the atmosphere with a symphony of the senses!" Our hearts are meant to pound with every beat of the hoof against Persia's dry ground. That's the response the narrator meant to elicit in Esther 8:10. Let's steady ourselves and talk about the timing.

What was the date of the new edict (v. 9)?

13th of Nisan	13th of Adar	23rd of Sivan

If you marked the third option, you are right, but if the two other dates sound familiar, you have a terrific memory. All three dates are crucial in Esther. Haman's edict of annihilation rode out on the 13th of Nisan (March/April). No coincidence on God's kingdom calendar, the news of impending slaughter hit the provinces on Passover. The date for the massacre was 11 months later on the 13th of Adar (February/March), affording ample time for psychological torment. The date introduced in today's segment is for the second edict. It was issued by Esther and Mordecai exactly 70 days after the first.

To help you keep the dates straight, please label the time line in the margin with all three dates and the corresponding event:

Many note the 70 days between first and second edict. Like the number seven, "the number seventy is often symbolic of completion and perfection in the Bible. But the reader must infer this, for the story makes no mention of the number seventy."[6] We don't know whether the number 70 is meant to carry significance here, but this we do know: God's timing is perfect.

In this day of instant messaging, we can hardly fathom the urgency of sending couriers on the king's fastest horses when the day of slaughter was nearly nine months away, but keep two factors in mind:

1. The Persian Empire was so vast that three months were required for a message to reach throughout its borders.

Nisan	March
Iyyar	April
Sivan	May
Tammuz	June
Ab	July
Elul	August
Tishri	September
Marcheshvan	October
Chislev	November
Tebeth	December
Shebat	January
Adar	February
	March

2. The Jews needed as much time as possible to prepare. They were not warriors. They were hardly even nationalists. Remember, the Jews were largely secularized in Persia. Their soft condition reminds me of another generation of Israelites many years earlier. Rewind the clock for a moment to a previous time in the nation of Israel when they'd finally settled in the promised land.

Read Judges 2:21-23. Why did God let some nations remain in Canaan?

Interesting, isn't it? As surely as the Jews in the promised land and Persia would have to learn to stand up and fight a physical enemy, we must learn to fight an invisible enemy (Eph. 6:10-17). Sometimes we're exactly where we're meant to be—right in the middle of our spiritual Canaans—yet God tests us there to teach us a new level of warfare.

One of the hardest parts of being a mother or a mentor is watching our children face a battle we can't fight for them. If God is going to raise our children to be mighty warriors of the faith, He must be free to teach them to fight. As hard as the process can be to watch, how can a person experience the exhilaration of victory in a battle they never had to fight? There, in the sweat and grime of spiritual war, I learned the realities of the following two verses.

Romans 8:37

Write the verses indicated in the margin. If you're overly familiar with either, write them from a different version of the Bible.

The Jews of Persia had no battle experience, but they were about to take a crash course. In Esther 8:10 we heard the king's mighty steeds pounding their way across Persia. Now let's take a second look at the orders they delivered.

Philippians 4:13

What message did the couriers carry to the provinces (v. 11)?

If you compare the edict in 8:9-13 to the original edict by Haman in 3:12-14, you'll see a similarity and difference. First note a very disturbing similarity. We were very likely both troubled by the apparent permission to attack not only the men but the women and children. While some things about war are too horrible to justify, we can at least attempt to come to some understanding about the force of this edict. Note the following factors.

First, it intentionally mirrors Haman's decree (that's why you see the same three words "destroy, kill and annihilate"). Simply put, the Israelites said to the Persians: "What you do to us, we'll do to you." The overriding difference is that Haman's command was to attack and Esther's command was to avenge. The Jews were not given permission to murder the Persians. They were given permission to defend themselves, to the death if necessary.

McConville points out a second factor. The passage may not mean that the Jews were authorized to destroy the women and children of the Persians but that they were to destroy any group that attacked the Jewish community. The women and children in the verse may be the Israelites, and the permission is to destroy any army that attacks them.[7]

Third, Esther may have feared that nothing would deter the Persian men unless they thought the lives of their women and children were at stake. Thus the women and children in the proclamation may have been a powerful threat. Either way, it's not pretty and it's going to get downright ugly in the next chapter. We'll save our discussions on overkill and holy war for that time.

As we conclude, let's draw some light out of this darkness as we draw a wonderful parallel from the edict of Esther.

Look carefully at verse 11. What were the Jews granted? Fill in the blank as your answer: "The king's edict granted the Jews in every city the right to _____ and _____ themselves."

Beloved, let those words soak into your spirit. The right to assemble. The right to protect themselves. They did not only have the responsibility. They had the right.

Please pore over the words of Hebrews 10:24-25 and describe the parallel in your own terms.

God's trying to make warriors out of us

The New King James makes the parallel blatant: "not forsaking the assembling of ourselves together, as is the manner of some, but exhorting one another, and so much the more as you see the Day approaching." We who call Christ Savior have the right to assemble in His mighty name. We are the blood-bought, Spirit-caught church of God and the gates of hell cannot prevail against us. The hordes of darkness have no greater agenda than the widespread destruction of Christ's bride and "so much the more" as His return draws near. Satan is furious because he knows his time is short (Rev. 12:12).

Some of us with little previous battle experience have no idea why God is allowing us to go through such difficult times in a place we thought was His will. He's trying to make warriors out of us, Girlfriend! Rise to the occasion! But we aren't meant to fight unseen forces alone. You and I have the God-given right to lock arms with our sisters and brothers in Christ and defend ourselves with the sword of the Spirit and the shield of faith. Here's the best part: When we do, we are guaranteed the victory. I said *guaranteed*.

"If you fully obey the LORD your God … the LORD will grant that the enemies who rise up against you will be defeated before you. They will come at you from one direction but flee from you in seven" (Deut.28:1a,7).

Day Four
Royal Garments

TODAY'S TREASURE

"Mordecai left the king's presence wearing royal garments of blue and white, a large crown of gold and a purple robe of fine linen." Esther 8:15

Since God's providence is the theme of Esther, the absence of His obvious activity invites us to imagine the divine activities behind the scene. If we could only see what is happening around us in the unseen realm, our eyes would nearly pop out of socket. Don't you wonder what transpires in the unseen realm when someone accepts Jesus as personal Savior? Luke 15:7 tells us heaven rejoices over a solitary sinner who repents. Think about it. Angels party over human repentance!

So much that would thrill us lies beyond our sight. Covenant children of God are marked—even dressed—in ways obvious to both heaven and hell but invisible to man. I'm not at all sure we don't bear an inscription on our foreheads somewhat like the one prescribed by God for the plate of the priest's turban. The engraving "Holy to the Lord" was the first thing people saw when they looked in the face of a priest. Ironically, one hint suggesting the possibility of such a mark is a counter reaction of the Evil One in Revelation.

What did the antichrist or "beast" demand in Revelation 13:16-17; 14:9-10?

How were God's sanctified ones identified (Rev. 14:1)?
          a white robe   a flame of fire   a name inscribed

Anything God does, Satan loves to counterfeit. A Christian may fret at times over lack of certainty concerning her salvation, but I don't believe the Evil One ever wonders who belongs to God and who does not. We are blatantly identifiable in robes of righteousness and garments of salvation.

As we open the Bible today and meditate on what happened to Mordecai next in our story, perhaps we can take a moment to imagine that something not entirely different has also happened to you and me. Read Esther 8:14-15.

Describe the way Mordecai left the presence of the king.   Principal Question

189

The narrator probably wasn't implying Mordecai hadn't left the king's presence since Esther 8:1. Though Esther and Mordecai undoubtedly acted quickly, they had to write the decree, summon royal secretaries, and have copies made for 127 provinces "in the script of each province and the language of each people and also to the Jews in their own script and language" (Esth. 8:9).

Even a rush order takes time. By the time the horses raced out of the city, Mordecai stood again in the king's presence. Perhaps the king and his new grand vizier even gazed from a palace window to watch the awe-striking sight of the couriers departing in thunderous clouds of dust.

Mission accomplished, Mordecai then "left the king's presence wearing royal _____ of _____ and _____, a large _____ of _____ and a purple _____ of fine linen."

Take stock of the significance. "No one else in the Book of Esther—not the seven eunuchs (1:10), not Queen Vashti (1:11), not the royal wise men (1:13-14), not Queen Esther (2:17), and not even Haman (3:1; 5:11; cf. 6:8-9)—receives these various honors that the king extends to Mordecai (8:15)."[8] God inspired Scripture and He alone knows which subtle details He meant to bear great significance to the searching student, but we may have happened on something more beautiful here than meets the eye. Obviously, Mordecai's royal garb was a profound investiture but perhaps, from heaven's gaze, something even more meaningful to the threatened nation of Israel was implied in his dress.

Please read Exodus 28:1-6. For whom were these garments prescribed?

- Priests
- Princes
- Kings
- Heads of 12 tribes

Record every similarity in Exodus 28:1-6 to Esther 8:15 whether in event, item, or color.

Whether or not Xerxes had any such intention, he dressed Mordecai as a royal priest then presented him to the people much like Aaron and his descendants presented themselves to the Israelites after serving God in the temple. Dr. Jon D. Levenson explains, "It should … be noticed that the garments and colors mentioned in Esth. 8:15 are reminiscent of the vestments of the priesthood in the Torah. Given the substantial overlap of the royal and priestly offices in ancient Israel, this is not surprising. [It] is probably right that Mordecai is here viewed as a kind of secular priest celebrated for his service on behalf of his threatened people. The joy with which the city of Susa cries out in Esth. 8:15 is the joy of salvation. It parallels the response of the worshipping community upon learning that their sacrifices have been accepted (Lev. 9:24)."[9]

A servant of God is no secular priest in God's estimation. His devotion to God's will automatically sets him apart from the common to the sacred. Mordecai himself may never have grasped what he represented as he stood between the king and the former captives of Israel, but we need not miss it.

Please read each of the following passages of Scripture. Record the era, the people to whom they applied, and any insight you receive into the overlap of royalty and priesthood.

TEXT	ERA	PEOPLE	ANY INSIGHT
Exodus 19:1-6			
1 Peter 2:9-10			
Revelation 1:6			

One of many elements fostering confidence in the inspiration of Scripture is its flawless thematic consistency from Genesis to Revelation. God wasn't forced to think up something new when the Book of Malachi rolled to a close and the Gospel of Matthew pounded on His door. God's plan for Israel hadn't fallen through the cracks between Testaments. To the contrary, events have unfolded throughout history like a sacred scroll in the high priest's hands in seamless keeping with God's prophetic plan. The theme of redemption arches like a brilliant rainbow of divine promise from the genesis of Scripture to its consummating end. The thunderings and lightnings reverberating from the Bible's dark and ominous clouds only hail the rainbow's coming.

> Scripture is consistent from Genesis to Revelation.

Like the scarlet yarn in the priestly garment of Exodus 28:6, the blood of perfect sacrifice runs from the river of Eden all the way to Revelation's "river of the water of life" (Rev. 22:1; see also Gen. 2:10). Our great High Priest who sat down at the right hand of God will stand once again to holy feet scarred by love but triumphant in glory. His royal robe will be dipped in blood (Rev. 19:13). His eyes will blaze like fire and upon His head will be many crowns (Rev. 19:12). He will mount the fastest horse in the King's stables and burst through the barriers of human sight and sound with the armies of heaven "following Him, riding on white horses and dressed in fine linen, white and clean" (Rev. 19:14). "On His robe and on His thigh" He will have "this name written: KING OF KINGS AND LORD OF LORDS" (Rev. 19:16).

Oh, the majesty and glory of His name! Jesus Christ, the Priest-King! The blending of royalty and priesthood is a hallmark of blessed consummation in Scripture. Many of us have heard Isaiah 6:1 so many times that we've missed a glorious oddity.

Search Isaiah 6:1 and see if you can find the least hint toward a royal priesthood. Record what you find.

Isaiah saw the Lord "seated on a throne" in "the temple." Not the palace, mind you. In Isaiah's vision, the throne of God was in a *temple*. What's the big deal? The temple was the place for priests, not kings; hence, a royal priesthood. John 12:38-40 makes reference to this very encounter quoting the words God said to His prophet. John 12:41 gives an astonishing summation of what Isaiah saw.

Read John 12:41 and record it here.

From Genesis to Revelation, the people of God have been members of a royal priesthood with none other than Jesus Christ, the Messiah, as their heavenly reigning Priest-King. Every single time we pray the familiar words, "Your kingdom come, Your will be done on earth as it is in heaven," we are praying for Christ to return in all His majesty. We are calling for Christ to be acknowledged by every inhabitant of earth as He is acknowledged by every inhabitant of heaven: All hail King Jesus!

All hail King Jesus!

Until then, every time the Devil looks at you and me, maybe he gets a stark reminder through our spiritual ensemble that every title of honor, authority, and supremacy in both church and state belong to the Christ we serve. I have a sneaking suspicion that, to the gaze of heaven and hell, we are somehow dressed to reflect the glorious dual identity of the royal priesthood bearing our citizenship.

Personal Question   What differences has Jesus made in your life that are outward signs of your new identity as a member of the royal priesthood? (List in margin.)

Just maybe we're dressed a little like Mordecai who "left the king's presence wearing royal garments of blue and white, a large crown of gold and a purple robe of fine linen." Then again, there's one monumental difference. We never have to leave the King's presence.

Jesus came near and said to them, "All authority has been given to Me in heaven and on earth. Go, therefore, and make disciples of all nations, baptizing them in the name of the Father and of the Son and of the Holy Spirit, teaching them to observe everything I have commanded you. And remember, I am with you always, to the end of the age" (Matt. 28:18-20, HCSB).

Day Five
A Time of Happiness

"For the Jews it was a time of happiness and joy, gladness and honor."
Esther 8:16

I'm not sure why but my eyes are filled with tears and my lip is quivering ridiculously as I stare at the words of *Today's Treasure*. Life is so hard. I know so many people who are suffering. I know so many women with broken hearts. I sat in my car in the grocery store parking lot a few hours ago and watched a darling young woman, tall and thin, saunter into Kroger with a shiny bald head and I prayed for God to heal her … and to make sure she knows Jesus.

My coworkers and I went face down to the carpet yesterday at staff prayer time and petitioned God's speedy aid for a pastor's wife under severe temptation, for an adolescent who has just finished chemotherapy, for a man dying with liver disease yet who remains resistant to Christ, and for many others just as needy. And for ourselves. We need Him desperately.

Sadness doesn't always come from earth-shattering events or even occurrences that other people would find disheartening. Not long ago I told you that I'd lost my little canine shadow of so many years, my Sunny, to cancer. What you don't know is that only 13 days later our delightful bird dog, Beanie, fell terribly ill and was also diagnosed with cancer. We tried to do everything possible to save that dog, but the disease went straight to her brain and she was gone before we could even collect ourselves.

Beanie was fodder for countless teaching illustrations and a constant source of laughter and company to my man and me. The four of us—Keith, Beanie, Sunny, and I—did everything together. We've stayed in cheap motels all over the nation just to travel with those silly animals. To these two dog people, our house feels like a morgue.

I realize this seems silly to many who just don't get the whole pet thing, but I cannot even tell you the tears my man and I have cried in the last month. I'm forcing myself not to stop and bawl right now.

One reason losing two constant companions in 21 days hurt so badly is because life is already hard. They just provided some welcome respite. Keith and I have a good marriage, but we still have fights. I still get my feelings hurt. Brood over something he said. Wonder if he'll always love me. We have terrifically serious and demanding extended family problems. Our lives also collide regularly with several close loved ones who battle mental illness. At times I feel stressed beyond human capacity and other times profoundly lonely. Sometimes I feel so frustrated I could scream and other times so ill-equipped I could panic. And those are only the things I feel free to tell you. The far more challenging conditions are too private to share. I venture to say that for this brief season I'm possibly living life as good as it gets … yet even *it* is hard. So when a time of happiness comes, I think we ought to take it and run.

Please enjoy Esther 8:15-17; then explain what happened.

Lock in on the word "happiness" because you're liable to enjoy what it means. The same Hebrew word is translated a different way in Psalm 139:12.

Read the verse; then fill in the following blank: "even the darkness will not be dark to you; the night will shine like the day, for darkness is as _____ to you."

The Hebrew word translated "happiness" in Esther 8:16 also means "lightness." In other words, the Jews in Susa celebrated a time of lightness! The day never seems brighter than when we walk out of a pitch-black room, does it? Can you remember a time when you experienced the first rays of warm sunlight after a very dark season?

If so, what were the circumstances? If you can define it, what did God use to bring lightness?

> When God intervenes and we get a chance to know we're blessed and to *feel* blessed, nothing is more appropriate than seizing the happy moment.

Beloved, when a moment like this comes, we need to take it. We often speak of happiness as a less noble term than joyfulness because the former is circumstantial and the latter less conditional. I won't argue with that, but when God intervenes in our circumstances and we get a chance not only to know we're blessed but *feel* blessed, nothing is more appropriate than seizing the happy moment. "A time of happiness" can come like a shot of B-12 to the soul to boost your system when darkness spreads once again like a virus.

One of the hardest challenges about taking advantage of a God-given time of happiness is the guilt of knowing that it coincides with someone else's sadness. No, we don't flaunt our light in someone else's darkness, but surely we can find a way to dip ourselves in the bubble bath of a second's bliss when it comes. Even if all we do is lean our heads back in the sunshine of our soul's Sabbath and take a minute to feel the glad emotion, it is meant by God to be medicine for our weary souls. Times of happiness are glimpses of heaven until we get there. Homesickness doesn't always feel sick. Sometimes it's a quick flash of happy that makes us long to find and keep it.

What made Israel's time of happiness supremely ideal is that it infected everyone who caught it. Is anything more exhilarating than sharing in something divinely happy with a large group of people?

When was the last time you had such an experience?

Several months ago my pastor, Gregg Matte, announced to a packed congregation how much money we'd raised for our long-overdue renovation campaign. The figure was above and beyond the budget, enabling us to pour lavishly into countless mission churches. Confetti fell from the ceiling like a heavy rain and the praise team sang their hearts out while we, a conservative congregation, jumped up and down in the name of our God and cheered in the aisles.

A whole passel of little girls and I caught confetti in the air and danced in circles, laughing and squealing. I'll never forget it as long as I live. It was a true time of happiness and much the sweeter because we experienced it all together. Imagine how the celebration would have intensified if the stakes were much higher and we'd gotten our lives back! I can't wait to show you something. Glance back at Esther 4:3.

What are the four recorded responses of the Jews to Haman's edict?

Now look back at Esther 8:16. This verse states that it was "a time of" four different conditions in Susa.

Please list all four.

Beloved, you are staring in the face of one of Esther's most glorious reversals! God took His children's mourning, fasting, weeping, and wailing and turned them into happiness, joy, gladness, and honor.

Meditate on this miraculous process by drawing a diagram depicting the four-fold reversal in this space:

What you see before you is a continent from coincidence. Remember, all Scripture is God-breathed. Yahweh, the faithful covenant God, reversed every negative of His threatened people into a positive. These mirrored terms in Esther 4:3 and 8:16 are more than narrative art. They are joyful cries from the streets of Susa exclaiming the enduring love and limitless grace of God!

I'm going to offer you several scenarios to see where you relate most. First, have you walked with God long enough to see Him do something similar to Esther 4:3/8:16 for you? Mind you, God's people didn't suddenly acquire perfect conditions. They still lived on planet earth and had fierce battles to fight, but He'd indeed done the unfathomable and turned their misery to victory. Have you ever experienced a work of God that ushered in such polar opposite conditions that the result was more of a reversal than a restoration?

Before ...

If so, in the margin please offer four words that describe your "before" and four words that describe your "after."

If you were able to complete the preceding exercise in reference to your own life, you've experienced an Esther-reversal. If not, please don't be discouraged. The joyous theme of today's lesson is that God can reverse every negative element in His child's life and turn it into a positive. He doesn't just diffuse the circumstance. He transfuses it.

After ...

Every blessed reversal will ultimately come to completeness in heaven, but often we live enough life with Jesus here on earth to see some tables turn along the way. Maybe you've never experienced a total reversal but you could certainly use one right now. Hence, a second scenario you may find more fitting at this season of your walk.

If your life is presently characterized by negatives, please offer four words that describe it:

Now, Dear One, as you look back upon those four descriptions, how do you wish God would reverse them? What conditions of soul, in the same general vein as Esther 8:16, do you wish He'd enact in you instead?

Please write four words representing changes you yearn to see Him bring. Jot them opposite the original descriptions above.

Are any of them unbiblical? I'm imagining not. Unless you're asking something ungodly and vindictive, I want to challenge you to turn those descriptions into petitions. Right this moment stop and pray in Jesus' name for God to bring a great reversal in your life with these exact results. Confess to Him aloud the negative conditions you've suffered, then express your deepest heart's desire for Him to turn them around. Date the request beside the words of reversal.

OK, humor me through one last part of this exercise by listing a few ways God could be glorified by accomplishing what you're asking.

Beloved, take these simple words to heart no matter how many times you've heard them: your God cares about you! He wants to show you what He can do with your life and your negative conditions, but He wants you to know without a doubt that He alone is the author of reversals. Wait like a watchman on the wall and when the first sign of reversal comes, don't dream of calling it coincidence. Raise the roof with praise and ask the One who has begun a good work in you to complete it! He is not only glorified through our suffering. He can also be supremely glorified through our celebrating.

Let's spend our last few minutes in verse 17. Please relish (no pun intended) the reversal from fasting to feasting. What's a great celebration without food anyway? Aren't you thankful God dictated food to taste good and not just be good for you? Let's remember amid this out-of-kilter culture that food is not the problem. Gluttony is. Feasting is not an unspiritual way to celebrate. If our worship is in the right place, we really can bless the food and mean it. (See 1 Tim. 4:4-5.) Note the last statement in Esther 8.

What kind of impact did the turn of events have?

How does Jeremiah 33:9 relate to the events described in Esther 8:15-17?

Note one commentator's intriguing perspective on Esther 8:17: "A final element in the mirror-image which these verses form with things that have gone before is that non-Jews (presumably those who have been hostile and now feel endangered) *pretend to be Jews*. This is the likeliest understanding of verse 17b. Where once Esther, inspired by Mordecai, had hidden her Jewish identity and thus effectively made herself like a non-Jew, non-Jews now contrive to be mistaken for Jews. The new royal standing of Esther and Mordecai (for Mordecai is hardly less "royal" now than his cousin, v. 15) is matched by an ascendancy of the Jews in general in Persia. The people that seemed doomed has not only escaped destruction, but come to occupy a place of privilege, the envy of the Empire. All this has happened because of their reliance on God alone and because of their willingness (exemplified by Esther and Mordecai) to make it known."[10]

He may be exactly right. Then again, some of the people of other nationalities may not have pretended to be Jews. Their souls may have genuinely envied a people whose God is the Lord. No witness is more effective than an undeniable observation that God is with us and has worked wonders in our behalf. Take it from the psalmist who said, "He lifted me out of the slimy pit, out of the mud and mire; he set my feet on a rock and gave me a firm place to stand. He put a new song in my mouth, a hymn of praise to our God. Many will see and fear and put their trust in the LORD" (Ps. 40:2-3).

And let a bystander take it from you.

esther 9:1-4

Today's chapter explicitly states the Book of Esther's most pronounced theme—the reversal of destiny. We will glance ahead to Esther 9:19-22 and then focus on verses 1-4. Esther 9:1 says, "but now the tables were turned." The Hebrew transliteration for "the tables were turned" is hapak *which means "to overturn, to overthrow, to tumble."*

Premise for Today's Session

God can't _____ _____ _____ that was _____

_____ _____ _____.

Seeing purpose in tough scenarios increases the trust required for a turnaround.

Turn Around Scenario #5

It's tough being a woman in the tight fist of fear.

• The Jews weren't just _____, they were _____. (See Deut. 33:29; compare Neh. 4:10-14.)

• See Esther 9:2: "The Jews assembled in their cities." The power wasn't just _____. It was all of _____.

• Every time you're in a _____ _____ of fear, remember you're in something much _____. Isaiah 49:16 says, "See, I have _____ _____ on the _____ ____ ____ _____."

Turn Around Scenario #4

It's tough being a woman thrown a giant-size weight.

• God always has the _____ _____ _____. Exchange the

_____ for a _____ (1 Pet. 5:7; see Deut. 23:3-5).

"However, the Lord your God ... turned the _____ into a _____

for you, because the Lord your God _____ ____ " (Deut. 23:5).

Ahab—"Implies an ardent and _____ inclination of the mind and

a _____ of _____ at the same time."[17]

Consider the unique metaphor in Hosea 7:8

"Ephraim is a _____ _____ not _____ _____."

Turn Around Scenario #3

It's tough being a woman in a mean world.

• In a _____ world, New Testament believers are called

to a _____ _____.

"I give you this instruction in keeping with the prophecies once made about

you, so that by following them you may _____ ____ _____ _____,

holding on to _____ and a ____ ____ _____. Some have

rejected these and so have shipwrecked their faith" (1 Tim. 1:18-19).

Consider the following excerpt from *The Queen and I*:

"When, because of your _____, your life too becomes perceptibly

different; when your reactions are quite _____ to what the

situation seems to call for and your activities can no longer be explained in

terms of your _____; that is when your neighborhood will sit

up and take notice. In the eyes of the world, it is not our _____

with Jesus Christ that counts; it is our _____ ____ _____!"[18]

week nine
The Tables Turned

As the daughter of a veteran, I am radically aware that

some wars are worth fighting. The holiest war of all, however,

has already been won by Jesus on the cross.

Principal Questions

1. What good reasons might Esther have had for asking a second day to avenge their enemies?
2. Why did the Jews in Susa feast and celebrate on a different day than the Jews outside the citadel (Esth. 9:16-19)?
3. What specific things were "turned" in Esther 9:22?
4. What one-sentence synopsis completes the entire Book of Esther? The Book of Esther is about …
5. What are the last glimpses we get of our Jewish protagonists, Esther and Mordecai?

Day One
No Plunder

"The Jews in Susa came together on the fourteenth day of the month of Adar, and they put to death in Susa three hundred men, but they did not lay their hands on the plunder." Esther 9:15

Our purposeful God allowed this final week of Esther to follow a ministry event that reminded me afresh what a beautiful thing women studying together can be. Amanda told me a group of eight young women who'd been communicating online were meeting at the event and spending the weekend together. She knew I'd want to meet them. They have a deep bond none of us would hope to share. Each has buried a cherished infant in the last year. They met through a ministry blog and bonded not only in their loss but in their profound determination to glorify God through their enveloping grief.

They were about my own daughters' age, and I could have held and rocked each one back and forth for a solid hour. Many of them entrusted me with pictures of their darling ones who are now safely and vivaciously in the playful, nurturing hands of Jesus. Those pictures are just to my left now as I peck away at the computer. I asked them what they'd have me pray over them, then invited them to their knees so I could lay hands on them and intercede.

How blessed we are to be women. By nature we like to do things together. Work and play. Laugh and grieve. Eat and pray. Live and die. A large measure of enjoying womanhood is enjoying a heart connection with other women.

I want you to know I respect you so much. You have diligently studied God's Word amid real life. Real pain. Real confusion. Real hormones. I would not trade journeying with you through the pages of Scripture for anything in this world. You are highly esteemed by God, and He has seen you sow His Word in your tears. Please sit back for just a moment, take a deep breath, and bask in the affection and approval of your God. He knows you and loves you so much. All of your toil is ever before Him.

Today we turn to Esther 9. In session 8, you'll recall we examined the first four verses. Please read Esther 9:1-4, hopefully as a review.

According to verse 1, what happened when the enemies of the Jews hoped to overcome them?

What has been happening ambiguously throughout the Esther story is now stated explicitly: *the tables were turned* for the advantage of the Jews! Dr. Levenson says the key is not that the Jews destroyed the enemy but that they assumed a new status of honor and dominion.[1] As the NASB translates verse 1, the Jews "gained the mastery over those who hated them."

Can you relate his point to your own spiritual battles? Like Mordecai in 9:4, you and I want to become "more and more powerful" in the honor and dominion Christ won for us, but to do so we must become more and more trustworthy with that power. Don't think for a moment that just because God gave us our status and dominion we can't abuse them. We've all seen it and, Lord help us, at some point probably done it. Our primary text today is longer than those of recent days. Please read 9:5-15.

How many men were initially killed in the citadel of Susa (v. 6)?
 500   5,000   50,000

Aren't you relieved to see no reference to women and children among the dead? This supports the theory that the wording of Mordecai's edict in 8:11 was an intentional reversal of Haman's exact wording and not a call to slaughter.

Who are the men listed in verses 7 and 9? (See v. 10.)
 The king's advisers   Haman's cohorts   Haman's sons

An unpleasant reality of ancient kingdoms was the killing of the sons of an assassinated ruler. This radical measure ensured that no one would be left to usurp authority or avenge the father's death. Ironically, by requesting the public impaling of the sons' dead bodies, Esther treated Haman as if he'd been king. Had Xerxes not been so quick to hand off his responsibilities, he might have taken offense. Once again his cluelessness worked to Esther's advantage.

OK, are you ready for something wild? Give this quote a good look: "The names of Haman's sons attract attention … Some appear to be *daiva* names—old Persian names of pagan gods or demons. This may underscore their evil nature or cultic affiliation."[2] Would you be surprised? Me neither!

Susa was undoubtedly Satan's focus on planet Earth in the bloody month of Adar many years ago. When Satan has much to gain, he also has much to lose. His every scheme against a child of God is a gamble. A cast of the lots, you might say. Let's continue unfolding the events in Esther 9.

What rather disturbing request did Esther make of Xerxes in verse 13?

How many additional men were killed (v. 15)? _____

Esther's reputation among commentators through the centuries has suffered no small hit over her request for a second day to avenge their enemies. Why do you think she made this request? Since we have no definitive answers, we'll offer some conjecture. First, let's give Esther the benefit of the doubt.

In the margin offer a few good reasons why she might have asked for a second day to avenge their enemies. Then offer a few bad reasons.

A good reason might be Esther's awareness that fierce enemies had escaped the first day and would be a continuing threat. The poorest reason would be spite. If she killed a few hundred more just because she could, she abused the crown. Based on what we've seen of her, however, I tend to think that if Esther's actions were out of line, she was motivated by panic more than spite.

I once killed a large tarantula in a cabin full of sixth graders at summer camp. I was so scared and felt so protective of the girls that I kept smacking the thing long after it was dead. Somebody finally had to say, "Beth, you can stop now!" Spiders and humans don't compare, but when I hear of overkill, I can't help but think of that tarantula and associate the overreaction with fear.

Bad reasons ...

Now for the heart of the lesson. What piece of information was the narrator very careful to tell us repeatedly in Esther 9:10,15,16.?

Glance at the last phrases of 8:11. Keep in mind when Mordecai wrote the new decree, he deliberately used language from Haman's decree to reverse it.

What did the edict give the Jews permission to do to their enemies?
- plunder their property
- behead them
- burn Susa to the ground
- impale the sons of Haman

You see the edict permitted the Jews to plunder the property of their enemies yet three times we read that they refused. Why? We have just stumbled on evidence that the Jews viewed this fight in sacred and scriptural terms. "The Jews understood the execution of Mordecai's decree as governed by the ancient command of holy war *against the Amalekites*."[3] Keep that thought in mind as we study the history of God's directive at specific times to keep their hands off the plunder. The practice originated through Abraham.

Read Genesis 14:17-23. Why wouldn't he receive from the king of Sodom?

God didn't always insist on the Israelites refraining from the plunder. In fact, He sent them to the promised land with their hands full of Egyptian treasures. When He said no, however, He meant NO! One example of disobedience to

His command has enormous ramifications in the conflict between Haman and the Jews. Don't forget that Haman was an Agagite, a direct descendant of Agag, the king of the Amalekites. The tie is critical to our understanding of Esther 9. Please read 1 Samuel 15:13-23.

What question did Samuel ask Saul regarding the plunder in 15:19?

What excuse did Saul give in 1 Samuel 15:21?

Saul's excuse is tantamount to one of us robbing a bank and claiming we wanted to give the money to the church. As Dr. Karen Jobes explains, "There was to be no personal profit in holy war because the destroyers were acting not on their own behalf but as agents of God's wrath."[4] In Esther the refusal of the Jews to lay hands on the plunder indicates strongly that they viewed the battle as a continuation—a correction—of the earlier battle with the Amalekites.

In 1 Samuel 15, plunder was not just *a* problem. It was *the* problem. The Jews in Esther intended to succeed where Saul failed knowing full well that, if Israel's first king had done what God told him to do, Haman's evil line would have been cut off at the root. In view of these things, was Esther right or wrong in her insistence on a second day of vengeance? Only God knows and He purposely remained silent.

In the following paragraph from Dr. Karen Jobes, underline the thoughts that most help you deal with the concept of retributive violence.

> Retributive violence appears all through the Old Testament but Jesus teaches love of enemies in the New. These two ideas seem completely contradictory. The death of Jesus, the Messiah of Israel, "provides the only basis for the cessation of holy war, and the infilling of the Holy Spirit provides the only power by which one may love one's enemies as oneself. … The vengeance due to us for our sins against others and due to them for their sins against us has been satisfied in Jesus' body on the cross."[5]

Personal Question   In the margin share your thoughts about retributive violence.

Distinguish holy war from war in general. As the daughter of a veteran, I am radically aware that some wars are worth fighting. The holiest war of all, however, has already been won by Jesus on the cross. Matters of religious vengeance are reserved for Jesus Christ both now and in the coming day when He will judge the hearts of all humankind. We have something our predecessors under the old covenant didn't have. As Jobes so eloquently remarks, "God's strategy against sin and evil was awaiting a perfect warrior, who could execute divine justice with clean hands and a pure heart. His name is Jesus."[6]

Day Two
A Day for Presents

TODAY'S TREASURE

"A day of joy and feasting, a day for giving presents." Esther 9:19

Dive in by reading Esther 9:16-19. Then continue with this paragraph. I'll organize our lesson in three elements from our Scripture: *the victory, the celebration,* and *the commemoration.* Let's get straight to the victory. Some wins are tallied on scoreboards. This victory was calculated in casualties. Before we total the deaths throughout the Empire, recall that the death count in Susa totalled 800 (vv.12,15) men. Remember Esther's request for a second day to avenge their enemies was limited to Susa (v. 13) which adds credence to the theory that known enemy forces slipped through Esther's fingers the first day.

In the margin explain why the Jews in Susa feasted and celebrated on a different day than the Jews outside the citadel (Esth. 9:16-19).

The second day of fighting explains why those in the citadel observed their celebration 24 hours later than the rural Jews. Verse 16 notes 75,000 died in total. If you're like me, you have to remind yourself that the loss of life was limited to those who raised their hands against the Jews. Remember, the edict only gave them the right to defend themselves.

The following comparison greatly affects my perspective: In 1941 the Nazis forced the Jews in Poland into the Warsaw Ghetto. This became the unlikely breeding ground for an insurrection against Hitler's Nazi forces in 1943. The vastly outnumbered and overpowered Jews actually held the evil giant back for a time. The story of Esther and Purim were not lost on the Nazis, who killed any Jew in the prison camps possessing a copy of Esther. Yet the incarcerated Jews wrote copies of it from memory. The story of Esther was most precious to the Jews facing mass death, because in it they found assurance and hope that they, not their enemy, would triumph.[7] Had Hitler had his way, the Jews would have been completely exterminated. That I've had the privilege of observing two Purim holidays on the happy streets of Jerusalem is a personal reminder that the true archenemy of the Jews did not succeed.

Hauntingly like the posting of Haman's edict, the Nazis began with an attack on Passover-eve. S.S. troops entered the ghetto with a vengeance and, after 23 days of stunning resistance, blew it to oblivion, block by block.[8]

The result of the Warsaw Ghetto Uprising was what some historians call an *heroic failure*—an effort with great sacrifices but an unrealized goal. It can also be a term for winning the moral upper hand while still losing the battle.

Here's the parallel to the insurrection in Esther 9:16. What if the Warsaw Ghetto Uprising hadn't been a case of heroic failure? What if the persecuted Jews had risen to their bare feet and fought back, taking 75,000 of their attackers' lives? Would we have cheered them on? We'd have immortalized them with an Oscar-winning movie. We'd teach our children the story and replay our favorite parts, clapping and cheering like we'd never seen it before.

No, that kind of underdog victory didn't happen in Warsaw, but it did happen when the Jews rose to their feet and defended themselves successfully against the mighty Persians. Haman's edict called for genocide. To skeptics, Mordecai's edict called for suicide. The landslide victory surely caused countless Persians to recognize that an unseen hand fought for Israel. Isn't a divine work through ordinary means what we've called Providence? Isaiah 28:5-6 reminds me of these exact events in Esther 9.

Do you see any connection between Isaiah 28:5-6 and our Esther narrative? If so, explain.

Based on Isaiah, who wore the real crown in the Jewish victory?_____

We've looked at the victory in Esther 9. Now let's look at the celebration and its significant timing. Fill in the following blanks based on Esther 9:17-18.

This happened on the thirteenth day of the month of Adar, and on the fourteenth they _____ and made it a day of feasting and joy. On the thirteenth and fourteenth, and then on the fifteenth they (the Jews in Susa) _____ and made it a day of feasting and joy.

Note something profound I would have missed had Jewish commentator Adele Berlin not made an issue of it: "the Jews did not commemorate the day of their victorious battle, but the day on which they rested from their enemies."[9] The Jews did not make an anniversary of their war but of their rest.

Can you think of a few reasons why this mentality could be healthy? Please share them in the margin.

We rarely take time to rest, reflect, and celebrate after a victory. We need to learn from Purim. "Purim 'was a spontaneous celebration of the joy of finding oneself still standing on the day after an irrevocable death decree was executed. The day of death had come and gone and God's people were still alive! Thus, Purim is in this sense a Sabbath, a joyous rest after evil and the threat of death have passed.'"[10]

"At that time the Lord who commands armies will become a beautiful crown and a splendid diadem for the remnant of His people. He will give discernment to the one who makes judicial decisions, and strength to those who defend the city from attackers."

ISAIAH 28:5-6, NET

206

Oh, Beloved, surely you've found yourself still standing after a time when the enemy came seeking your slaughter! Testify here of his foiled plans:

I wish I could read what you wrote, but, by faith, I'm going to clap my hands and give God a shout of praise on your behalf. We've taken a few minutes to center on the victory and celebration in our Scripture. Let's spend the rest on the commemoration. We'll highlight specific ways the Jews observed their celebration of victory. Read Esther 9:19.

Note that the day was set aside for joy. What could be more healing to our weary, war-torn souls than setting aside "a day of joy"? Because Christ has overcome sin and the grave, any day can be a day of joy, but can you imagine the impact of becoming deliberate about it?

The Jews were told to commemorate the victory through feasting. Praise God, feasting is not a sin in our celebrations! Of course I'm not advocating gluttony, but I'm proposing that God is not more glorified by denying yourself everything but an unsalted celery stick on a day set aside for celebration. OK, we've just got to go here for a second.

What is your favorite menu for a celebration?

Mine is a big rump roast covered in fresh garlic, salt, and coarse ground pepper, offered with sides of fluffy mashed potatoes and dark brown gravy, green bean casserole, and homemade yeast rolls with cold butter. You can keep the dessert. I'll take some more mashed potatoes. Man, I'm hungry.

Let's distract ourselves with a look at the final act of commemoration in 9:19. It was a day for giving presents to each other. Don't you love it?

You're going to love it even more after we do a little exposition on the word translated *presents*. A more literal rendering of the Hebrew *manot* is *portions*. Several times in Scripture we see it used of something that can be eaten. In other words, the present itself is some kind of special food much like we'd gift someone with a box of Godiva® chocolates. You've seen the word used in the context of food earlier in our narrative. Please read Esther 2:8-9.

What did Esther win from Hegai? _____ With what did he "immediately" provide her? _____ and
_____ .

The word translated *presents* in 9:19 is translated *special food* in 2:9. Keep in mind that the *present* could be something much broader and more significant than food. I can't wait to show you the ultimate use of the same root word. Read Psalm 16:5-6 as a cohesive whole and take it personally.

What did the psalmist say that the Lord had assigned him?

In this context, the word translated *portion* has strong ties to the concept of destiny. One author explains: "Here the 'lot' or 'portion' is an allusion to the way life has worked out; the psalmist is thinking of all the signs of God's providence which have marked his pilgrimage ... the word had within it suggestions of destiny."[11] In our own words we might say something like, "Lord, in all the chaos and crisis, all the threat and doubt, You caused my life to work out. Instead of me falling apart, the lines of my life have fallen together. Truly, I can say that You have given me a delightful inheritance."

Stare at *lot* in Psalm 16:5. What did the psalmist say about his *lot?*

You are very familiar with the word *lot.* Take another look at it in Esther 3:7 and describe its context.

Yep. Same Hebrew word. And this is the way the three terms—*favor, portions* (or presents), and *lots*—tie together. No matter what life—or Satan himself—hands us, the favor God has on His children causes that "lot" to tumble out on the table in such a way that, instead of destruction, the child will discover that her portion turned into destiny one trusting step at a time. When all is said and done, she will see that the portion God assigned her was good. Right. Rich. Full of purpose. The English Standard Version translates Psalm 16:5 best of all. Read it out loud and let it sink in. "The LORD is my chosen portion and my cup; you hold my lot."

Personal Question   What does that verse say to you personally?

Here you are, Beloved, Satan tried to destroy you along your life's path, but clearly, he didn't get his way. You're still standing, aren't you? Instead of falling apart, your lines are all starting to fall together. Piece by piece. Glimpse by glance. What a beautiful inheritance you have!

Once you wrap your mind around the favor God has had on you and the richness of the portion He assigned to you even through disaster, you can't help but share your portion with others. Hence, Esther 9:19. "The Jews send these 'portions' of food (*manot*) to one another to celebrate their 'portion' or destiny (*manah*) allotted by God."[12] They gave portions of their portions.

Oh, that we'd wake up to the goodness of our God and the crushing defeat of our enemy! The day we do will be "a day of joy and feasting, a day for giving presents to each other" (Esth. 9:19, NIV). I think we had better grab us some wrapping paper, Darling One. We've got some gifts to give.

Day Three
An Annual Remembrance

TODAY'S TREASURE

"Mordecai recorded these events, and he sent letters to all the Jews ... to have them celebrate annually the fourteenth and fifteenth days of the month of Adar." Esther 9:20-21

I got a letter yesterday from a young friend I sit near at church. Her name is Abigail and she's one of the cutest, most precocious first graders you've ever seen in your life. She wanted me to know that she'd fallen and cut her chin and had to have stitches. She also wanted me to know that she'd gotten a new arm so she could take golf lessons.

When God fearfully and wonderfully made Abigail, He allowed her the challenge of missing one hand. You hardly notice because of her irresistible charm. Her parents tell me she insists on praying for me almost every night. I've thought that she could pray for me to be like her: (1) confident in who God made me and (2) undeterred by small matters like a missing hand.

If I've ever seen a girl I believe God destined to impact women, it's Abigail. Let's follow her philosophy today: Missing a hand? Sign up for golf lessons.

Do we feel we lack what it takes? Somebody else would be better at our job? I just got off the phone after laughing and talking with an expectant mom quarantined to a hospital bed until her baby is born. When I prayed for her, I reminded her she was God's first and only choice to birth that baby boy.

You may have no trouble applying "chosen-ness" to an expectant mom but think you defaulted into your position. Esther shows that ordinary events are never coincidental in the lives of God's people. Our text today invites us to continue in the flow of yesterday's lesson. Then it leads us to a new stream.

Record every new bit of information Esther 9:20-22 offers:

You have a sharp memory if this segment rings a bell from session 8. We touched on Esther 9:22 alongside 9:1 as our narrative's only explicit references to the splendid theme of reversals. The wording in 9:22 states it best.

What specific things were "turned"?

Principal Question

I will exalt You, O LORD, for You

and did not let my enemies gloat over me. O LORD my God, I called to You for help and You

O LORD, You brought me up from the grave; you spared me from

You turned my wailing into dancing; you removed my sackcloth and clothed me with

that my heart may sing to you and not be silent. O Lord my God, I will give you praise forever.

We've deliberately pounced on this theme in our last several chapters so as long as we live we'll remember the most celebrated message in the whole Megillah. I've asked you to recount turnarounds in your life so you'll make a lasting connection and view Esther's story as your own. As our journey narrows toward its end and while our remembrance is piqued, let's offer God the praise He's due. The psalmist put wonderful words in the mouth of every grateful worshiper who wishes to express praise for a divine work of reversal.

Read Psalm 30:1-3 and 11-12; then in the margin complete the sentences based on your experience.

If you have not yet experienced what the psalmist described, fill in the gaps by faith with words you hope will become your testimony. In the spirit of Romans 4:17, call "things that are not as though they were"!

God has worked such outrageous turnarounds in my life, my family, and this ministry that I can hardly proceed without sobbing. Oh, Darling One, He will be faithful to you. Do not fret. "Trust in the LORD and do good." (Ps.37:3) In the midnight hour or when you least expect it, God can turn it all around.

At first glance, Esther 9:20-22 seems redundant, but it records the proclamation that turned a one-time celebration into an annual affair.

Some occasions are simply worth celebrating every year. Name a few:

You may have listed personal occasions like birthdays, but surely you recorded Christmas and Easter. Purim probably reminded you of Christmas. Though we don't know the exact day Christ was born, taking one season a year to observe, savor, and celebrate our most wonderful gift is profoundly appropriate. The commercialism and secularism of Christmas is revolting, but the gift-giving is terrifically fitting. God gave His one and only Son as His portion and we who receive Him have the joy of giving to others out of that lavish portion.

A glance at Leviticus 23 tells us that God is a huge proponent of annual remembrances. I particularly love one author's explanation of annual Jewish remembrances: "The very writing of the Book of Esther recognized the ever-present danger that people—even those of the household of faith—would look upon the world and conclude that there was no God. … Corporate remembrance, solemn and joyful, is essential to the healthy life of the Church."[13]

Try to grasp that we are the only reminder some people ever get that God lives, forgives, loves, and remains in control. As the end of our journey challenges us to consider what to do with all we've learned, the thought may occur that perhaps the church should celebrate Purim. Beloved, you and I don't need to celebrate the Jewish Purim. We each have our own to celebrate. God tells us what action we can take when we're overwhelmed by His kindness.

We can celebrate our deliverance and call upon His holy name. Check out the New English Translation of Psalm 116:12-13 in the margin. Fathom it, Dear One! We glorify God when we celebrate our deliverance.

Purim for us can be the deliberate remembrance of all God has done to set us free. Like the Jews of Persia, we have been delivered from a sweeping sentence of death, but our decree was engraved with nails on the cross of Christ and bears a crimson seal. If you're like me, you've also been delivered from a stronghold Satan intended to destroy you. These victories are meant to be joyfully treasured and greatly celebrated. That, my Sister, is Purim to us. I don't ever want to go back to that old oppression. Do you? Then you and I need to go out of our way to remember the wonderful works God has done.

I have a friend God set free from a long-term lesbian lifestyle. She knows the date she made the decision to do anything necessary to cooperate with God to get out. Her complete deliverance took months, but she rightly views that first day as a her anniversary. She celebrates that same day every year. I often get a card asking me to rejoice before God in her grateful behalf.

I wish I knew the exact anniversary of my deliverance, but Resurrection Sunday can represent that day to me each year. Easter is the celebration of my blood-bought freedom. No, this Gentile doesn't need to celebrate the Jewish Purim, but I am making a commitment to celebrate my deliverance at a specific time every year, calling upon the name of my faithful God. How about you? Take another look at Esther 9:22 and compare it to 9:19.

> "How can I repay the Lord for all His acts of kindness to me? I will celebrate my deliverance, and call on the name of the Lord."
>
> PSALM 116:12-13

What additional practice was added for an annual observance?
gather at synagogues   fast before feasting   give to the poor

My family had little tolerance for disrespect toward the poor. My grandmother had been the wife of a state representative who died just before the economy collapsed. In a moment the china on her table fell to the floor in scattered pieces of a shattered life. We were reminded regularly that a solitary disaster stood between us and the streets. Still, it wasn't until recent years that God began troubling me to make a life-practice of giving to the poor.

We might occasionally make the grave error of feeling heady when we give to the poor, but nothing is more humbling than when the poor give to us. Over and over as a young woman speaking in small churches, I marveled that the most giving fellowships seemed to be the ones that had the least. One example, however, left me speechless. Keith and I joined a small team in Angola to check on remote villages with feeding programs and others desperately needing them. Nothing is more disturbing than starving children.

We visited a village where the feeding program had for a year operated a one-meal-a-day school program for the children. The bad news is, they don't have the money to feed anyone over age 14 except expectant mothers. The good news is, the dull faces we'd seen on the children in our last visit had been transformed into what looked like happy masks of shiny milk-chocolate.

Just before we prepared to leave, I was summoned by a team member who told me that the village wanted to present me a gift on behalf of the organization I represented. I could instantly tell that something formal was about to take place as the villagers gathered.

I was ushered before the head of the community and his wife, who was dressed in a traditional brightly colored, ankle-length dress. Her white teeth gleamed in the African sun as she smiled ear to ear. She then proudly thrust a bowl toward me that rocked with small eggs. Eggs they needed and that I didn't. I was taken aback. I wanted to shake my head and insist she keep them, but she was so exuberant in her offering that I couldn't. With untamed joy they gave a portion of exorbitant expense out of the portion God had given them. I have rarely experienced a more humbling moment.

Personal Question   Have you ever been profoundly humbled by a sacrificial gift someone gave to you? If so, in the margin describe the situation.

On the long ride back to a sparse motel room, I felt a deep and painful sense of my own poverty. I knew I was poor in my giving. Poor in my sacrificing. Poor in my daily expression of God's giving heart and woefully rich in all things *self*.

That day on the edge of the world's nowhere, God wrote His signature on the sandy ground in the shape of a circular arrow. I was stricken by the absurdity of an unexpected turnabout. The scattered pieces of their lives jumped from their dirt floor to a lavish table and a wooden bowl of eggs became like bisque in fine china.

There before my eyes, the rich became poor and the poor became rich.

Day Four
These Days Were Called Purim

TODAY'S TREASURE

"Therefore these days were called Purim, from the word pur." Esther 9:26

Keith called my attention to an obituary in our newspaper. It was the fourth anniversary of the death of a very-successful businessman in Houston. His picture appeared and underneath his tribute was a picture with the label: "Installment IV." Call me brilliant, but I'm assuming they'd published installments II and III on the second and third anniversaries of his death. We'd never seen a miniseries in the obituaries. I don't mean to be disrespectful, but

I thought, *the public has probably moved on*. The ongoing annual tribute was a wonderful remembrance for family and close friends but an eye-opening reminder to the rest of us that life goes on whether we want it to or not.

Today's Scripture segment is a synopsis of the events in the all-but-otherwise-forgettable kingdom of Xerxes. It tells why an annual celebration called Purim exists and, in many respects, why we have a Book of Esther at all. Ultimately, Esther's beauty did not make her memorable. Every generation has beauty queens. Her way with people did not make her memorable. Every generation has voices touting how to win friends and influence people. Esther is memorable because God remembered a people who'd all but forgotten Him. Please read Esther 9:23-28.

In the margin create a one-sentence synopsis of the Book of Esther by completing this phrase: The Book of Esther is about …

Check every person or group mentioned in the six-verse synopsis (vv. 23-28) and mark an X by anyone who is not.
    Haman   Mordecai   the Jews   the King   Esther

That's one last irony for your PURIM acrostic. It's tough being a woman. Don't worry though. We haven't heard the last of our queen, but her absentia in the segment of Scripture devoted to the holiday's explanation offered its own one-sentence lesson: Getting the credit is the wrong reason to do the right thing.

I'm anxious to show you something in the wording of Esther 9:27 (NIV), "The Jews took it upon themselves to establish the custom … and … without fail observe these two days every year." The Hebrew repeats very significant wording from the Esther narrative that isn't identifiable in the phrase "establish the custom." One of my Jewish commentaries translates the original language this way: "the Jews undertook and irrevocably obligated themselves and their descendants … to observe these two days."[14] The word *irrevocably* is a rendering of the Hebrew wording we first saw back in Esther 1:19.

What did we learn in Esther 1:19 about the laws of Persia and Media?

One of the most maddening twists in the entire narrative is the irrevocability of the Persian laws. Had a law been alterable in Xerxes' kingdom, Haman's decree would have easily been revoked and presumably 75,800 lives saved.

The repetition of the Hebrew in the synopsis is very deliberate. With the blessing of Xerxes, the Jews seemed to be saying, "You want irrevocable? I'll give you irrevocable! We'll never stop observing the date of this deliverance. Call this the law and mark it down as irreversible." That we're told the Jews "took it upon themselves to establish the custom" (9:27) tells us that Purim is not in the same echelon of holy days as the Levitical feasts prescribed by God.

Don't get me wrong. That doesn't mean God doesn't recognize the celebration. He had no greater priority on earth than the deliverance of the Jews in Persia.

Compare Purim with the Jewish observance of Hanukah, which also fell outside the feasts of Leviticus 23. The New Testament calls Hanukah the "Feast of Dedication." In John 10:22-24 Christ Himself participated in it.

Think of the difference like this: Some holidays, like the Levitical feasts, were prescribed by God to bless man. Other holidays, like Hanukah and Purim were prescribed by man to bless God.

The Persians "took it upon themselves" to establish some laws that were irrevocable. The Jews "took it upon themselves" to follow suit. Long before God set the plan of man's redemption into motion, He took it upon Himself to establish laws of His own that were irrevocable.

In the margin list the irreversible edicts of God that bring you comfort.

With those in mind, please pore over Romans 11:25-29. You don't have to make perfect sense of this segment to be awed by it.

What does verse 29 call irrevocable? _____

How is this irrevocable "law" of God significant to our narrative?

The following excerpt makes me catch my breath each time I read it. Ryle says of the continued existence of the Jews:

> Why is it that … this singular race still floats alone, though broken to pieces like a wreck, on the waters of the globe… as separate and distinct as it was when the arch of Titus was built at Rome? I have not the least idea how questions like these are answered by those who profess to deny the divine authority of Scripture. ... among the many difficulties of infidelity there is hardly any one more really insurmountable than the separate continuance of the Jewish nation. ... God has many witnesses to the truth of the Bible, if men would only examine them and listen to their evidence. But you may depend on it there is no witness so unanswerable as one who always keeps standing up, and living … That witness is the Jew.[15]

Anne Rice, sometimes called "the vampire novelist," came to a similar conclusion and it brought her to a head-on collision with 30 years of atheism. She wrote: "I stumbled upon a mystery without a solution, a mystery so immense that I gave up trying to find an explanation because the whole mystery defied belief. The mystery was the survival of the Jews … It was this mystery that drew me back to God. It set into motion the idea that there may in fact be God.

And when that happened there grew in me for whatever reason an immense desire to return to the banquet table."[16]

Hebrews 1:3 pounds in my chest like a bass drum: Nothing in the universe's order—no kingdom, no nation—is sustained through the millennia except by Christ's powerful word … whether or not they acknowledge Him. It is this unexplainable survival that the Jews celebrated during that first Purim.

In large part the Jews have kept the tradition they "took it upon themselves to establish." A handful of customs surrounding Purim remained the same. Some Jews still fast the day before Purim as a symbol of Esther's three-day fast preceding her courageous approach to Xerxes. Many give presents to one another and money to the poor. Other practices have evolved through the centuries. In synagogues they read whole Megillah on Purim. Many children dress in costumes reflecting the characters. You should see the lovely little Esthers!. The reading of the Megillah is a raucous affair with whooping and hollering and the rattling of noise makers every time the evil name "Haman" is said. Purim is set aside as one of the happiest days of the Jewish year.

As is often true in our Western celebrations, many "help" themselves get happy by drinking themselves into a stupor. One commentator puts in words what I learned from a disapproving rabbi in Jerusalem. "Celebrants are permitted—even encouraged—by a later Jewish writing to give themselves enthusiastically to revelry until they cease to be able to distinguish between cries of 'Cursed be Haman!' and 'Blessed be Mordecai!' "[17]

Somehow the Purim observance has evolved into a day for loosening the limits and blowing off steam. To symbolize Esther's great theme of reversals, some men dress up like women and some women dress up like men. Everything possible is turned upside down to make the point.

Like Purim, many of our holiday observances have veered from their original intent. In the margin offer a few ways:

One of the practices that evolved through centuries, however, is especially delicious and hardly licentious. Jews all over the world bake cookies for Purim called *Hamantashen*. The term is foreign to us, but you should well recognize a name within it. The name of the cookie literally means "Haman's Pockets" or "Haman's Hat," but in Israel they are gleefully tagged "Haman's Ears." The name comes from a legend describing the evil Haman as a man with ugly, twisted ears (perhaps for not listening to God!). Others say the cookies are shaped like Haman's hat. They have no real biblical basis except in reference to the gifts of food, but as you can imagine, the custom brings great delight.

I ate "Haman's Ears" first in Jerusalem and thought obsessively about them until I found a bakery in Houston that serves them. They are prepared much like round sugar cookies but with traditional fillings (poppy seeds or apricot preserves) folded into the center. Before baking, the dough is folded over the fruit-filling on three sides giving the cookie a triangular shape. You'll

"The Son is the radiance of God's glory and the exact representation of his being, sustaining all things by his powerful word."

HEBREWS 1:3

find the recipe for Hamantashen on page 224 with hopes that many groups will bake and serve them at the last session like we did in Houston after the taping. It was unforgettable fun.

Coincidentally, I'd planned to direct you this very day to create a triangle-shaped diagram to help you remember our New Testament references to this marvelous thing we call providence. This is perfect timing! When you make the cookie, perhaps you could see both representations. What a shame it would be to let this series end without a fresh and deliberate last visit to our most blatant references to divine providence.

Read each of the following Scriptures and write the phrase beside each that best depicts divine providence. I'll supply the first example.

Ephesians 1:11 _works out everything_____

Philippians 2:13 _____

Romans 8:28 _____

Now draw a triangle in the margin, making sure the horizontal line is on the bottom. Ephesians 1:11 speaks in broadest terms concerning God's providence, so let's label the outside of the triangle's bottom line with the phrase I supplied for you. In this way we'll view the biblical claims of Ephesians 1:11 as the foundation for the other two. Outside the diagonal line on the left, write the phrase you recorded from Philippians 2:13. Outside the diagonal line on the right, write the phrase you recorded from Romans 8:28. Complete the diagram by drawing a "P" in the center of the triangle to represent "Providence."

Let this simple diagram become a visual aid to represent the balanced sides of God's providence. Please don't let familiarity cheat you of these priceless truths: God not only promises that He "works out everything" (Eph. 1:11) "according to His good purpose" (Phil. 2:13). He promises that "in all things God works for [our] good" (Rom. 8:28). In other words, every time He shifts us here or moves us there on this earthbound chessboard, He's not just fulfilling His own pleasure regardless of its impact on you. He's also working every detail—even the dreadful ones—to your and my good.

In three sides of one perfect whole, Ephesians 1:11 tells us God's providence is at work universally, Philippians 2:13 tells us God's providence is at work personally, and Romans 8:28 tells us God's providence is at work beneficially … and not just for Him but mercifully for us too. Providence cancels out every coincidence.

As we draw our journey to an end, what has this truth come to mean to you through this nine weeks?

A few days ago I waited anxiously for one of my beloved daughters to call me after she heard from her doctor regarding a malady that could have been frighteningly serious. My consolation was the overarching message of this nine-week Bible study: God knows. God sees. God acts. His providence is no less evidence than the openly miraculous.

We'll conclude now with a great recipe for Haman's Ears (p. 224). Make them, ponder them, then eat them! Nothing could be more delectably fitting than seeing a dual representation in these triangle cookies. No matter what our unseen Haman plots and schemes against us, God is for us. He will work it out, work it in, and work it well. We've got His Word on it. He who has a twisted ear, let him hear.

Day Five
With Full Authority

TODAY'S TREASURES

"So Queen Esther, daughter of Abihail, along with Mordecai the Jew, wrote with full authority to confirm this second letter concerning Purim."
Esther 9:29

I can hardly believe my eyes. We've reached our final lesson. It's time to gather up our things and say good-bye. For a while I honestly won't know what to do without you. You've spent nine weeks with me. but I've spent 18 months with you. At the compulsion of the Spirit, I've held you on my heart and written to you almost every weekday for a year and a half.

Your fellowship in this journey has been crucial. I might have studied Esther without you but never with this intensity. I would not know Christ or His Word remotely the same way if not for you. You encourage and challenge me so. I have such a long way to go in my pursuit of God, but I'm not where I was before I learned to live life from the pages of Scripture with sisters like you. Thank you, Beloved One, for allowing me this exquisite interaction.

When it's tough being a woman, God makes your camaraderie a comfort to my soul. When I'm appalled at how women treat one another, God brings you to mind and shields me from cynicism. Hear my heart: I dearly love you. Please take a deep and bittersweet breath then read the remainder of our marvelous narrative: Esther 9:29-10:3.

"The Jewish Passover
was near, so Jesus
went up to Jerusalem.
In the temple complex
He found people
selling oxen, sheep,
and doves, and [He
also found] the money
changers sitting there.
After making a whip
out of cords, He drove
everyone out of the
temple complex with
their sheep and oxen.
He also poured out
the money changers'
coins and overturned
the tables. He told
those who were
selling doves, 'Get
these things out of
here! Stop turning My
Father's house into a
marketplace' And His
disciples remembered
that it is written: Zeal
for Your house will
consume Me."

JOHN 2:13-17, HCSB

Describe the last glimpses we get of our Jewish protagonists:
ESTHER   MORDECAI

So the story ends. The banquet tables turned in the provinces of Persia and the same woman who'd lived her life at the mercy of decrees issues what Scripture plainly calls "Esther's decree" (9:32). Mordecai, the overlooked, is now Mordecai, the overseer, second in rank and highly esteemed. Hands wrung. Villains hung. Songs sung.

Do you think the saying's true, "All's well that ends well"? Why or why not?

The Book of Esther wasn't the last time in Scripture that tables were turned. Fast-forward 400 years to the opening pages of the Gospels. As surely as God overturned the tables of Persians in Xerxes's kingdom, He overturned the tables of Jews in Herod's Jerusalem. John 2:13-17 tells the story (margin).

Tables turn both ways. God isn't just partial. He's zealous for His house. When all history is written, the only tables left standing will be those He set. As the Gospels unfold, we find Jerusalem not only rebuilt, but a grand sight to behold: a city set on a hill that cannot be hidden.

Not unlike Esther in the early part of the narrative, Jerusalem's beauty, for the most part, was skin deep in those days. The Jews in the early first century did what most religious people do when they lack a fresh work of God. They turned to legalism. Their temple was one of the most imposing displays of human architecture in the world, yet it lacked something profound. Something Solomon's temple would have only been a shell without. They lacked the divine presence ... so they settled for profit. One unsuspecting day, the divine presence sauntered onto the temple grounds wearing a cloak of human flesh. Tables flew, but only to set a new one.

Luke's Gospel describes the banquet like this: "When the hour came, He reclined at the table, and the apostles with Him. Then He said to them, 'I have fervently desired to eat this Passover with you before I suffer. For I tell you, I will not eat it again until it is fulfilled in the kingdom of God. ... And He took bread, gave thanks, broke it, gave it to them, and said, 'This is My body, which is given for you. Do this in remembrance of Me.' In the same way He also took the cup after supper and said, 'This cup is the new covenant established by My blood; it is shed for you'" (Luke 22:14-16,19-20, HCSB).

That fateful night God instituted the new covenant and set a table big enough for every nation, tribe, and tongue. He rang the first dinner bell 50 days later at the Feast of Pentecost. Are you wondering what all of this has to do with the Book of Esther? I'm dying to show you. Please read Acts 2:5-24.

From where had these God-fearing Jews come according to Acts 2:5?

Check the first three nationalities of God-fearing Jews in Acts 2:9.
Arabs   Parthians   Cretans   Medes   Elamites

As veiled as it seems, you're staring the connection in the face. Scholars tell us that residents of Susa were likely among the Parthians, Medes, and Elamites who witnessed the first outpouring of God's Spirit.[18] So descendants of the generation Esther and Mordecai served made their pilgrimage to Jerusalem for the great Feast of Pentecost on its most significant year. They may have been those of Jewish blood or among those "of other nationalities [who] became Jews because the fear of the Jews had seized them" (Esth. 8:17).

Fathom the significance with me: God met them in Susa. Then He drew them to Jerusalem. Right there in the holy city the wandering Jews stretching from Xerxes's kingdom came to faith in Jesus Christ, the Son of God. The apostle Peter explained the signs that accompanied the big event: "This is what was spoken by the prophet Joel: 'In the last days, God says, I will pour out my Spirit on all people. Your sons and daughters will prophesy, your young men will see visions, your old men will dream dreams. Even on my servants, both men and women, I will pour out my Spirit in those days" (Acts 2:16-18).

Sons *and daughters*. Men *and women*. Mordecai's *and Hadassah's*. That day when pilgrims "from every nation under heaven" gathered for Pentecost, Esther's crown came full circle. The beauty of the princess bride of Christ would not be skin deep. It would be Spirit-deep. Beaten, bloody, and scattered, she would draw strength from Rome's persecution, rise to her royal feet and write with "full authority to confirm" (Esth. 9:29) the gospel of Jesus Christ. Testify, they would, until the canon of Scripture was complete.

It would rumble. It would shake. The bolts would threaten to give way, but the gates of Haman's hell would not prevail. I've lived too long and seen too much to believe that all is well that ends well in human terms. Much carnage can take place between crisis and the crown. In Christ, however, all's well that ends well because He emphatically does *all things well*.

Moments have passed since I wrote the preceding words. I suppose I'm trying to delay the ending. The fact is, that's the whole Megillah and little is left but good-byes. Mind you, I'll see you in our final session, but I can't draw the print to conclusion without asking you this question:

What have you savored most about our nine-week journey? Take some time and think then write your response in the margin.

"That which was from the beginning, which we have heard, which we have seen with our eyes, which we have looked at and our hands have touched—this we proclaim concerning the Word of life. The life appeared; we have seen it and testify to it, and we proclaim to you the eternal life."

1 JOHN 1:1-2

I've savored so many things about the Book of Esther but nothing more extravagantly than the pure element of story. That's what God used to captivate my imagination for months on end. Eugene Peterson explains the wonder of "story" in words beyond what I can express: "Story doesn't just tell us something and leave it there, it invites our participation. A good storyteller gathers us into the story. We feel the emotions, get caught up in the drama, identify with the characters... Honest stories respect our freedom; they don't manipulate us... They bring us into the spacious world in which God creates and saves and blesses... they offer us a place in the story, invite us into the large story that takes place under the broad skies of God's purposes."[21]

Based on Peterson's eloquent description, name one very specific way the Book of Esther offered you "a place in the story."

Everyone has a story, you know. No one is just skin deep. I learned that fact recently in a way I'll never forget. After my father's death last year, my stepmother, Madelyn, sought to put her loneliness and grief to good work by compiling what he'd written concerning his life story.

Sadly, none of my brothers and sisters and I knew those accounts existed until, around the first anniversary of his passing, she gave copies to us as gifts. I sat riveted and read every word. By the last page, I buried my face in my hands, and sobbed, "I never even knew you, Dad. *Why?*"

My gregarious father never met a stranger. yet oddly, those of us closest to him felt like we never cracked the surface of who he really was. My husband, the deep thinker, always surmised that Dad kept to the exterior because so much pain brooded underneath. Military orders placed him on the front lines in two wars, entrusted him with secrets, and caused him to see and experience some unspeakable things. One intense encounter, however, became a heart-wrenching beacon of hope to him. I'll recount the event the way my stepmother introduced it.

Several years ago she and Dad were browsing in a small shop. He called her to his side, a look of astonishment on his face. He pointed to a plaque etched with words he'd ironically not seen in over 50 years. With uncharacteristic emotion, he explained that he'd seen them before, etched on a prison wall in the Nazi concentration camp he helped liberate. These were the words:

I believe in the sun, even when it is not shining.
I believe in love, even when I do not feel it.
I believe in God, even when He is silent. (Author unknown)

My father wrote, "I will always believe I saw the very place where this was [first penned]. No one will ever know if [the prisoner] survived... The conditions were so horrible and the prisoners so near death. My unit, a part of the 45th Infantry Division (*The Thunderbirds*), took this German concentration

camp, within days of the end of World War II in Europe ... This was the final thing we did at the end."

Read those words etched on that prison wall again because there you have it: the Book of Esther in a nutshell. Those three simple lines preach with atomic power the timeless message of providence. And, not coincidentally, they come from a Jew desperately seeking a Deliverer.

My friend, the Rabbi in Jerusalem, framed the holocaust this way: "Our Deliverer did indeed come. He just came a little later than we expected. Had our enemy had his way, none of us would have survived. Yet here we are." I fight back the tears almost every time I replay those words in my head. Make no mistake. Deliverance always comes for the people of God. He can cause mountains to quake or simply keep kings awake.

God never writes a story without a good ending. That includes yours, Sweet One. Nine weeks ago we opened with Miss Potter's whimsical words. "There is something delicious about writing the first words of a story."[22] But, when God is the author, nothing is so delicious as the last word.

One day on the hillside of the New Jerusalem, surrounded by a crowd of glad hearers, the divine Narrator will tell the story of one woman's life. It will not be Esther's. It will not be your teacher's. It will be yours.

The story will begin something like this: "Once upon a time, in the days of the great and glorious Jesus, King of the vast empire of heaven and earth, there was a little girl who thought she was forgotten. Her name was _____ but the king called her _____. ... This is the story of how she won His favor." And with all the drama and emotion a great storyteller can muster, the Rabbi will read the congregation your whole Megillah. The listeners will groan. Bite their nails with suspense. It will be a raucous affair. With every mention of the villain's name, the crowd will heckle and jeer. Then at the height of the story, when hope seems lost and her life and loves most threatened, He will say these words to the crowd:

"But if she'd only known, she had come to royal position for such a time as this!" By faith alone, to her face she will fall… then to her feet she will rise, ready to do what deliverance demands. Then the Rabbi will quote her resolve: "And if I perish, I perish" and the crowd will stand and cheer! For what if she does perish? Is that the worst this world's wicked Haman can threaten? On the day that she does, this is what will happen: She will put on her royal robes and stand in the inner court of the palace, in front of the King's hall. The King will be sitting on his royal throne in the hall, facing the entrance. When he sees his queen standing in the court, he will be pleased with her and hold out to her the gold scepter that is in his hand (adaptation of Esth. 5:1-2).

And she will approach.

And cast her crown at His feet.

"God rewrote the text of my life when I opened the book of my heart to his eyes" (Ps. 18:24, The Message).

221

viewer guide ❦ session nine

*As the inspired writer puts the finishing touches on the
book, we will put the finishing touches on our approach
to its overarching theme—reversals of destiny.*

Interestingly, a book called by Esther's name and showcasing her beauty and
courage begins and ends without her. So, who is the the Book's real hero?
Who is the truest protagonist?

Consider the following thoughts:

*Neither Esther nor Mordecai had the power or position alone to deliver
their people. It was only as they acted in _____ _____
and _____ that they were able to lead God's people through
the crisis of death and into deliverance. Neither of them _____
to the role; perhaps neither of them _____ it. It was thrust on
them by a series of improbable circumstances largely beyond their control.
Nevertheless, their _____ _____ accomplished
God's ancient promise, and the Jewish race was preserved until in the
fullness of time, God entered history through this people as the
_____. How marvelous are God's inscrutable ways!*[19]

Recall Scenario #2

It's tough being a woman in a world where _____

____ ____ _____.

Before we locate and record our "turn around" Scripture, consider some of the possible implications of Genesis 3:16. Two different Hebrew words are translated "man." They are *adam* and *ish*. When a distinction exists between the two, *ish* denotes "man as the

_____ of woman and/or _____ in his

_____."[20] The word is first used in Genesis 2:24. In the KJV, *ish* is translated "husband" 69 times and "man" or "men" 1212 times.

Turn Around Scenario #2

It's tough being a woman in a world where beauty is a treatment.

"He has made _____ _____ ____ ____

_____" (Eccl. 3:11).

In man's realm, _____ _____ _____.

In God's realm where we will spend forever, _____ _____

___.

Turn Around Scenario #1

It's tough being a woman in another woman's shadow.

"He who dwells in the _____ ____ ____ _____ _____

will rest in the _____ ____ _____ _____" (Ps. 91:1).

On the "Turn It Around!" page, write concise descriptions of each scenario over the top of each corresponding box.

Hamantashen (Haman's Ears) Cookie Recipe

2 sticks butter or margarine (softened)
2 cups sugar
2 large eggs
2 tsp. vanilla
4 tsp. baking powder
4 cups wheat flour *OR 2 cups white all-purpose flour and 2 cups wheat (All white works well too.)*

FILLING: I use apricot preserves. You can use any fruit butters, jam, or pie fillings. Traditional fillings are poppy seed and prune.

1. Cut butter into sugar. Blend thoroughly. Add eggs and vanilla, blending thoroughly. Add baking powder and then flour, ½ cup at a time, blending thoroughly between each.
2. Put the batter in the refrigerator overnight or at least a few hours.
3. Roll it out to about ¼-inch thickness and then cut circles with a cookie cutter or drinking glass. (From Beth: Make them at least 3 inches in diameter so you have room to fill and fold them over!)
4. Put a tablespoon of filling in the middle of each circle. Fold up the sides to make a triangle, overlapping the sides as much as possible so only a little filling shows through the middle.
5. Bake at 375° for about 10-15 minutes, until golden brown.

A Note from the Editor About Endnotes and Extras

Producing a book is a bit like building an airplane. It involves a series of compromises. If you want an airplane to go fast, it won't carry as much. In several studies we've struggled with competing needs of type size and word count. So with *Esther* we've made readability the top priority. To do that required some compromises.

Faithful Beth students will note response to many learning activities in the margins. Not my preference but it preserves space. Beth did a phenomenal amount of research for this study, but with the priority of readability, I didn't have space for the endnotes. So we're putting the endnotes online. You'll find them at *www.lifeway.com/bethmoore*. You will also find the "Turn It Around" form there along with viewer guide answers, the Christian Growth Study Plan form, and various promotional items. We pray that you are blessed by the study as your LifeWay team has been in bringing it to you.

And we hope you'll enjoy the larger print. We love you.